A Catholic Guide to
Caring for Your Aging Parent

A CATHOLIC GUIDE TO

CARING

FOR YOUR

Aging Parent

MONICA DODDS

✝

LOYOLAPRESS.

CHICAGO

LOYOLAPRESS.

3441 N. ASHLAND AVENUE
CHICAGO, ILLINOIS 60657
(800) 621-1008
WWW.LOYOLABOOKS.ORG

Cover and interior design by Kathryn Seckman Kirsh

Library of Congress Cataloging-in-Publication Data
Dodds, Monica.
  A Catholic guide to caring for your aging parent / Monica Dodds.
    p. cm.
  ISBN-13: 978-0-8294-1872-9
  ISBN-10: 0-8294-1872-5
  1. Caring—Religious aspects—Christianity. 2. Caregivers—Religious life. 3. Aging parents—Care. 4. Aging parents—Family relationships. 5. Catholics—Family relationships—Handbooks, manuals, etc. 6. Adult children—Family relationships. 7. Caregivers—Family relationships. I. Title.
  BV4910.9.D63 2006
  259'.3088282—dc22
        2006010525

Printed in the United States of America
06 07 08 09 10 11 12 Versa 10 9 8 7 6 5 4 3 2 1

To my parents,
Russ and Terry Faudree

To my husband,
Bill

To my children,
Thomas, Carrie, Andy, and Tom L.

To my grandson,
Dominic

Contents

Introduction: Caregiving Is Personal   xv

PART ONE: YOU ARE A CAREGIVER

1 The Realities of Growing Old   3

     "Not *My* Parent"   3

     Understanding Aging   5

2 Welcome to Caregiving   9

     The Sandwich Generation   9

     Stages of Caregiving   11

     The Basics of Catholic Caregiving   14

3 The Spirituality of Caregiving   17

     God Knows   17

     The Role of Spirituality in a Caregiver's Life   20

        A Prayer for a Greater Awareness

        of the Presence of God   22

     How to Nourish Your Spiritual Life   23

     Praying as a Caregiver   25

     Responsibilities of the Church and Your Parish   28

     How Your Parish Can Support Caregivers   30

4   What to Expect . . . and What to Do about It 33

Handling Unexpected Emotions   33

Anger   34

Guilt   35

Exhaustion   38

Respite Care   40

The Need to Talk   43

5   Caregiving Is a Family Affair   45

You and Your Siblings   45

Preparing Your Children to Visit Your Parent   47

When You're Married to the Caregiver   50

Caring for an In-Law or a Stepparent   51

PART TWO: CARING FOR YOUR PARENT

6   Conduct an Assessment   57

Physical Condition   59

Mental Ability   60

Emotional and Social Health   61

Spiritual Life   63

From an Evaluator's View   64

Choosing the Best Solution   65

7   Understanding Your Parent   67

Your Parent's Generation   67

Independence, Control, and Self-Determination   71

Losses 73

Grief 75

Confusion about Role Reversal 79

"I Don't Want to Be a Burden" 80

Always a Parent: Worries about Adult Children 82

Challenges of Communication 83

8 Doctors and Hospitals 87

The Doctor 87

Getting a Second Medical Opinion 90

When the Professionals and Your Parent Disagree 92

At the Hospital 93

9 Physical Well-Being and Decline 97

Vision Loss 97

Hearing Loss 100

Dental Problems 102

Poor Nutrition 104

Problems with Mobility 106

Wheelchairs, Walkers, and Canes 108

Incontinence 109

10 Mental Health 111

Mental Illness 111

Dementia and Alzheimer's Disease 115

Depression and Suicide 119

Alcoholism 123

Tobacco Use 125

11 Emotional and Social Health — 129

The Need to Have Fun — 129

The Danger of Isolation — 131

Celebrating Birthdays and Anniversaries — 133

Grandparenthood — 136

Writing Memoirs — 137

Leisure-Time Activities — 140

12 Spiritual Matters — 143

Spiritual Health — 143

Helping a Parent Find Forgiveness and Peace — 147

Welcome Back to the Church — 149

The Gospel of Life — 150

The Sacraments — 151

Penance and Reconciliation — 152

The Eucharist — 154

The Anointing of the Sick — 156

13 Your Parent's Safety — 159

Home Safety — 159

Personal Safety — 162

In Case of an Emergency or a Disaster — 164

14 Is It Time for Your Parent to Move? — 169

Housing Options — 169

Choosing a Nursing Home — 171

Should Mom or Dad Move In? — 174

When Mom or Dad Moves In   176

Saying Good-Bye to the Family Home   178

Finding Help for Your Parent   180

Hiring a Case Manager   181

When Mom or Dad Doesn't Want Help   183

15 Finances and Other Paperwork   185

Financial Management   185

Health Care and End-of-Life Decisions   188

Personal Affairs   190

16 Some Special Problems   193

Helping Your Parent Give Up the Car Keys   193

Long-Distance Caregiving: Talking on the Phone   196

Long-Distance Caregiving: Visiting Home   198

Keeping Secrets, Telling Lies   200

Dealing with Your Parent's Racial and
Ethnic Prejudices   203

Euthanasia and the "Right to Die"   204

Taking Care of a Crabby or Formerly Abusive Parent   206

Refereeing Fights between Mom and Dad   209

17 Dying and Death   213

Preparing for Death   213

Talking to Your Children about Death   216

Words That Sting, Words That Comfort   218

Hospice   219

Sorting Out, Moving On, Remembering   221

18 The Church and Dying   225

    Funerals, Memorial Services, and Cremation   225

        The Vigil   229

        The Mass of Christian Burial   230

        The Committal Rite   231

    The Communion of Saints   232

PART THREE: APPENDIXES

Appendix I: Resources for Caregivers   237

    Caregiver   237

    Catholic   239

    Critical Issues   242

    Death and Dying   243

    Disability   244

    Diversity   244

    Government   245

    Grandparents   250

    Housing   250

    Legal   251

    Mental Health   251

    National Organizations   253

    Resource Information   257

    Support   260

    Suggested Reading   261

Appendix II: Assessment Guides, Checklists, and Reminders — 265

Tips for the Caregiver — 266

Caregiving Stress: Warning Signs — 267

An Assessment Checklist — 269

Home Safety Checklist — 275

Depression Checklist — 280

Driving Skills Checklist — 282

Legal and Financial Paperwork Checklist — 284

Elder Abuse Checklist — 288

Evaluating Housing Options — 290

Evaluation of Assisted-Living Facility — 292

Evaluation of Nursing Home — 298

Appendix III: Traditional Prayers of the Catholic Church — 303

Sign of the Cross — 303

Apostles' Creed — 303

Lord's Prayer — 304

Hail Mary — 304

Glory Be to the Father — 305

Memorare — 305

Angelus — 306

Magnificat — 307

Hail Holy Queen — 308

Peace Prayer of St. Francis — 308

Prayer to the Holy Spirit 309

Act of Contrition 309

Prayer to My Guardian Angel 311

Grace before Meals 311

Grace after Meals 311

The Universal Prayer, Attributed to Pope Clement XI 311

Eternal Rest 314

Rosary 314

Index 329

Introduction:
Caregiving Is Personal

Over the years, a lot of caregivers have told me their stories. Some caregivers—still in the thick of it—share what they're experiencing right now. Others—their duties completed—reflect on what that relationship, that role, has come to mean to them since the death of their loved one.

Some caregivers take care of an aging parent or another senior family member. Others care for a spouse or a son or daughter. In any case, caregiving is always personal. It's one person providing for another, and that other accepting care. Both the giving and the receiving have their challenging moments.

I've discovered that while every caregiver has his or her own story, in many ways every caregiver's story is the same. It's always a unique blend of successes, regrets, frustrations, fears, and fatigue; a combination of laughter and tears, love and grace.

My stories are no exception. In 1970, as a senior in high school, after months of helping my grandpa remain at home as his cancer slowly advanced, I rode in the back of an ambulance with him as he was being transferred from his apartment to the hospital for the last time. Then, a few years later, I stood at my grandma's bedside on the last day of her life and assured her, "It's OK to let go now."

I've been a caregiver a number of times over the years, but, I must confess, it wasn't until recently—when caring for a senior family member in failing health—that I began to truly understand just how complex the task of caregiving can be. It was only then that

I began to realize the most powerful support I have is an awareness of the presence of God as I go about my daily caregiving tasks.

That's what I bring to this book. It's what I want to hand to you. It's what separates *A Catholic Guide to Caring for Your Aging Parent* from the many other fine books on caregiving on the market today. For me and—as I've found from the stories I've had the privilege to hear—for many others, the spirituality of caregiving is not incidental. It's fundamental. This is true even when those grace-filled moments—moments of awareness of God's infinite love for this person whom I so dearly love and of God's gratitude for the work I am performing—are fleeting.

The truth is that you have been chosen. God has asked you to help his beloved son or daughter. This is true even if your response, like mine, hasn't always been enthusiastic—if, unlike Mary at the Annunciation immediately saying, "Your will be done," you've done your share of muttering and grumbling.

I'm reminded of the Gospel parable of the two sons asked by their father to go work in the vineyard (Matthew 21:28–31). The first answered, "No way!" but then went out and got the job done. The second said, "Sure thing" but didn't budge. "Which of the two," Jesus asked, "did the will of his father?" The answer is obvious. The answer is encouraging for those of us in the vineyard who still mutter and grumble from time to time.

In This Book

Because of the complexity of caregiving, this book has three layers.

First, there's some basic, real-life, practical information: ideas you can use day in, day out, to provide care and to better understand what you and your loved one are going through.

Second, there's information about the support offered by the Catholic Church. This includes the church's teaching on life and death, Pope John Paul II's encyclical *The Gospel of Life,* and the sacraments available to your parent and to you.

And third, there's discussion of the role of spirituality in the caregiving experience. Spirituality is blended into this book, intertwined in the chapters, just as it is in your daily life. That spirituality may be under the surface, or dramatically above it, staring you in the face, ready to catch you when you feel like you're falling or hold you tightly when you feel like you're going to break apart. At the end of each section, you'll find a prayer to help you slow down and reflect on your caregiving experience. You'll also find some basic principles and guidelines reflecting the underlying values of caregiving.

I've included three appendixes in the book:

Resources for Caregivers

There is a wealth of information available to you as a caregiver, and it would be impossible to go into great depth about that information in a guide of this kind. The resources appendix will give you a running start as you look for the assistance your parent or family member may need and the support you may need. It is critical for a caregiver to get current and accurate information. Do your research, and always remember to check your sources.

Assessment Guides, Checklists, and Reminders

Everyone gathers information in a way that's most efficient for him or her. I've found checklists helpful, so I've included some that might make your tasks easier. The lists in this appendix will help you assess your parent's needs, look at safety issues in the home, and evaluate a nursing home, among other tasks.

Traditional Prayers of the Catholic Church

This section features traditional Catholic prayers. You may discover that, at this point in your life, they speak to you—and for you—in a new way. Then, too, you can use them if your loved one would like to pray in a formal way or would like to say with you some of the prayers he or she learned as a child. My favorite prayer is the rosary. You'll find it here.

About the Author

My experience with the elderly and with caregiving has been professional as well as personal. With a degree in social welfare, I've worked with the active, well elder as a program coordinator at a senior center; with the independent needing some assistance as a case manager for in-home care; and with the neediest, the homebound, as the manager of Meals on Wheels for Seattle/King County. I've also served as an officer on the Council on Aging for Snohomish County, Washington, where my role included examining policy issues related to the field of aging.

My husband, Bill, and I write columns on family life for Catholic News Service and *Columbia* magazine, published by the Knights of Columbus. We edit a devotional magazine, *My Daily Visitor*, published by Our Sunday Visitor. Together we wrote *The Joy of Marriage: Inspiration and Encouragement for Couples* (Meadowbrook Press) and *Caring for Your Aging Parent: A Guide for Catholic Families* (Our Sunday Visitor), now out of print. I also had the wonderful experience of writing (with the help of St. Thérèse!) *Praying in the Presence of Our Lord with St. Thérèse of Lisieux* (Our Sunday Visitor).

In 2004, I began the Web site YourAgingParent.com. I invite you to visit me there. It offers spirituality, information, and resources

for Catholic caregivers. In 2006, I launched CatholicCaregivers
.com, an online community and a resource for parishes and dioceses.
That same year I started the Friends of St. John the Caregiver
(FSJC.org), an association that is the parent organization of both.
Its fundamental purpose is promoting care for the caregiver.

Why St. John? Who better to be the patron saint of caregivers
than the one Christ chose from the cross to care for his own mother?
"When Jesus saw his mother and the disciple whom he loved standing beside her, he said to his mother, 'Woman, here is your son.'
Then he said to the disciple, 'Here is your mother.' And from that
hour the disciple took her into his own home" (John 19:26–27).

You, too, have been chosen. Under whatever circumstances, for
whatever reasons, God has asked you to become a caregiver.

I hope you find this book helpful as you face the many challenges of caregiving and as you travel along on your spiritual journey.
My prayers are with you and your loved one.

—Monica

St. John, patron of caregivers, pray for us.

Part One

You Are a Caregiver

†

1

The Realities of Growing Old

"Not *My* Parent"

Everybody gets older. Everybody dies. But this isn't "everybody." This is different. This is *your* parent.

You're not the only one feeling this way. Members of the baby-boomer generation are facing the undeniable fact that as they enter and pass through middle age, their parents are marking their seventieth, eightieth, or even ninetieth birthdays. Likewise the adult children of these boomers are assuming caregiver duties more and more frequently. And suddenly—it always seems sudden—the people who cared and nurtured and taught and provided are the ones who need help. Suddenly Mom isn't as independent as she used to be. Suddenly Dad is neglecting tasks he's been handling faithfully for more than half a century.

The realization that a parent needs help is a realization that gnaws at the heart and begins with self-doubt. Soon after, guilt, panic, frustration, and grief fight for dominance. If you're an adult child living near your aging parent, you probably blame yourself for not noticing the gradual deterioration. Maybe Mom had a small stroke and fell on the kitchen floor and lay there all night until a neighbor happened by. Why didn't you drop in more often? Why did it take something big to make you see what was going on?

If you and your aging parent live in different parts of the country, you may not notice the small and not-so-small changes adding up. Perhaps a visit home to Dad—a visit you've put off for how long?—brings a shocking revelation: the spunky, independent person you remember is no longer there. Why didn't you come sooner? Why didn't you notice the changes when the two of you spoke by phone? Why wasn't it obvious that his letters were more muddled and arrived less frequently? Why did you take that job so far away?

You start to feel panicky. You need to solve these problems *now!* But you can't. In fact, you shouldn't even try.

First, you can't solve *all* the problems now. Your parent didn't reach this condition overnight, and it will take time to make changes. There are no quick fixes.

Second, *you*—singular—shouldn't solve the problems. If you swoop in and begin giving orders, you may be not so pleasantly surprised to see that the proud, self-reliant (some might say stubborn and cantankerous) person you thought had gone is not gone entirely. Not by a long shot. The more your parent is involved in finding solutions to the problems, the more cooperative he or she will be.

Gradually you realize that you are a caregiver. Frustration mounts. Why does it take a dozen phone calls to find the right agency to deliver the service your parent needs? Why do you always feel as if you're either not doing enough or doing too much? Why don't you have the energy or time or money to properly take care of your spouse, your kids, and your parent?

In the dead of night, grief wins. There's the icy realization that your parent is going to die. As you try to cope and solve and assist, you can't help feeling this is the beginning of the end. You can't help the grief you feel because you know someday your mother or father will be gone.

You lie there and pray, "Please, God, not yet. Not *my* parent."

Dear God, time is just passing too fast. The thought of my life after my parent dies scares me. What will it be like? I know I need to trust in you. Help me accept your timeline. Amen.

Understanding Aging

Throughout our lives, our bodies change. As long as a human body is living, it's growing older. So how can you tell if your parent is developing a new and potentially serious health problem, or if what you see is simply part of what could be called the natural aging process?

The temptation is to assume that a new problem your parent develops is one every older person experiences and that nothing can be done about it. Not necessarily.

Take being confused, for example. Doesn't everyone, if he or she lives long enough, develop some form of mild dementia? Yes, the chances of developing a form of dementia (Alzheimer's disease being only one of the possible diagnoses) increase with age, but there are other reasons a parent might be confused. Maybe Dad's metabolism has changed, and a medicine he's taken for years is now causing side effects. Or the problem is a new medicine combined with what he's already taking. Maybe, without your knowledge, Mom is drinking more than she used to. Maybe she has had a small stroke.

It's a good idea to do some research and then ask your parent's primary physician about the "normal" aging process—what, in general, is to be expected—and keep the doctor up to date on what's happening with your mother or father. If you see something new, ask the doctor about it. It's a good idea to consult with the physician even if you think what you see is to be expected with any chronic condition your parent may have. (And it's important for you to know the usual progression of that condition as well.)

For example, Mom has arthritis, and she's having more pain and more difficulty using her hands. Yes, her condition may grow worse over time, but perhaps a more effective medicine or treatment will help as the inflammation reaches this new stage. Would physical therapy help her feel better, and is it available? Would occupational therapy or an adaptive device make it easier for her to perform daily tasks like holding a fork or using a zipper? Ask about these things.

Don't compare your parent's condition or symptoms with another older person's. Maybe your best friend noticed that her father was growing hard of hearing, and he now wears a hearing aid. You notice your father's hearing isn't what it used to be, but you hesitate to bring up the subject with Dad or his doctor because you're fairly certain getting your parent to accept a hearing aid would be a tremendous battle. At the same time, Dad has noticed the trouble he's having, and he's worried but too frightened to say anything about it.

While you both tiptoe around the subject, the source of your father's problem may be nothing more than wax buildup in his ears. His doctor's nurse could quickly and easily take care of it and give both of you tips on how to avoid the problem in the future.

In other words, don't assume that you understand what you are seeing, and don't assume that there's little to be done about it. Remember that while you and your parent may become very good at spotting and diagnosing a change or a problem, that's not the same as having an objective health-care professional evaluate what's happening. Let that person be the one to decide if it's an inevitable part of the aging process.

My Lord, so many people are afraid to grow old. Give me wisdom to understand the aging process. Keep me alert to the changes in my parent's life. Make me an alert caregiver. Amen.

2

Welcome to Caregiving

The Sandwich Generation

Caregivers can feel like the "sandwich generation": there's pressure from your children on one side and your aging parent (or even grand-parent) on the other, and sometimes it gets messy in the middle. Add in a spouse and a job, and it's no wonder you often feel that you don't have nearly enough time and energy for all you have to do.

Pressure comes from expectations. Maybe your parent took care of Grandma or Grandpa. Your spouse took care of your mother-in-law or father-in-law. Your friends or coworkers seem to be able to handle their situations. But you are having trouble. Then comes guilt. When you realize that you can't do all the things you're supposed to do, you think you're letting everyone down. If you just worked a little harder, slept a little less, sacrificed a little more, then somehow . . .

If you find yourself in that situation, these suggestions might help:

Remember that there is no single "right" way to do this. Trying to mimic what another person has done probably isn't going to work for you. Each case is unique because the personalities and problems in each case are unique.

You need to take care of yourself. If you don't, you will burn out quickly and be of little use to anyone, including yourself. The situation in which you find yourself is not a sprint; it's a marathon. Yes, someday it will end, but that may be a long, long time from now. In the meantime, if you do not pace yourself—or sometimes even pamper yourself—you won't be able to keep going. That's not because you're weak; it's because you're human.

The big picture can look and feel overwhelming. Sometimes it helps to break it down into the many tiny pieces that make up the whole: what you have to do for your parent, your children, your spouse, your job, yourself. The lists may be long, but somehow no single item is overpowering.

Prioritize your tasks. Making those lists helps. Obviously, getting Mom to her doctor's appointment is more important than vacuuming her apartment.

Give away some of the low-priority duties. Someone can be hired to do the apartment cleaning. Someone else—the bakery at the local grocery store, for instance—can supply the brownies you're supposed to send to the next Cub Scout den meeting.

Get support for yourself. Groups for caregivers and organizations that focus on your parent's particular illness or condition can help you deal with what you are facing. Doctors, social workers, and your region's Area Agency on Aging can give you local contacts.

Write it down. Take notes on all the information from doctors, therapists, pharmacists, teachers, coaches, your boss, your spouse, your kids . . . There's no way you can remember all the things you need to remember without help. It may seem like the day is completely packed, but if you jot down your own to-do list, you may discover there's half an hour free here, twenty minutes there. A little oasis like that gives you something to look forward to—a short break to at least partially recharge your batteries before you have to go, go, go again.

> Jesus Christ, sometimes my life feels like a tug-of-war, and I'm the rope. Keep me strong so I won't break. I need you right here next to me. Amen.

Stages of Caregiving

> Start by doing what's necessary, then what's possible, and suddenly you are doing the impossible.
>
> —St. Francis of Assisi

There is no single, tidy, all-encompassing definition for *caregiver*. Rather, it's a job that includes multiple responsibilities that vary not only from family to family, and not only from one family member to another, but also from caregiver to caregiver. The caregiver you are today may not be the caregiver you were six months ago, because the care your parent needs has changed. In the same way, the caregiver you are now may not be the caregiver you will be in six months. If your parent's health improves, you may be less involved. If it worsens, you may be more involved.

Nevertheless, the caregiving role is typically a continuum that you move through as your parent's needs change. Generally, the role of a caregiver follows a particular identifiable pattern. In other words, it's possible to identify where you are right now on that "continuum of caregiving." Recognizing where you are on that spectrum can help you better understand why you feel as you do. You may be more tired because your duties as a caregiver have crept up incrementally and now demand more of your time, energy, and patience.

One aspect of caregiving is that it has many stages. A list of these stages can not only help you identify what parts of a caregiver's vast "job description" are in the forefront for you right now, but also better prepare you for what may soon lie ahead. These are the stages that can be identified, although they don't necessarily follow this sequence:

Pre-caregiving: The caregiver is a helper, beginning to lend a hand with a limited number of tasks but not identifying him- or herself as a "caregiver."

Self-identifying: Those caregiving tasks have increased to the point that the caregiver realizes and says, "I am a caregiver." The caregiver now defines the role for him- or herself or continues to "just do it."

Studying and researching: Adopting the role of a student, the caregiver wants to know about and understand a parent's condition or illness, including the symptoms and prognosis, and begins to look for resources for stress management and for informal support, such as family and friends.

Acting like a caregiver: The caregiver is actually doing the work—increasing the number and frequency of tasks, learning new skills and improving on others—and, as his or her parent's health deteriorates, begins to feel more stress.

Recognizing challenges: The caregiver sees the impact of the situation: the emotional strain for both the parent and the caregiver, the parent's resistance to accepting help, and the caregiver's own exhaustion, anxiety, and anger.

Getting help: The caregiver acknowledges the need for help. The spirituality of the role of caregiving becomes more apparent, and the caregiver incorporates prayer and the awareness of God into daily activities. The caregiver locates and accepts formal support from social services and expands informal help to include the extended family, more friends, and the parish community.

Managing the role of caregiver: With the added help, the caregiver begins to be more proactive in his or her approach to the role. The caregiver may decide on a game plan, learn about and use new coping strategies, and begin to feel more in control and more confident.

Preparing for the end of caregiving: The caregiver understands that the role of caregiving will end with the death of Mom or Dad. In many ways the caregiver begins to grieve the loss of both the once-healthy parent and the parent who now needs care. This is when the caregiver most clearly sees the true value of caregiving and the love and respect he or she has for the parent.

Moving on after death: The caregiver experiences shock, even if death was expected, and grieves the loss of his or her loved one. There may be an empty period in the day, a feeling of *"Now* what do I do?" This is a good time to rest and reminisce. Acceptance and appreciation of the experience will gradually come.

In a perfect world a caregiver would move step by step through the list. In the real world, in your world, that might not happen. The next time you're feeling overwhelmed, review this list to see if one of the steps gives you some ideas for helping you to feel more in control.

See the information fact sheet about caregiver stress on page 267.

Most Holy Spirit, guide me on my journey as a caregiver. Each step of the way I need you. I don't know how long this trip will last. Please give me comfort and rest when I'm done. Amen.

The Basics of Catholic Caregiving

Some underlying themes of caregiving are repeated throughout this book. They can be used as basic principles and guidelines while you care for your parent. When you, the caregiver, are facing a particular issue or concern, it can be helpful to keep these in mind. Consider how your idea, plan, or solution corresponds—or doesn't correspond—with these themes:

Love and respect: No matter how old you and your parent are, you will always be child and parent. The lifetime bond between you is like no other. As an adult, you probably realize that this relationship is seldom ideal and never perfect, and yet it is tremendously important. As the adult child of an aging parent, you're now being given the opportunity—the challenge—to honor your mother or father in a new, different, and more demanding way.

Self-determination: It's still your parent's life, not yours. You're there to assist, not take over. As long as your parent is mentally competent, he or she should be included in decisions, and his or her choices should be respected.

Normalization: A basic goal for you is to help your parent continue to lead the same lifestyle he or she has been leading and wants to keep leading (provided, of course, that lifestyle is not undermining his or her health or safety). The fewer the changes in his or her daily routine, the better.

Individualization: Just because your friend did this or that for her parent doesn't mean it's best for your parent. And what was good for Mom may not be what's good for Dad. Each life is unique, and therefore one's care must be tailor-made.

Communication: Planning early and talking often, even about difficult subjects will help you and your parent avoid having to work things out in the middle of a crisis.

Support: A number of support systems are available for both you and your aging parent. In addition to the informal support of family, friends, neighbors, and members of the parish, you can access the more formal support of professional counseling. A support group, for example, can be extremely helpful. You don't have to reinvent the wheel. Others have been here before. You can learn from them.

Use of resources: Many resources and services are available. Research can be challenging, but it's worth the effort. (Remember that there are resources and services for both your parent and you, the caregiver.) The aging network is growing rapidly. Keep looking for whatever you need. Don't assume that the help you need isn't out there.

Solutions: Try not to panic. Most often there is no quick fix to your parent's increasing needs, no simple answer. Keep in mind that even the best solution is only temporary. As your parent's situation changes—and it will—even the best answer will have to be reviewed and reworked.

Minimum to maximum: Change is difficult for all of us, and sometimes little steps at a time make it easier to accept. If you meet with resistance from your parent, start with the most basic and critical help needed. Stick with that and keep it limited. Then, gradually increase services to cover more needs. This approach helps your parent stay within his or her comfort zone, and it also helps you evaluate how things are going and what more may be needed. The challenge is to begin with the minimum amount of help or change that's necessary and then, as needed, gradually increase it.

Ongoing process: The aging process is ongoing, and each step along the way brings new challenges for both you and your parent. As your parent's health deteriorates, you and your parent's traditional roles as child and adult—the one who needs help and the one who has always provided that help—may continue to fluctuate or reverse. These changes are new for both of you and can seem overwhelming. Remember, neither you nor your parent has to be an expert at this. You can learn together.

Prayer: As is true when facing so many of life's challenges, the best coping strategy includes turning to prayer. Pray for your parent, that he or she can accept what is happening and find comfort. Pray for yourself, that you will have the strength to do the many tasks before you. Pray that both you and your parent will have wisdom when decisions need to be made. Pray that you both will feel the love of God, our heavenly Father. Pray for your fellow caregivers. Pray—right here, right now.

Father in heaven, I want to be a good caregiver, the best, because I know you want this for my parent. Gently remind me that I have a responsibility to you to care for my parent. I accept the assignment you have given me. Amen.

3

The Spirituality of Caregiving

God Knows

God knows caregiving is hard. God knows caregiving is work. God alone knows all the particular circumstances—the feelings and emotions, the life experiences and personality quirks, the baggage and hot buttons—that can make taking care of another person hard work.

And knowing all that, God has chosen you to play a central role in providing that care. Just as from the cross Jesus asked St. John— the patron saint of caregivers—to take care of the Blessed Mother, God asks you to help take care of someone else he so deeply loves. But that doesn't mean providing care for a spouse, a parent or grandparent, an aunt or uncle, a sibling, or any other family member or friend is simple or easy. (Although this book uses the terms *adult child* and *aging parent* and focuses on that particular relationship, the same material can be adapted and applied to other caregiving relationships.)

You know—or have quickly been discovering—that caregiving is hard work. You know—or have quickly been discovering—that caregiving can take a toll physically, emotionally, mentally, financially, and spiritually. What you may not know, or at times not recognize, is that you are not the only one facing these challenges. While you may be the only one in your family providing care (or the primary person providing it), there are other caregivers in your workplace, in your parish, in your community, in your city or town, in your state. The number of caregivers continues to grow rapidly, because the number of seniors needing care continues to grow rapidly.

As in your case, often the work they do and the services they provide—the loving care they offer—is unknown and unseen by others. That's so because caregiving is personal. That's so because caregiving is not a role one accepts and sticks with to earn glory and praise. That's so because caregivers aren't interested in tooting their own horns (even if they had the time or energy to do so).

In each case, in every case, a caregiver needs workable options that can easily be tailored to meet specific needs and circumstances, not a one-size-fits-all, time- and energy-consuming "answer." A caregiver needs up-to-date information on, and access to, afford-able services, not programs that are out of touch with reality or out of reach financially. A caregiver needs the support of others, not a hands-off attitude from the workplace, the community, the state, or the church. And a caregiver needs solid spiritual nourishment, not pie-in-the-sky platitudes.

More than needing all that, a caregiver deserves all that . . . and much, much more.

You deserve all that . . . and much, much more.

God knows you do.

One of the basic teachings of Catholic spirituality is that throughout our lives each of us is personally called by God to use a particular talent, to meet a particular need. For you, now, that vocation is taking care of a loved one.

Our Catholicism also tells us that in all things, at all times, we're never alone. God doesn't send us on our way. He walks with us. That's not to say there aren't times when we feel alone—or abandoned. Countless saints have testified to that experience. From the cross, Jesus himself cried, "My God, my God, why have you forsaken me?"

When you are caught up in the many everyday details and demands of caregiving, it's easy to overlook the spiritual side of what you have been asked—called—to do and what you are doing. That's why this book is sprinkled with small prayers. They're there as reminders that what you're doing is a prayer, and the path you and your loved one are taking is a spiritual pilgrimage.

It is the Father calling his beloved child home. It is the Father asking you to help his son or daughter along the final stages of that journey.

It is his Son whom you are tending. It is the Son who told us that whatever we do for those in need we do for him.

And it is the Spirit who is with you right now. It is the Spirit who will never leave you, even during those times when it seems he has gone away and taken his gifts—wisdom, courage, knowledge, and the rest—with him.

May God the Father, the Son, and the Holy Spirit richly bless you and your loved one in this life, and in the life to come. Amen.

The Role of Spirituality in a Caregiver's Life

> When Jesus saw his mother and the disciple whom he loved standing beside her, he said to his mother, "Woman, here is your son." Then he said to the disciple, "Here is your mother." And from that hour the disciple took her into his own home.
>
> —JOHN 19:26–27

One of the last things a caregiver wants or needs is pious platitudes about the spirituality of caregiving. Those saccharine, greeting-card sentiments with a religious spin often fall flat. Some of the "spiritual" things that get said to caregivers make matters worse.

Let's be honest: there are times in our lives when our spirituality is on the back burner at best. Spirituality—God, prayer, sacraments, and all the rest—may not make the top-ten list of our concerns when we're caught up in life's many demands. But there is some good news.

If you haven't been too spiritual before now (or if it's been awhile), it's a small step for your "Oh dear God!" to be transformed from an exclamation muttered in fear and frustration to a quick prayer . . . muttered in fear and frustration. It's God's presence that not only lets you take that small step but also makes you aware you've done so.

How did that happen? Grace. Amazing grace.

A prayer that begins, "I know I haven't talked to you in a long time, and there are a lot of things I've done that I shouldn't have and a lot of things I didn't do that I should have. . . ." is a very good prayer. So, too, one that begins, "I know I haven't believed in you in a long time . . ." or "I know I've been mad at you for a long time . . ."

What if your spiritual life is strong and active? When you find yourself in a caregiving role, you might feel as if you have to put your spiritual life on hold. You can't make it to weekday Mass. You can't attend the prayer group meeting. You can't head to the retreat house for your annual weekend away.

But you don't need to "go there" to experience God in a very particular and personal way. God has come to you. Or, more accurately, God—present with your parent at this time in his or her life—has invited you to join him.

Now your spiritual life may consist of receiving Holy Communion from a Eucharistic minister who has come to visit your parent. Now it may be saying prayers and reading Scripture with Mom or Dad—for the first time in a long time, if ever. Now God's presence may help you realize that a bedside, a car, or a doctor's office has replaced the retreat house this year.

Now you may realize that you and your parent are on a pilgrimage. The bedroom, the car, the doctor's office—all are holy ground, because the two of you are making a truly sacred journey. Together, you are preparing for what is to come: one of you will continue into the next world, and one will remain behind. On that day, one will grieve, even as she knows her parent is rejoicing. And one will rejoice, even as she knows that—for a time—her child is grieving. This is a once-in-a-lifetime experience: a walking with God that can never be duplicated or repeated.

These aren't pious platitudes meant to gloss over the realities of caregiving. You know the truth: Caregiving is exhausting. Caregiving is maddening. Caregiving is frightening. Caregiving is frustrating. But the truth is also that, in the middle of all this, you can experience an awareness of the presence of God.

Whether you feel it or not, God is constantly present with you in your new role. And whether you like it or not, you've been given an assignment, a mission, a vocation: you are a caregiver. ("Oh, God help me!" That's another good prayer.) This is God's will for both you and your loved one. He has prepared you for this all your life. By loving you, God and your parent have taught you to love. And love is the essence of caregiving.

St. John, patron saint of caregivers, pray for me. You know how important caregiving is. Jesus himself asked you to take care of his mother. Intercede with God the Father to help me in this role. Please help all our fellow caregivers and their families. Amen.

A Prayer for a Greater Awareness of the Presence of God

Heavenly Father, help me better understand and believe that I can do what you ask me to do.

Forgive me for the times, even now, when I question your judgment.

As I go about the many daily tasks of caregiving, give me energy.

As I watch Mom walk so slowly across the room, give me strength.

As I answer Dad's repeated question just one more time, give me patience.

As I look for solutions to whatever is the most recent concern, give me wisdom.

As I sit and reminisce with Mom about the "good old days," give me a moment of laughter.

As I get to know Dad in a new way, seeing both his strength and his frailty, give me joy.

As I sit beside Mom's bed waiting for her pain medication to take effect, give me comfort.

Lighten my burden, answer my prayer, and give me the strength to do what so often seems impossible. Give me a quiet place to rest when I need it and a quieting of my anxieties when I'm there.

Change my attitude from tired, frustrated, and angry to loving and compassionate.

Remain my constant companion as I face the challenges of caregiving, and when my job is through and it's time for me to let go, help me remember that my parent is leaving my loving arms to enter your eternal embrace. Amen.

How to Nourish Your Spiritual Life

Caregiving includes a strong spiritual component. Here are some suggestions for ways that you can nourish your spiritual life in your role as a caregiver:

- Pray every day. Make an effort to spend quiet time with God.
- Read Scripture.

- Ask for prayers from your parish community for your parent and for you as a caregiver.
- Prayerfully reflect on your unique role as a caregiver and realize the special gift you have been given.
- Use the basics of Catholic caregiving (page 14) as a foundation in decision making.
- Provide comfort and compassionate care.
- Accept God's will for you and your family.
- Take time to be aware of God's presence.
- Share your thoughts and feelings about your caregiving experiences with a spiritual director or a trusted friend who can honestly support and guide you.
- Ask God to reveal the meaning in your life as a caregiver.
- Seek forgiveness for your mistakes and offer it freely and completely to those who have hurt you.
- Use the Internet for prayers and do an online retreat.
- Attend Mass, and go with your parent if at all possible.
- Write down your thoughts, prayers, fears, and joys in a journal. Review your experiences as a caregiver to become more aware of the presence of God in your daily life.
- Listen quietly to music as a way to slow down and hear the sweet whisperings of God.
- Join or become active in a parish community and draw on the strength of others.
- Read the Liturgy of the Hours and realize God is with you from the moment you wake up to your last thoughts at night.

Oh Lord, I know you are with me these days. I want to be more aware of you in my daily life. Show me how, and if I forget, gently whisper in my ear, "I am here." Amen.

Praying as a Caregiver

It's not surprising that an aging parent and an adult child can be drawn together toward prayer. Still, praying can feel awkward if it hasn't been a central part of your parent's life or your life. Just the thought of praying can make you feel uncomfortable. Even if you're accustomed to praying, it's likely that prayer with your parent won't come easily. Where to begin?

Prayer has been defined as lifting the mind and the heart to God. That's easier to do when your mind is filled with concern for a loved one. Praying isn't complicated. There are no formulas that have to be followed. "Thee" and "thou" aren't necessary. Praying is telling God: "This is what's on my mind." "This is why my heart is aching." "This is what I'm so grateful for." It's turning to the One who created your parent, to the One who *loves your parent even more than you do,* and asking for help, for comfort, for strength.

Your prayers may change as your parent's condition goes through stages. The focus of your prayers may shift. For a time it may be "Heal Mom." And that might happen. At another time it may become "Yes, I know she's going to die, but just not now. Please. Later." And you may reach a point in your prayers when you say to God, "Let her go peacefully. When it's her time, let her go and welcome her into heaven."

There may also be periods when what is happening is so overwhelming—so frightening, so awful—that your own words just won't come. Many adult children in that situation have discovered that silently repeating the prayers they learned as children—the Our Father, the Hail Mary—can bring comfort. Some who haven't said the rosary for years are surprised to find that it can be especially helpful.

If your parent wants to pray out loud with you, then saying those same childhood prayers—an Our Father, a Hail Mary, or a rosary—can be a good place to begin. If you are worried about coming up with the "right" words or avoiding the "wrong" ones, you can find prayers on audiotape or CD at Catholic bookstores. (Some of the traditional Catholic prayers can be found in the back of this book beginning on page 303.) Your parent may surprise you with the number of prayers and hymns he or she remembers. It's not uncommon that someone with significant short-term memory loss can easily, and happily, recall what he or she memorized as a child.

A personal shared prayer doesn't have to be long or complicated: "Heavenly Father, bless Dad and me. Thank you for letting us be a part of each other's lives. Give us strength for whatever lies ahead." Even if your family has never been the touchy-feely type, holding hands with your parent as you pray may feel right, and may be very comforting, for both of you. Read Scripture together. Try something from one of the Gospels: Matthew, Mark, Luke, or John. They're filled with Jesus' words of love.

There may be times when it helps to pray privately in silent prayer. Hold Mom's hand or sit beside Dad's bed as he sleeps, and silently tell God what you're thinking and what you're feeling. Ask for God's comfort and encouragement.

What if your parent wants to pray together and you don't want to? Do it anyway. It probably means a lot to your parent. And later, after your mother or father is gone, having done it may mean a lot to you. Are you being hypocritical if you turn to prayer now? No. Just the opposite. You're being true to how you feel.

In Catholic tradition there are three expressions of prayer: vocal prayer, meditation, and contemplative prayer. Vocal prayer combines body and soul: we express outwardly the interior prayers of the heart. Saying the Our Father is an example of vocal prayer. Meditation uses thought, imagination, emotion, and desire. It is the meeting of our faith and the reality of our own life. Contemplative prayer expresses the true mystery of prayer. It is a most intimate relationship with God achieved through a faith-filled gaze, attentiveness, and silent love.

Reflect on these words of Pope John Paul II about the "art of prayer":

This training in holiness calls for a Christian life distinguished above all in *the art of prayer*. . . . But we well know that prayer cannot be taken for granted. We have to learn to pray: as it were learning this art ever anew from the lips of the Divine Master himself, like the first disciples: "Lord, teach us to pray!" (Luke 11:1). Prayer develops that conversation with Christ which makes us his intimate friends: "Abide in me and I in you" (John 15:4). . . . This reciprocity opens us, through Christ and in Christ, to contemplation of the Father's face. Learning this . . . and living it fully, above all in the liturgy, the summit and source of the Church's life, but also in personal experience, is the secret of a truly vital Christianity, which has no reason to fear the future, because it returns continually to the sources and finds in them new life. (*Novo Millennio Ineunte*, 2000)

Jesus Christ, teach me to pray. I want to learn more than just words. I want to be close to you. I want a personal relationship. Just you and me! Can we really be friends? Amen.

Responsibilities of the Church and Your Parish

While dioceses and parishes are doing a better job of addressing the needs of seniors, in general the scope of that service has not yet broadened to include support for caregivers. Simply put, the church hasn't caught up with you yet. You are a pioneer—a trailblazer. Where you are leading, the institutional church is beginning to follow. There will come a day when every parish will offer support for caregivers. When that day arrives, pro-life offices will offer material on caregiving, including how to help caregivers. Respect Life Sunday sermons will feature this unique ministry, and at those Masses caregivers will be remembered in the prayers of the faithful.

This will happen in large part because of the work you are doing today. Your legacy will include helping not only families, communities, and the workforce find ways to assist caregivers, but the church, too. You are making the challenge of caregiving less daunting for future generations of caregivers.

Here is what the American bishops have said about caregivers, along with some suggestions for how a parish can help its caregivers right now. This is from the United States Conference of Catholic Bishops' "Blessings of Age: A Pastoral Message on Growing Older within the Faith Community" (1999):

> We know that caregivers themselves need care. The responsibilities of caregiving can be emotionally and physically exhausting. Some of you are simultaneously caring for children and older relatives. Many of you are employed; some

of you have had to adjust work schedules. Finances can be a serious concern. Some of you who are priests and religious are also dealing with these issues. You have a right to expect support from: . . .

Your Faith Community

The parish has a responsibility to provide spiritual and other support for caregivers, for example, by helping to form support groups for caregivers, referring you to community resources, sponsoring adult education programs that deal with issues of particular concern to caregivers, or periodically recognizing and blessing caregivers.

Too often, however, as a Church and as a society we have not provided adequately for the needs of caregivers. As more people provide care—and as more people receive care for longer periods of time—we must respond to this new reality. We must look for ways to support caregivers who are themselves growing older, who are trying to balance multiple responsibilities, and who can expect to provide care for a number of years. Respite care is one possibility to explore.

"Blessings of Age" is available through the publishing department of the United States Conference of Catholic Bishops (USCCB) by calling (1-800) 235-8722; from outside the United States or in the Washington, DC, metropolitan area, dial (202) 722-8716. The text of "Blessings of Age" is also available on the USCCB Web site at www.usccb.org/laity/blessings.

Holy Spirit, inspire the church to fulfill its mission to serve the elderly and their caregivers. With the support of the church, help caregivers recognize the spiritual role of caregiving. Amen.

How Your Parish Can Support Caregivers

Any parish beginning to establish a ministry for caregivers would be wise to keep three basic points in mind.

First, parish members who are caregivers may not use that word to describe themselves because they truly don't see themselves as that. It's not uncommon for a caregiver to define his or her role as "just helping Mom [or Dad] with a few things." What this means is that when the parish announces a new service or program for caregivers, the caregivers themselves may not realize it applies to them and that it is being offered to help them.

Second, because caregivers have extremely busy schedules and little or no energy to spare, it can be difficult for them to attend a meeting or other event, even one designed just for them.

And third, because caregiving is very personal and no caregiver is in it for the glory, the caregivers in a parish may be uncomfortable with any form of public recognition.

With those points in mind, here are some suggestions for starting or enhancing a ministry to caregivers in a parish:

- Get and read a copy of the United States Conference of Catholic Bishops' "Blessings of Age." Purchase copies and make them available for parishioners.
- Survey the parish to identify the needs of the caregivers in your community.

- Collect and distribute information from the local Area Agency on Aging, diocesan programs, the Internet, and other sources.

- Start a caregiver support group.

- Talk about caregivers in homilies and remember them in the prayers of the faithful at Mass.

- Provide caregiver information on a regular basis in the parish bulletin and school publications and on the parish Web site.

- Instruct parish pastoral ministers making visits to the homebound to also offer assistance and encouragement to their caregivers.

- Host a "Caregivers Day" to honor your families' caregivers with an event that recognizes their contributions, offers them information to help them in their tasks, and gives them an opportunity to meet and pray with fellow caregivers. (Include respite care as part of the event for those who need it.)

- Get parish groups—such as the Knights of Columbus—interested in finding ways to help.

- Sponsor educational presentations for pastoral ministers and parish staff to increase their awareness of a caregiver's roles and needs.

- Set up a prayer chain so that fellow parishioners can remember the needs of caregivers in their prayers.

Lord, help parishes find ways to support family caregivers. Inspire new, creative, compassionate services to address their needs. Then help parishes share and learn from one another. With your help the parish community can truly give care to caregivers. Amen.

4

What to Expect . . . and What to Do about It

Have patience with all things, but chiefly have patience with yourself. Do not lose courage in considering your own imperfections, but instantly set about remedying them—every day begin the task anew.

—St. Francis de Sales

Handling Unexpected Emotions

Caregiving is stressful work. It can unleash a torrent of unexpected emotions. It brings many challenges that often have no clear solution. Here is a sketch of some of the emotional and physical challenges you may encounter, along with some ideas about how to handle them wisely.

Anger

At times, anger can be a dominant emotion in the relationship between aging parent and adult child. Both people are drained, physically and emotionally. Your mother sees so many losses that her life seems out of control. Dad can feel angry because he thinks you owe him something in return for all his years of parenting, and he may not think he's getting a fair shake.

You're angry at what's happening to your mother or father, whose health continues to deteriorate. You want to reverse the deterioration, or at least stop it, but you can't. You might be mad at Dad for getting old. Mad at Mom for fighting you when you try to help. Mad at health-care professionals who don't seem to understand that this is *your* parent, and that makes it different. Mad at your siblings, who seem to be doing nothing or doing only the wrong thing. After you get mad at all these people, you get mad at God for letting all this happen.

Perhaps, after helping your parent, you come home and find that your spouse and children are angry at *you*. They resent the time you are spending with Grandma or Grandpa. You just don't have any energy left, and you've used up all your patience. At work, at home, and out in public, the slightest problem makes you clench your teeth and seethe.

Identifying why you and your parent are having these feelings can be an important first step. It may also help you as a caregiver if you do the following:

- Remember that Mom or Dad is not necessarily mad at you. You may simply be the target because you're there or because you make him or her face all those fears head-on.
- Try to find some time for yourself.

- Look for a support group where you can "dump" some of that anger, or turn to a friend for support.
- Forgive yourself.
- Keep in mind that getting angry with your parent doesn't mean you don't love him or her.
- Go back and apologize. Don't let guilt over that anger eat you up. You can start over again.

Dear God, I'm sorry for the times I'm angry. I seem to run out of patience before my work is done. Give me the gift of patience so that I will be able to always give compassionate care. Amen.

Guilt

The problem with guilt is that sometimes we deserve it. We've all made mistakes; we hurt people; we're lazy or arrogant or selfish and we feel bad about that. Guilt can goad us into being better people. In the same way that the body uses pain to signal an injury that needs attending, the conscience can send a message of guilt that forces us to examine our actions. Guilt makes us consider what we have done and what we have failed to do.

All too frequently for the adult child caring for an aging parent, that guilt alarm never stops ringing. That examination of one's actions becomes perpetual. The feelings of frustration and inadequacy and doubt never cease.

Sometimes it helps to realize that no matter what you do, the guilt is likely to be there.

You feel *guilty* because you don't stop in and see Mom every day. Or you feel *guilty* because you're spending too much time helping her and you think you're neglecting your spouse and kids.

You feel *guilty* because you don't live closer to Dad now that he needs extra help. Or you feel *guilty* because you're the sibling who does live close by and you're resentful that the others don't know the day-to-day hassles you're facing.

You feel *guilty* that Mom gets out of bed and walks to the living room when your sister visits her but refuses to do that for you. You must be pampering her, doing too much. Or you feel *guilty* that she isn't doing well right now. You must be pushing her too hard.

You feel *guilty* that sometimes you get mad at Dad because he won't listen to your suggestions. Or you feel *guilty* that you're not more involved in helping him decide what to do and helping him get it done.

You feel *guilty* because Mom wasn't very good at being a parent and sometimes you just don't like her very much. Or you feel *guilty* because she was a super parent and now she needs your help and you're not coming through for her the way she did for you.

You feel *guilty* because you've been a pretty good son or daughter all your life, but now, when Dad is really relying on you, you're just not making it. Or you feel *guilty* because you were pretty wild when you were younger and you didn't listen to him and you know that hurt him.

You feel *guilty* that you didn't go into nursing or some other career that would really benefit Mom now. Or you feel *guilty* that you can help all kinds of people at work, but Mom just drives you up the wall.

You feel *guilty* about feeling *guilty* all the time. Or you feel *guilty* for giving yourself a break and not feeling *guilty*.

And maybe hardest of all, you feel *guilty* because sometimes you imagine what a relief it will be when Dad has died. And then you can't believe you feel this way.

As if your emotions aren't already stirred up, overworked, and muddled enough, your parents, siblings, spouse, and kids might not be blameless in this area, either. Mom or Dad knows what buttons to push—with a phrase, a gesture, a sigh, a stare—to make you feel like a guilty little kid. Your brothers and sisters likewise haven't forgotten your emotional weak spots, and at times they're not above exploiting that knowledge. Your spouse can pour on guilt. Your children—even the little ones—can be masters at using guilt to manipulate you. And society would have you believe all the elderly are poor, lonely, forgotten people because of an adult child's selfishness. And, it claims, placing a loved one in a nursing home—or even considering such a move—is always cruel and immoral.

While your head may realize these things aren't so, sometimes your heart seems to believe them. The truth is that even after a parent dies, the guilt can live on in a flurry of: "I should have . . ." "I shouldn't have . . ." "Why did I . . . ?" "Why didn't I . . . ?" Guilt can easily become a constant companion, and if left unchecked, if allowed to race freely, it continuously feeds the twin fires of exhaustion and anger.

You're unlikely to eliminate guilt from your mind, but there are some strategies you can use to keep it under control.

Remember that *you are not perfect*. You will always fall short. You will make mistakes. This is something you need to accept.

Remember that *you don't have to do everything* for an aging parent. It is not required that you meet all of Dad's needs yourself. Give away some of that work. If there isn't enough time to clean his house and make all his meals, or if you can't bring yourself to give Dad a bath, there are very competent, qualified people who can do those things. Instead, use your time and energy to do those things with him that you really want to do—the things that mean the most to you and to him. Who ever heard of a grieving caregiver saying, "No, I didn't get to talk much to Dad near the end, but I'm just so thankful I kept his kitchen floor spotless"?

Remember that *you can set limits*. As Mom's health continues to fail, she's going to need more and more attention, but that does not mean you will be able to continue to meet that need. Permit yourself to say, "I can't do that."

Remember that *sooner is better than later*. Don't wait for a crisis to arise before getting supplemental help.

Remember that *there are others who are facing the same insurmountable challenges you are*. There are support groups available whose members will listen and understand.

Finally, remember that *no matter how much you do for an aging parent, his or her health is going to deteriorate*. Your parent is going to die. And it's not your fault.

> My dear Father in heaven, I'm sorry for my mistakes. Please remember my good choices, times when I acted just as you would want, and forgive the rest. Amen.

Exhaustion

Exhaustion is more than just being tired. It's being tired for weeks, for months. The people around you can't help but notice if you've become exhausted. It's not unusual for them to comment on it. The typical response from the exhausted caregiver is to deny it. "If I say how tired I am, I feel disloyal to my parent." Or if you admit the problem, you may be expected to somehow change your behavior, and change seems impossible. At the same time, exhaustion can bring on a sense of helplessness.

The symptoms of exhaustion aren't hard to spot. They include

- Extreme fatigue: even when you do get the chance to sleep, it isn't a restful sleep
- More intense emotions: you get angry more quickly and are less patient; you feel a deep sadness that may lead to depression
- More arguments with your spouse, your children, your siblings, even your parent
- A change in your eating habits
- A haggard appearance
- Poor judgment
- Trouble remembering things
- A constant feeling of being overloaded and stressed
- Fear of "crashing," breaking down and then not being able to care for your parent, or yourself

Here are some strategies for dealing with exhaustion:

Don't deny the problem. Admit that being exhausted isn't good for you personally or for you as a caregiver. An exhausted caregiver can't be a good caregiver.

Give yourself a tiny break. A minute or two. Go into the bathroom, shut the door, and wash your face with cool water. Or walk out onto the porch by yourself and take a few deep breaths. Taking a day off may seem impossible, but you can take a one-minute break. And you can build on that.

Get help. If you have a sibling who lives in another part of the country, this would be a good time to ask him or her to come back home for a week or two and give you a break. Look into respite care (see the next section). Even a few hours once a week can help a lot.

Try to get some exercise. A daily walk around the block will make a difference.

Remember that it's better to prevent exhaustion than to reach that point and have to come back from it. You're not being selfish if you take breaks, get some exercise, eat right, get your sleep, and ask for help.

Consider joining a caregivers support group. Many caregivers find it extremely beneficial. Some groups offer care for your parent while you attend the meetings.

Realize that the best way to be a good caregiver, to be good to your parent, is to be good to yourself. If you continue to take care of yourself, you can continue to provide the first-rate, loving, compassionate care you want your parent to have.

Gracious God, I'm so tired. I don't think I can do any more. Please let me be with you, to have a place to rest, to find comfort, to regain my energy, to be the caregiver I want to be. Amen.

Respite Care

Come to me, all you that are weary and are carrying heavy burdens, and I will give you rest. Take my yoke upon you, and learn from me; for I am gentle and humble in heart, and you will find rest for your souls. For my yoke is easy, and my burden is light.

—MATTHEW 11:28–30

Human beings weren't created to be responsible for someone else twenty-four hours a day, seven days a week, fifty-two weeks a year. Our bodies and our minds simply can't maintain that grueling schedule. But in many ways, that's exactly what many primary caregivers try to do. And it's not good for them or for the people in their care.

Respite care is a term that's becoming more common. It is a break for someone who is taking care of an ill person. In some instances, the caregiver is a mother taking care of her child who is severely disabled; in others, it's an adult child caring for a sick parent. In still others, it's one senior taking care of his or her ill spouse. No matter what the particular circumstances may be, the basic truth is the same: a primary caregiver needs to take breaks or will soon be unable to take care of anyone, including him- or herself.

These are some points to consider:

Caregiving is physically and emotionally draining. Often caregivers experience a tremendous sense of responsibility coupled with strong feelings of guilt: *I'm not doing enough. I'm not doing this well. Sometimes I don't want to do this and I wish someone else would.* We need a break from this. Without a break, anger may surface, along with an increased risk of physical and verbal abuse directed at the one being cared for. If abuse is happening already, it's a clear indication that respite care is not only needed but also overdue.

Respite care needs to be regular and frequent. It does not mean a week off every six months or a free weekend every few months (although those types of breaks are also very helpful and healthy). Good respite care means several hours once or twice a week away from the situation, with someone else assuming the role of caregiver. You may need to work to accomplish this. It can be hard for you, a primary caregiver, to allow someone else to do your job, even for a short while. Family members may not understand why you need to get away. And the person in your care may not understand either. He or she may add to your guilt by apologizing for being such a "burden."

Don't be surprised if you feel guilty when you're taking a break. You need to remember that respite care will help you be a better caregiver. Taking that short step back from the immediate situation will help you see it better. It will give you a moment to catch your breath.

Use the respite wisely. Don't fill the time running errands for the person in your care, going grocery shopping, getting the car fixed, and so on. Do something for yourself. Have lunch with a friend. Check out a support group for people facing the same situation you are. Go bowling. Play a round of golf. See a movie. Visit the library. Sit in a coffee shop and read the newspaper. Do what you used to like to do but no longer have the time for.

To find someone to help you with respite care, consult the local Catholic social service agency. Call Senior Information and Assistance, a program run by the local Area Agency on Aging. Ask for help from siblings, fellow parishioners, friends, neighbors, the community, and social service professionals. Many people would like to help but really don't know what you need, so they offer a vague "Just let me know what I can do." Believe them. Let them know specifically what they can do. Keep in mind that there may be state money available to cover the cost of respite care, *even for people who are not considered low-income.*

One final point: if your spouse or sibling is the caregiver, he or she may be reluctant to say, "I need some time off" and may be waiting for a push from you to begin to take those vital breaks. Take the initiative in suggesting some time off.

Lord, I need to take a break. I need to be away from the responsibilities of caregiving. Help the caregiver who will be filling in for me. Take good care of my parent for me. I know you will. You've been doing it longer than I have. Thank you. Amen.

The Need to Talk

When you're taking care of an aging parent, you may think that no one else in the world understands what you're going through. To a certain extent, you're right. No one else in the world has the same history with their parent as you have with yours. But don't assume that no one else can even come close to comprehending what you're going through. No matter where you are on that broad "continuum of caregiving," other people have been there, too. You can talk to others about it. In fact, you *need* to give words to emotions that are filling your mind and your heart.

Resist the temptation to remain silent. Unless you unburden yourself, that inner turmoil will only get worse. Talking to others might mean overcoming a lifelong reluctance to seek help for emotional distress. It's the same as seeking medical attention for a physical problem. If you had appendicitis, would you simply tough it out?

But where can you go for help? You have many choices:

A professional counselor in the field of aging. This person will not supply "the answer." Rather, a counselor will help you find the most workable solution. He or she can help you identify and label some of the feelings you're having and explain how typical, and normal, these emotions are for a person going through all the things you're experiencing.

A professionally run support group. This is a good place to express your feelings without listeners jumping in with solutions or judgments. Sometimes it's easier to "unload" when surrounded by concerned strangers rather than family and friends. A group like this also offers a feeling of support from the sharing that takes place. And you can learn from other people's experiences. However, this may *not* be the best choice for you if you feel like a "caregiver" to everyone; if you begin to pick up on their troubles and worry about their problems, it doesn't help them or you.

Your priest. Remember the spiritual support available from your parish priest. He can listen to you, pray with you, administer the sacraments, and remind you that God is always available for comfort and support.

A friend. This needs to be someone to whom you can say, "I don't want answers, advice, or solutions. I just need to talk." Some individuals, however well-intentioned, can't help offering advice. That doesn't mean they aren't good people or good friends. They just aren't the right ones to meet your needs in this area. A good way of telling if someone is the right person is the way you feel after you've talked to him or her. You shouldn't feel worse.

Holy Spirit, I need to talk to someone, to share my feelings and experiences. Help me find someone who will listen without judging. Someone who will support without taking over. Someone who will understand. Amen.

5

Caregiving Is a Family Affair

You and Your Siblings

As a child, you probably didn't like it when others compared you to your siblings. Now, as an adult caring for an aging parent, you may find that those differences and similarities between you and your siblings have a greater impact: they can affect the task you have in front of you. You and your siblings each have a unique relationship with your parent. You've each played particular roles in the family, roles that have been shaped over your lifetime and that, not surprisingly, you fall back into when everyone gathers together. You each have unique abilities, life experiences, and training. You each have your own way of handling things and your own strengths and weaknesses. It's a small wonder, then, that when it comes to helping your mother or father, there may be some differences of opinion, even some friction, among you and your siblings.

The best way to begin to handle a potential conflict or difference of opinion is to sit down and talk things over with your siblings before there's a medical crisis or other emergency. Here are some guidelines for a successful meeting:

The meeting doesn't have to be formal. Plan a conference call to chat. Or you may just want to make some time at the next family get-together. Be sure to include your parent in the meeting.

Take time to prepare for these meetings. Gather information that will be shared and that will help in decision making. You might even get input from a professional who can lend expertise that the family doesn't have.

Together, make a list of the what-ifs and come up with some workable solutions. The important thing is that everyone has an opportunity to talk and to help in any decisions that need to be made. This means that everyone must respectfully listen to each other. Assign someone to stay in touch with the doctor, handle the finances, see to it that home care is provided, and all the rest. Schedules can be set up: Who's driving Dad to the doctor when? Who's going to be with Mom on what days? (Or, for out-of-town siblings, who's going to call her when?)

Work together. Sometimes siblings just can't be in the same room with each other without arguing. There may be a lot of family dynamics at work here: feelings of anger or resentment, disagreements over money, a history of abuse or alcoholism, and so on. If that's the case, try to find someone respected by the family members to facilitate the meeting. This may be a time when it's necessary to set aside differences and call a temporary cease-fire.

Here are some things to remember when working with your siblings to care for your aging parent:

It's a time for everyone to learn. Out-of-towners (long-distance caregivers) and those who live nearby are going to have different perspectives.

A visit home can give a long-distance sibling a chance to offer the primary caregiver some time off. And the local sibling should make sure the long-distance brother or sister has some time alone with Mom or Dad.

If you are the primary caregiver, don't be shy about asking your siblings for help. They may not know what to do. They may feel a little intimidated because you seem to be doing everything so well. Sometimes it helps to offer a couple of choices: "Can you take Mom to the doctor on Tuesday afternoon or stay with her Saturday morning?" And when they help, remember that how they perform a task might not be how you would do it, but both ways may be right.

There can be incredible strength and comfort in numbers. Common concern for Mom or Dad doesn't have to splinter a family; it can bring members closer together.

Thank you, heavenly Father, for my brothers and sisters. Help us work together to make our parent's life better. We want our parent to be proud of us, to see what a good job he or she did raising us. Amen.

Preparing Your Children to Visit Your Parent

Do not disdain one who is old,
  for some of us are also growing old. . . .

Do not ignore the discourse of the aged,
>   for they themselves learned from their parents;
from them you learn how to understand
>   and to give an answer when the need arises.

—SIRACH 8:6, 9

Visiting an elderly grandparent who is ill and dying can be tough for your children, whether they're youngsters or teens. There are things you can do before that visit to make their time together less stressful and more rewarding for both generations.

Explain things. Give your kids the basic information about their grandparent's condition in words they can understand. For example, *emphysema* probably means nothing to them. Tell them Grandma may have trouble breathing and some difficulty talking. She may need some oxygen. Describe what an oxygen mask does and how it helps her breathe. Talk about what equipment is being used if, for instance, your parent is on an IV or has a catheter bag hanging beside the bed. Kids are amazingly curious, and just looking around may be a way for them to pass the time. Let them know you'll answer their questions after the visit with Grandma.

Explain what kind of behavior is appropriate to the setting. There's no running around. Like a library or a church, it's a quiet place, and we use our "quiet voices." Warn them that all visitors may need to step out of the room if Grandpa has to take care of some personal business with a nurse or an attendant.

Warn them about confusion. If Grandma has dementia, talk about what symptoms the children might see. Explain how she might not recognize them—or you—and might speak as if a long-dead relative is still living.

Talk to them about how to relate. Remind your children that when they aren't feeling well they tend to be cranky, and explain that the same is true with grown-ups. Grandpa may seem angry or get upset easily, but it's not because he's mad at them. Offer some suggestions for what they might talk about with their grandparent. They can talk about school, their sports team, or their pets. Suggest that younger children prepare some homemade gift, maybe a drawing to hang on the wall. Explain to older ones that their visit is a gift, one that can mean a great deal to their grandparent.

Fill in the story. Your children may have very few, or no, memories of this person, especially if you live a distance from your parent and, over the years, visiting has been limited. Your father may seem to them to be only a little old man lying in bed. Tell your kids some of the stories of his life. Help your children understand why it's so important that they see him. It might help to dig out the old family photo albums. Let your kids see pictures of Grandpa when he was young.

Talk about death with your children. Prepare what you want to say. Don't just wing it. This may be especially difficult, but just as you talk about how life begins when there's a newborn around, you can talk about how life ends.

Remind your children that this is an important event. Tell them you hope that years from now they will remember this day, this visit—this person who has meant so much to you.

Holy Spirit, I know this visit isn't going to be easy for my children. But I know it's important. I'm so proud of my kids and of my parents. I want them to realize how fortunate we are to be a family. Be with us all. Amen.

When You're Married to the Caregiver

If you're the spouse of an adult child who is taking care of an aging parent, it can seem that no matter what you say or do, it's the wrong thing. You may suddenly find yourself an outsider as the immediate family closes ranks. You may feel tremendously frustrated about your powerlessness: you cannot make everything all right; you cannot stop the pain your spouse is feeling.

Just as your spouse has assumed a new role, you have a new, special, and vital role as well: taking care of the caregiver.

Here are a few points to consider and a few suggestions that may make this time easier:

You don't have the same relationship with your in-laws as your spouse has with his or her parents. This is simply human nature. No matter how close you may have become to your mother-in-law or father-in-law, your experience is not the same as your spouse's. So while you may feel that the two of you are doing more than enough to help, your spouse may not feel that way at all.

Understand that every immediate family has its own little quirks. Maybe Dad has always had a short fuse. Maybe Mom has never been able to relax if there is one speck of dust on one stick of furniture. Maybe family members never talk to one another; they yell. Maybe they never yell . . . or talk. Whatever their characteristics, they may be intensified under the present, stressful circumstances.

Don't take it personally if you are suddenly outside the loop. You may feel that no one really wants to hear your opinion because this is a "family" matter. At the same time, you may very well be affected by the decisions being made by your spouse and the other siblings. It's not uncommon for sons to decide what's best for Mom or Dad and the daughters-in-law to provide almost all the care. Or your spouse's siblings are no help, so it is up to your spouse and you to do everything.

Sometimes you will become the target for your spouse's emotions. You'll get the anger, the fear, the sadness, the frustration, the guilt. Again, try not to take it personally. The emotions are about something else—the disease or medical problem that is taking the life of your spouse's parent.

It's temporary. This situation will not go on forever.

In the meantime, your spouse is being pulled in many different directions: between his or her parent, you, the children, the job. This is a time when he or she especially needs your help and your understanding. A spouse also needs to hear, "You're doing a good job helping your parent, but *you can't do everything.*" It's hard to hear that. It has to be said gently over and over again.

> Father, Son, and Spirit, bless my marriage. Be with us as we face the challenges ahead. Help me be supportive, understanding, loving, and comforting to my spouse. Thank you for the love we share. Amen.

Caring for an In-law or a Stepparent

Being the caregiver of an in-law can be very different from taking care of your own parent. It brings out unique emotions and requires good communication skills. The same can be true when taking care of a stepparent, especially if he or she is someone who joined the family after you reached adulthood or if there has always been friction between you.

Every newlywed soon learns that you don't marry an individual; you "marry" a family—a family that may be very different from your own family of origin. But even newlyweds may not realize that a promise to stick by each other "in sickness and in health" can include a family member's sickness, too.

Being an in-law's caregiver is a task that's both easier and harder than being your own parent's caregiver. It's easier because you probably don't know your mother-in-law or father-in-law as well as you know your parent, and the roles of caregiver and care receiver may feel less awkward. You have no memories of being cared for by this person. And your in-law probably isn't able to push your buttons the way your own family members can. With an in-law, it's sometimes easier to feel one step removed. This doesn't mean you aren't concerned or you don't provide compassionate, loving care, but no matter how close you are to your in-law, it's just not the same as your relationship with your own mother or father.

On the other hand, it can be harder because you may feel you've been forced into this role. It's not uncommon for a son to want to take care of a parent but the daughter-in-law to provide the care. You may have little interest in taking care of an elderly person—especially someone who is pretty much a stranger. The relationship you've had with your in-law changes; you become the caregiver, and your in-law is the care receiver. In that situation, you can't help but invade your in-law's privacy. Now you see your mother-in-law disrobed and need to help her with a bath. Now you know your father-in-law's financial situation. It can lead you to feel resentful. Why are you putting so much of your time and energy, so much of yourself, into helping your spouse's parent?

These are some suggestions for how to cope with your new role:

From the very beginning, involve your spouse as much as possible. What you're doing is a wonderful gift to your spouse, but it's also something that can be extremely hard on your relationship. Your spouse may have unrealistic expectations about what you can do. You can become the focus of your spouse's anxiety as your in-law's health continues to deteriorate.

Get your spouse's siblings involved. Plan ahead and talk early and often with the family. If they live out of town, maybe they could help with finances (if that's needed) or with keeping extended family members up to date on what's happening. They can offer you some respite time.

Set limits when necessary. With emotions running high, your spouse or a sibling may say, very emphatically, "I *can't* do that." Your silent response, with equal passion, may be: "And what makes you think I can?" Be honest. You can do some things, but you can't do that. Don't hesitate to bring in as much outside help as you need, even if the family frowns on that because it just "isn't the way we do things." Their way of doing things may be stepping back and letting the burden of being primary caregiver fall on your shoulders. No one can carry that load alone.

> Jesus, bless all my family. Help me offer gentle compassionate care, help me love as you showed us to love, and help me always trust in you. Amen.

Part Two
Caring for
Your Parent

✝

6

Conduct an Assessment

The first step in caring for your parent is determining what help he or she really needs. You probably have some vague, anxious impressions: "Mom used to be so active." "Dad's just rattling around that big old house." "My parents are eating less than what I feed my preschooler." Take a step back. Look at the situation the way a concerned but objective outsider would. How is your parent *really* doing?

Here are the central questions: Is your parent safe in his or her present situation and able to do the things he or she wants to do? If not, what steps need to be taken to make that happen?

"Able to do the things he or she wants to do" brings up the issue of quality of life. You need to remember that it's your parent—not you, not your siblings, not your parent's siblings, not a concerned neighbor—who determines what that life will be. If Dad refuses to go to the senior center anymore and prefers to stay home and watch *The Young and the Restless, All My Children,* and *General Hospital* every day, do you need to step in? Maybe. Maybe not.

Conducting an assessment will help you determine how to handle such situations. It requires looking carefully at each piece of the jigsaw puzzle and adding them together to get the complete picture—not simply focusing on one or two pieces. The complete picture needs to include information from four basic areas: physical, mental, emotional and social, and spiritual.

Try to look at each area objectively. It can be hard to put aside emotions, and there's always the temptation to gloss over some area or need because the truth can hurt so much ("Well, yes, Mom doesn't seem to hear everything that's said, but . . ."). Base your assessment on what you see your parent doing or not doing *now*. Don't worry about what he or she used to be able to do. Be careful not to dismiss an apparent problem with a handy excuse ("If he weren't tired today, I'm sure he could . . .").

It's best to begin any assessment by reviewing some good, basic information on the aging process to get an idea of what's normal. Should you worry that Dad seems to be forgetting things lately, that Mom's feet have gone numb? Mom is sleeping later than she used to. Dad has trouble reading the newspaper. Your parent's doctor is a good resource for basic information about the process of aging. So is your local Area Agency on Aging and it's Senior Information and Assistance program.

If your parent has been diagnosed with a particular illness or disease and you want information of a more specific nature, visit the Web site of the national association that focuses on it. Often there's also a toll-free number you can call. Or call information, at (1-800) 555-1212, and ask for any listing under that particular topic—for example, "Parkinson's disease" or "stroke." (Many associations are included in the list of resources in the back of this book.)

Once you have a basic idea of the aging process and any diagnosed conditions that your parent has, you can better assess his or her situation. For more information, see the checklist section in the back of this book.

> God, help me step back and get a clear look at what's happening with my parent. Please give me the skills to be a good observer, an observer who is aware of what a mind, body, and spirit need. Amen.

Physical Condition

Your parent needs to see a doctor for a complete physical examination and hearing and vision tests. You both must listen to what the physician recommends.

You need a clear diagnosis of problems. "It might be this or it might be that or it might be something else" isn't going to help. You may not get an exact answer the first time. Keep asking, report any changes in symptoms, and be persistent. You also need to ask about the prognosis. The diagnosis is the identification of the disease from tests and symptoms. The prognosis is a forecast of what's going to happen because of that particular problem. For example, how long will a symptom last? Will other complications and problems follow? How soon? Will there be a rapid deterioration in health or a gradual one? And so on.

Take a look at your parent's daily routine. How is Mom sleeping? Has she lost weight recently? Is she smoking? Has she been drinking more? Should she be drinking at all with the medication she's taking?

What medications is Dad on now? If he has more than one doctor prescribing more than one medication, does each doctor know what the other has given him?

What about mobility? Can Mom get up from a chair and walk around? Does she need some adaptive equipment, such as a walker or a cane?

Is your parent experiencing a problem with incontinence, the loss of bowel or, more commonly, bladder control? This is difficult to talk about. Although many television ads praise the benefits of adult protective wear, the subject is still taboo in many households. Yes, it can be extremely embarrassing to have to ask or answer questions about incontinence, but it needs to be done. And done respectfully.

Finally, listen when your parent tells you his or her symptoms. It may be that day after day, week after week, it seems to be the same litany of minor aches and pains or problems already being addressed, but there could be something new in there that needs immediate attention.

Holy Creator, I know you formed this amazingly complex human body. So many parts working together to live and love. Make me aware of any physical ailments my parent may have. Amen.

Mental Ability

How is your parent's memory, both long and short term? Does Dad seem confused? Does he remember Christmas 1955 but forget to eat? Can he still handle his own finances? Can he make and stick to a decision, or does he seem to say yes and no in the same sentence and mean both?

Is Mom showing poor judgment? Did she leave the front door wide open all night—in a very unsafe neighborhood—because it was hot?

Does she know what day it is? What time of day?

Can she follow a conversation? Does she seem to have trouble with her receptive language ability (the ability to understand words and follow the general train of thought in everyday conversations)? Is there a problem with her expressive language? For instance, does she use the wrong word or seem unable to come up with a word for which she's searching?

Is she aware of her mistakes, and does that make her feel frightened and angry, or is she oblivious to them?

Is there evidence of dementia—a deterioration in mental ability? Do you need to arrange for a professional assessment?

Father, you gave us a mind so we can think, plan, understand, and remember. Help me see into the mind of my parent. Where there may be some loss, please fill that space with your peace. Amen.

Emotional and Social Health

What do you see? Is Mom depressed quite a bit of the time? Does she not want to get up in the morning? Does she complain of having no energy? Does she burst into tears?

Is she using "suicidal phrases"? Does she say things like "Life's not worth living anymore," "I don't want to be here,"

"What's the point?" "I hope it's over soon," or "It would be better if I just died"?

Is she grieving? Has she recently suffered a major loss (the death of a spouse, failing health, an amputation, or other loss)? Does she seem angry all the time? Frustrated? Resistant to any help?

Is she frightened most of the time? Is she generally anxious or agitated? Is she afraid to be alone at night or does she panic when you say you have to leave?

Has her mood been taking wide swings, from extremely angry to completely passive?

What about your parent's social life? Does Dad seem to be more and more isolated from the rest of the world? Does he get out and see other people as much as he wants to? Have telephone calls and letters replaced visits, and is he content with that?

How does he spend his leisure time? Does he just sit in front of the television for most of the day? Does he have any hobbies? Does he have a pet?

Is he just not interested in anything anymore, or has he adjusted his interests to match his abilities? (For example, he used to love gardening, and now he reads gardening magazines and watches gardening shows on TV.)

Does Dad know what he needs, and if so, can he get it for himself? If he wants to go someplace, can he figure out how to get there—by walking or driving, by taking a bus or taxi, or by arranging to have someone drive him? Is he still involved at his parish? Does he stay for donuts and coffee and visit with fellow parishioners? If he can't make it to Mass, can he arrange for someone from his parish to stop by the house for a visit and bring the weekly bulletin?

Jesus, give us peace of heart. Let us always remember the value of good times and good friends. Thank you for the gift of laughter. Amen.

Spiritual Life

How is Mom's spiritual life? Does she practice her faith as she has in the past, or has it faded away? Does she continue to attend Sunday Mass? Has she faithfully attended daily Mass but now can't or doesn't want to?

Does Dad have access to the sacraments? If he can't go to Mass, does he have a Eucharistic minister come each week?

Is his parish community involved in his life? Is he on the list of the sick in the parish for the prayers of the faithful at Sunday Mass? Does he still attend his monthly Knights of Columbus meetings?

Has he talked to a priest lately? Would he like to arrange for his parish priest to stop by for a visit?

Does he have a Bible nearby for reading? Would he like other spiritual reading, such as a lives of the saints or a daily devotional?

Do you and your parent pray together? Would he like to? Would he like to say the rosary?

Does he seem at peace with this time in his life, or is he frightened, bitter, angry, and confused? Does he ever express a desire to improve the spiritual part of his life?

Most Holy Spirit, come to me. Bring your gift of piety to my parent and to me. I want to live a holy life. Please show me the way. Amen.

From an Evaluator's View

You may have a major concern in one of the areas that obviously needs to be addressed first. It could be that nothing stands out, but there are a lot of little problems that, added together, may mean a parent needs some kind of help from you.

To evaluate a senior's living situation, consider his or her "activities of daily living." Without help, can Mom eat, walk, use the toilet, take a bath, and get dressed? You also need to look at "instrumental activities of daily living." Can Dad handle the finances, go shopping, drive the car or take the bus, do the housework and the laundry, prepare meals, and take the right medication, at the right time, in the right amount?

Once needs are determined—and sometimes it's best to do this with that outside, more objective help—then you can investigate how those needs can begin to be met by family, friends, neighbors, people from the parish, and professionals. But keep in mind that *those needs may fluctuate*. Mom may have to have someone in to help with the cooking and cleaning for a while after her surgery, but later she can resume those duties. Dad might have had no trouble writing the bills six months ago, but recently there have been a lot of extra charges for late payments.

Assessing a parent's need isn't a onetime task. It's a job that needs to be repeated periodically to make sure you're seeing all the little pieces and getting a clear view of the big picture: your parent's health, safety, and quality of life.

For more information, see the checklist section in the back of this book.

Dear Lord, how can I do this evaluation for someone I love? Someone I know so well? Give me the wisdom I need for this critical task. Amen.

Choosing the Best Solution

It's not unusual for an adult child taking care of an aging parent to discover that there are many possible solutions to a parent's needs. After looking carefully at your parent's needs and the various ways to meet those needs, it may become clear that there is no single right choice. There may be many choices, each with merit.

So which is best for Mom or Dad? The following are basic principles that can help a family trying to reach a decision:

You're dealing with a whole person, not simply one or two particular problems. Just because Mom has a safe place to live and is eating all right doesn't mean she's doing well. What about her health in general? Is she getting the proper care? What about her need to get out and socialize? Does she have the opportunity to be a part of the community? What about her spiritual needs? Can she get to Mass? Does she still feel as if she's part of the parish?

An elderly person still has the right to be treated with dignity and respect. A solution should not humiliate or embarrass Mom or Dad. Your parent's privacy should continue to be respected.

Your parent is a unique individual. Avoid any cookie-cutter approaches. Just because one particular choice worked best for your neighbor's aging parent doesn't automatically mean the same will be best for yours. Just because one solution was the best fit for Dad five years ago doesn't automatically make it right for Mom today. It's so easy for a family to fall into the trap of thinking, *This is how we did* *it with Grandma, so this must be how we need to do it with Mom.* Yes, it *may* be the best way, but then again, it may not. The best-fitting solutions, like the best-fitting suits, are tailor-made, not bought off the rack or handed down.

An open and honest approach is always best. It's important for your father to be involved in the decision making, and that means keeping him informed when information is being gathered. He should participate in the entire process. Don't keep secrets. At times a family may want to hide or disguise the cost of a particular service (home care, for example) because Dad won't like it. Invariably, keeping secrets, withholding information, or telling little white lies backfires.

Your parent has a right to free choice. Even if you *strongly* disagree with Mom, she maintains the right to make her own decisions. There are exceptions when intervention is necessary, such as if your parent has significant dementia or is suicidal, but remember that exceptions are rare, not the norm. Just because you don't like your Mom's choice doesn't mean she no longer has the right to make that choice.

Perhaps no solution will be perfectly aligned with all the principles, but often the best choice for your parent is the one that comes closest.

Show me the way you want us to go, my Lord. I know the right answer is one that is in accordance with your will. Your way is my way. Amen.

7

Understanding Your Parent

One of the most important tasks in caring for your aging parent is understanding how your parent thinks and feels. The more you get to know your parent, the more smoothly your caregiving role will go. The task begins with understanding your parent's generation.

Your Parent's Generation

Members of each generation who come from the same or a similar culture share common experiences that influence how they think, how they act, and what they see as rock-bottom truth. Look at your parent's life history to better understand him or her. Keeping Dad's or Mom's childhood, adolescent, and early adult experiences in mind will help when you're taking care of your parent now.

This is especially true for families with strong ethnic or cultural backgrounds. Adult children of immigrants need to be aware of the fact that life has changed dramatically from their parents' generation to their own.

For the generation raised in the United States during the 1920s and '30s, the Great Depression was a highly significant event. Few families were spared the hardships brought on by the Depression. In some families, the breadwinner lost a job. In others, siblings had to be split up because parents couldn't afford to take care of all their children. Children routinely had to drop out of school and take any job they could find to help support their families. Many family homes and farms were lost.

During the Depression and on through World War II, Americans learned to make do, to go without. They rightfully took pride in their ability to accept those hard times and to live through them.

It's difficult for the generations that have followed to imagine the spirit of patriotism and the spirit of sacrifice that swept the United States from 1941 to 1945. World War II touched everyone, from the young men entering military service to those they left behind. On the home front, women stepped forward to fill the gap in the American work force. Rationing was one way all private citizens were asked to contribute to the war effort.

Members of this senior generation have never forgotten the lessons those events taught them during their childhood and young adult years. On a scale that our country hasn't seen since then, American families learned firsthand what it means to be poor. They learned firsthand what it means to be at war.

Later came a generation raised during the 1950s, 1960s, and 1970s, decades that saw the beginnings of the cold war and nuclear threat, the Vietnam War and the protests against it, the civil rights movement, political assassinations, the decline in religious affiliation and practice, the increase in drug use, the push for greater equality for women, the coming out of homosexuals and lesbians, and the beginning of mind-boggling advances in technology. Just as their parents did, members of this baby-boomer generation carry their history into the present. It could be argued that they have a sense of entitlement. Throughout their lives, they have belonged to the largest demographic, and society made accommodations for them—from the growth of the suburbs to the building of more schools nationwide, for example.

Accustomed to the government adjusting to meet their needs, they—more than the generation ahead of them—may feel entitled. Now, if they're helping an aging parent, they expect—and even try to demand—assistance. Now, if they are the ones needing help because of their own diminishing health, they may expect their adult children to lead the battle to see to it that they get what is "rightfully ours," whether it be Medicare, Medicaid, veterans' benefits, Social Security, or services from state and local government.

In a sense, it's easier for a spouse taking care of a spouse (assuming both are of the same generation) or a sibling taking care of a sibling than it is for an adult child trying to help a senior family member. That's so because members of the same generation and background more easily know how their peers think, feel, and react—even if they have never analyzed, or even considered, why their generation tends to behave that way or where those deep-seated emotions come from. Common frames of reference mean they "speak the language" and have the mindset of their own Depression and World War II generation or their own baby-boomer generation.

Cross-generational caregiving can be more challenging because the one providing care has to consider what a suggestion (getting help from the state) or even a word (the "government") means to the one receiving care.

For a boomer helping her aging mother, the battle may be over getting Mom to accept any state help. If her mother's own family didn't accept "charity" during the Depression or "the War," she's certainly not going to want to "go on the dole" now.

For a boomer's son or daughter taking care of a parent, a part of the tension may be trying to explain why the government has come up short on its explicit or implied promises, or why Dad is not eligible for particular services. Most likely, that adult child can offer no satisfactory explanation and, in fact, the government itself may have a hard time justifying what it is doing now compared to what it said it would do during all those years that taxes and Social Security payments were deducted from a parent's paycheck.

What this means is that to understand a member of a particular generation, you need to understand the experiences that shaped that generation—whether it's a breadline, Woodstock, or the Internet.

Often those experiences are so much a part of who we are that we don't even recognize them as unique to our generation. We assume that all people see things the same way we do or that those who don't are somehow lacking in understanding, wisdom, or common sense. Intertwined in all this are differing views of society. The Great Depression/World War II generation tends to put the accent on the individual's responsibility to society. Most baby boomers stress society's responsibility to the individual.

The bottom line here? You and your aging parent were born and raised on the same planet but come from different worlds.

Jesus, my parent and I have our own history and our own life experiences. Help me understand what my parent has lived through—what has happened to mold and shape this person. Teach me so that I can give care to this most unique individual, my parent. Amen.

Independence, Control, and Self-Determination

Your parent values his or her independence. Many of the decisions you and your parent make revolve around this key concept. As you make decisions, try to follow these guidelines:

Encourage and allow independence. A part of growing to adulthood is accepting, and sometimes demanding, independence. Because of chronic illness or mental deterioration, growing old can mean the chipping away of that personal freedom. A goal for you as a caregiver is to delay or to minimize that erosion in your parent's life. Your role is to help Mom remain as independent as possible.

That means you don't take over tasks or make decisions Mom can still handle. For example, don't dress her in the morning just because it would take you only five minutes but it takes her twenty. Don't decide she needs a lifestyle that is as active as her health will allow when what she really wants is a quieter schedule, because she's lived a long and hectic life and now wants to rest.

Whenever possible, let your parent be in control. It's human nature for Dad to want to be in the driver's seat when it comes to his own life. Giving up control, or having it snatched from him, can make him angry and frightened. What you may see as a mere detail can be monumental to Dad.

For example, maybe he has always gone to the 8:30 Mass on Sunday morning, but now you're concerned about him getting there on his own. So you unilaterally decide the two of you will go to the 5:00 Mass on Saturday evening, and you can't understand why he's so upset. After all, you're the one making the sacrifice, aren't you? You're the one doing him a favor. But from your father's point of view, you're trying to ruin his Sunday morning routine. Now he won't be able to say hello to his fellow "8:30 regulars," the friends and peers he enjoys visiting with each week.

Letting him keep some control might mean mutually agreeing that one or two Sundays each month you'll take him to the 8:30 on Sunday. Let him pick which Sundays. Likely, after a while, he'll feel equally comfortable with the "strangers" at the Saturday Mass.

Remember that each of us has a God-given right to self-determination. We were created to make choices. We were given free will. This means that your parent has the right to determine what his or her life will look like. At some point, however, your parent's ability to make safe decisions may begin to fail. Mom or Dad may begin to choose what is dangerous or unhealthy or may lapse into self-neglect. That's still not a valid excuse for you to decide on your own that Mom is incompetent and to take over all decision making for her. It's possible to design a plan including any necessary precautions without losing sight of her independence, her need to be in control as much as possible, and her right to determine how she wants to live the remainder of her life.

Holy Spirit, please give my parent the wisdom he or she needs to make decisions. I want to be supportive and respectful. Help me offer options without taking control. Amen.

Losses

Quite often, what your parent is feeling is a tremendous sense of loss—in so many areas. The process of aging is a process of letting go bit by bit. It's losing many things and being forced to accept the fact that many of them—if not most—will never be replaced. Life is filled with losses, but we experience loss more intensely in later life.

Here are three examples:

A tooth: If I'm five years old and my front tooth starts to wiggle, I can hardly wait to show everyone. This proves I'm on my way to getting rid of my baby teeth and getting "big kid" teeth. If I'm elderly, it's bad news if my tooth begins to wiggle, if it aches, if my gums become inflamed. Where is it leading? To expensive and painful dental work? To dentures? To a change in my diet, to soft, boiled, mushy food? Maybe it would be best just to ignore it. Maybe the pain will go away.

A set of keys: If I'm twenty-five and I lose my keys, I mutter and fuss and fume because I might be late for work. It's a minor inconvenience. If I'm a senior and I misplace my keys, I can't help worrying that I'm exhibiting an early stage of Alzheimer's. Isn't this how it starts?

A friend: If I'm forty-five and I lose a friend it's probably because one of us has moved away. I feel sad and miss spending time with him or her, but we can still chat on the phone, send each other e-mails, and get together every few years. If I'm old and lose a friend, it well may be because that person has died. That's the end of our friendship. I have lost something that was irreplaceable. And it hurts so much.

As any human body ages, there are adjustments that have to be made. When I am young and strong, I can go mountain climbing.

As I get older, I have to limit myself to hiking. Then walks through the park. Then walks around the neighborhood. Finally, simply leaving the house may take more energy and strength than I have. Step by step, I have told myself, "That's all right. I can still . . ." But what now? What can I do if I cannot climb a flight of stairs? If I cannot cross a room by myself? If I cannot get out of bed?

In my heart, I still want to be climbing that mountain.

As a caregiver, you are helping your parent cope with a succession of losses. Now your father may think, *Here is my child trying to tactfully explain to me that I should wear . . . diapers! That's what they are. They may have a different name, but that's what they are. Even my grandchildren are old enough that they no longer wear diapers. This is so humiliating.*

Or *A hearing aid! I don't need a hearing aid. If young people today would just quit mumbling and speak up.*

Or *No, I'm not going to the eye doctor. Every time I go he gives me more bad news, and my eyesight is just fine.*

Realize that as Mom ages and becomes unable to perform the everyday tasks she used to love, she may feel she is losing a part of her identity. Your mother is no longer the "super housekeeper" with a spotless home. Her yard is no longer the prettiest one on the block. She can no longer bring her famous scalloped potatoes to family gatherings. And if she isn't that great housekeeper, gardener, or cook, what is she? Who is she?

At the same time, even with the absolute best of intentions, a grown son or daughter may seem to be taking over. Being downright pushy—or so it seems to Dad. "You think it's not safe for me to drive anymore? Just who do you think it was who taught *you?*" "You think I need help writing checks? Why, I was a vice president in one of the largest corporations!"

They make me so mad sometimes, a parent may think, *but what if I don't go along with them? Will they put me in a nursing home?* That may be the farthest thing from your mind but you're dealing with emotions, and emotions can be based on misconceptions.

How can you help your parent who is dealing with a loss?

- Acknowledge the loss.
- Avoid minimizing both what is gone and the impact the loss has on your parent.
- Allow your parent to grieve over that loss in his or her own way.

Lord, sometimes it's so hard to accept the losses that are a part of life. A part of my life. A part of Mom's. Help me comfort her, support her, and show her how much I love her. Amen.

Grief

It isn't simply that I've lost my spouse. It's that without that person, I'm lost.

—Anonymous

Some losses are permanent. Among the most difficult for an aging parent is the death of an adult child. That just doesn't seem right. Children are supposed to outlive their parents.

Usually the biggest loss of all is the death of a spouse: "This was my best friend, my lover, my confidant, my partner, my support in so many ways for so many years, and now that person is gone. Now I need him . . . now I need her . . . more than I ever did before, because I've never felt pain and loneliness like this."

To grieve after the death of a loved one doesn't mean experiencing a single emotion. Grief involves a host of feelings. It's commonly accepted that there are "stages of grief." But those stages don't necessarily follow a set pattern or stick to a particular time frame. Even after going through one stage, the griever may return to it. How one grieves, just as how one lives and how one loves, is unique for each individual.

With that in mind, it sometimes helps to understand that the stages can be divided into:

Shock and denial: Mom can't believe this has happened. She hopes it's all just a bad dream. She feels confused. Later, she may not remember some of the things she has said or done.

Anger and guilt: Dad is mad at Mom for dying and leaving him. Mad at God. Mad at the doctor or hospital staff. At the same time, he feels guilty. "I should have . . ." "If only I had . . ." Then, too, if death followed a chronic illness, he may feel even worse, because a part of him may be glad the ordeal is over. He feels guilty because sometimes, in the middle of being a caregiver, he looked forward to the day he could rest. At this stage in Dad's grief, others around him may seem so stupid, their concerns so petty.

Depression: Mom realizes there's no satisfactory answer to truly explain what has happened. She feels so lonely. She's so tired.

Adjustment or acceptance: One day, Dad notices he's getting on with his own life. He's starting to return to his normal activities. At times this brings feelings of disloyalty to Mom. Somehow his moving on is a betrayal. But he knows it's time to move on.

Elisabeth Kübler-Ross, a pioneer in bereavement ministry and the author of *On Death and Dying*, includes "bargaining" in her list of stages. If Mom promises to be very good, no one else she loves will die. If she vows to be perfect, maybe it will turn out that all of this is some kind of mix-up or mistake and her husband isn't really dead.

What can you expect from your parent if he or she is grieving? (What can you expect if you're going through grief?) It is an extremely stressful time. That wide, multilayered range of emotions can be constantly shifting.

Your parent's anger, loneliness, sense of loss, and even physical pain can be triggered by any number of things: By realizing the loved one's favorite television program is about to start. By even thinking about attending Sunday Mass without her (many a widow or widower finds it extremely difficult to go to the couple's Sunday Mass alone). By seeing an item in the newspaper that would have amused him. By coming up on Christmas, a birthday, or an anniversary without her. By catching a whiff of Old Spice aftershave. By smelling bacon cooking. By holding her hairbrush or his hammer. By hearing their song played on the radio. By so many things your parent sees or hears or touches or tastes or feels.

In grief's early stages it's not uncommon to feel anxious, vulnerable, and ill. Grieving people often experience tightness in the chest and throat, headaches, fatigue, and stomach problems. Mom may not be able to eat. Her sleep may be disrupted. She may not be able to stop crying. Dad may withdraw socially. He may want to be alone, or he may become more dependent on another family member.

What can you do to help your parent if he or she is grieving? (What can you do to help yourself?) Here are some points to consider:

How each person grieves is unique. Mom shouldn't compare how she grieves, or feels the need to grieve, with anyone else's method. The best way for her is whatever works best for her.

Dad should avoid making any major changes right away, like selling the house or moving to another part of the country.

Mom needs to take care of herself. She needs to eat properly and get enough sleep, even if she doesn't feel like doing either. It may help if, under a doctor's care, she takes medication for a time. Be sure to watch for signs of self-medicating with alcohol.

It may help if Dad "works" on his grief. When a feeling surfaces, he shouldn't automatically push it aside. He should let himself cry when he feels the need to cry, get angry when he feels mad, and so on.

This can be a rich spiritual time in your parent's life, and in yours. Encourage your parent to turn to God.

Mom may want to consider taking advantage of whatever bereavement ministry her parish or diocese might offer.

Dad may want to look into taking part in a support group. There are many groups out there, each with its own "personality." If one doesn't seem right, he could check out another.

Your parent may benefit from professional counseling. A therapist or grief minister can't take away the pain, but he or she may help make it more bearable. Watch your parent for signs of depression and/or suicide, and get help if needed.

Encourage Mom, when the time is right, to consider having her own ritual for saying good-bye to Dad. Maybe it's visiting the grave site alone, or writing a letter to him (as if it were going to be mailed), or doing whatever it is that fits her, that fits them, best. It shouldn't be surprising that she feels a need for a private and personal memorial. The relationship the two of them shared was one of a kind. It is irreplaceable.

Holy Trinity, there's no pain like the pain of grief. We know that our loved ones are no longer with us. But we haven't lost them. We know right where they are. They are with you. Please bring us comfort. Amen.

Confusion about Role Reversal

Cook. Chauffeur. All-around fix-it person. Financial officer. Problem solver. Protector. These are only a few of the roles parents play when they are raising children. Gradually, roles become reversed. You, the adult child, assume more and more of those responsibilities for Dad or Mom. You become the "parent." Mom or Dad becomes dependent on you.

This is rarely an easy transition. An aging parent may understandably have a difficult time giving up those favorite tasks. Maybe Dad is known for his beautiful garden, Mom for her wonderful family dinners. Now someone else will be clipping the hedge or making the pot roast, and your parent knows that person can't do the job as well as he or she did. It may seem to your parent that the other person isn't just doing it differently; he or she is doing it wrong! Your parent may argue, "Just who says I can't do that anymore? You? Why, I was doing that when you were in diapers. Doing it before you were born." Your help or another person's can sometimes be seen as interference rather than assistance.

Maybe you don't want to assume so many of those responsibilities but see that you must. Maybe you can't make everything just the way Mom did for dinners with the extended family. Maybe you don't know how to fix Dad's car, and so—heaven forbid!—you have to hire someone else to do it. ("A stranger? You're throwing away good money for a stranger to change the oil?")

These are two suggestions for how to handle confusion about role reversal:

Go slowly. Be gentle about taking over responsibilities. Don't suddenly charge in and take control. Start with small things. If at all possible, let your parent still play a part. Maybe Mom can't host Thanksgiving dinner but can still make her famous gravy for it. Maybe Dad can't go crawling around under the car but can accompany you when you *both* take it in for a thirty-minute oil change.

Be alert to the emotional undercurrents in your changing relationship. When you were growing up, Mom or Dad was the one who chased away the bogeyman and comforted you in times of trouble. Now it's up to you to comfort and reassure Mom. She is experiencing losses and understandably feels frightened. You've lost something, too. And as Dad grows old and loses his abilities, you are losing the person who once comforted you.

This is a special time in the relationship between you and your parent. It's a strange and confusing time that brings new challenges as it exposes new facets of the love you share. It's not the easiest of times, but it is a precious time.

Heavenly Father, you have given my parent and me our roles in life. We have performed them to the best of our ability. Now we need to change those roles. Please help us adjust. Amen.

"I Don't Want to Be a Burden"

Aging parents are often concerned about being "a burden." They live in a society that sees self-sufficiency as the greatest goal. If you can't take care of yourself, you are not of value. On top of Dad having his pride battered by being dependent on you, he also worries about adding more weight to your load. He sees the pressure that you are under. It seems to him that he is a burden.

Mom or Dad might say, "I don't want to be a burden" when you're feeling angry, upset, or frustrated. Typically, your immediate answer is "You're not!" Typically, your immediate feeling is one of guilt.

Here are some suggestions for how to handle the problem:

Admit that what you're doing is hard. Remember that this situation will not last forever. Fortunately, and unfortunately, it will end. Meanwhile, look for outside support. Try to avoid becoming so overloaded that your parent *does* seem like a burden.

Realize that Mom may need to be reassured more than once. Yes, you told her last week that she is not a burden. You need to tell her again.

See if there's some small part of a bigger task that your Dad can do so that he feels like he's helping out at least a little bit. Better still, see if there is something he can do for you, even if it's a token gesture to say thanks—setting the table or folding the laundry, for example.

Sit down with your parent during a calm time and talk about the idea of him or her being a burden. Let your parent know that providing care is something you *want* to do. Yes, there are hectic moments, but you see taking care of him or her as a privilege. It's a way of saying thank you for all your parent has done for you. You can also point out that you view your parent's acceptance of your help as a gift from him or her to you.

God, help my parent know that to be a caregiver is what I really want to do. It is my gift to you and to my parent. But I can't do it without your help. Give me the strength I need. Amen.

Always a Parent: Worries about Adult Children

Maternal or paternal instinct isn't something that can be shut off once a child reaches a certain age. In the midst of your concern for your parent, he or she is also worried about you. That concern, that love, has been a cornerstone in your relationship. It's not about to suddenly change now.

Your mother can't help but worry when she sees how much her problems and her needs stretch your patience, your strength, your schedule. She knows you're overworked, frightened, and sad. You can tell her not to worry, but she does anyway. She sees the truth.

Here are some things you can do to help ease your parent's mind—and yours.

Talk with your parent during a calm time. Let Dad know that if you feel there's some part of caring for him that you can't handle, you will admit it and get help from someone who can. Let him know that you're going to take care of yourself, too: by going to a support group or out with your spouse. Your parent will be happier knowing you're looking out for yourself.

Understand that Mom may suddenly seem like such a busy-body because you're around her more than you have been in recent years and she's more aware of your daily ups and downs. Maybe you're upset because your child was sent to the principal's office this morning or the car repair isn't going to be completed for three more days. Your mother didn't used to know about these things in any detail. Now she does. When you're down, for whatever reason, she wants to solve the problem or offer possible solutions. Gently thank her for her concern but let her know you can handle it.

Remember that you don't have control over your parent's worry. Even though you reassure your dad that he doesn't have to worry, he does. You'll say, "Don't worry," and he'll sit there and worry anyway.

> Father in heaven, please help Dad understand he's relieved of "active duty" as a parent. I know he worries about me. He always has and probably always will. Give him the gift of trust in you. Amen.

Challenges of Communication

The television is blaring. You went to all the trouble to get off work a little early so you could stop by and see your father, and now he won't even turn down the TV. He stares at the screen and ignores your attempts at conversation or answers you with a curt "Uh-huh" or "Huh-uh." Finally, to your amazement and confusion, he gives you a disgusted look, gets up, and storms out of the room.

What's going on here? Communication has broken down, and you need to figure out why. First, consider that your dad might have a hearing problem. Hearing is a complex function that involves a number of abilities. The mechanics of the ear have to work correctly, or Dad's not going to catch all that you're saying. Then his brain has to be able to understand and interpret your words. This is known as receptive language. He also needs to be able to use expressive language: he has to be able to call up the words he needs to use when he needs to use them. Finally, the mechanics that enable speech must be working properly for him to speak those words in an intelligible manner.

There may be breakdowns at any point here, and they can be brought about by any number of events. Sometimes it's very clear after a person has had a stroke that her ability to converse has been severely impaired. However, a gradual loss of hearing may go unnoticed. Then, too, the mechanics may be working fine but there is—or always has been—a problem when it comes to the two of you talking with each other. Why? Perhaps a basic personality clash. Perhaps a history of miscommunication or misunderstanding that goes back decades. In any case, as you well know, communication is a critical skill for all caregivers. Your goal is to express an idea clearly with understandable words while, at the same time, saying it with compassion and respect.

These are suggestions to make communication with your parent easier:

Be sure to face Dad when you're talking to him. Speak slowly. It may take him a little longer to come up with the right word. Don't jump in and finish his sentences for him.

Identify the problem. Begin by asking questions with only yes or no answers. Then ask questions that *can't* be answered with yes or no. Take note of how your parent responds. This will give you a better idea of your parent's cognitive abilities.

Don't try to communicate when you're angry.

Don't get distracted with unimportant details. Keep communication simple.

Plan what you will say. Not just the concept, but the words, too. This will help you hear what your parent is going to hear.

Remember: if the time comes when verbal communication is no longer possible, touch can be a form of communication.

If your parent has a form of dementia, learn from the experts. Research the field for help in communicating with a person who has dementia. For example, if you make a statement and don't get a response, it might be best to repeat the statement exactly instead of paraphrasing it. Your parent may be taking time to process a response, and a paraphrase will seem like a whole new thought.

Try to be patient. Remember that even in a world of PalmPilots, cell phones, microwave meals, instant replays, and the Internet, some things still can't be rushed. Conversing with your parent can give you a much needed opportunity to slow down, take a deep breath, and remember, once again, what's really important in life.

Lord, my parent and I are in this together. I understand that we need to communicate in new ways. It's just one more new challenge. We have to be patient with each other. We need to talk. Show us the way. Amen.

8

Doctors and Hospitals

The Doctor

When you are caring for an aging parent, it's easier for everyone concerned if your parent has a primary doctor he or she trusts. Your parent doesn't necessarily need a physician who specializes in geriatric care, but he or she should have one who is comfortable working with the elderly. It's also a good idea for the doctor-patient relationship to be established before your parent needs to hear bad news. Dad is going to be much more likely to believe what he's being told, and to do what his doctor asks him to do, if he already has faith in his physician.

Here are steps to take when choosing and visiting your parent's doctor:

How do you find the right doctor for your parent? Ask. Ask Mom if she would prefer someone younger or older, male or female;

then do some research. Find a doctor whose office is accessible to you and your parent, if possible. Ask the doctor if he or she is accepting new patients and which hospital he or she is affiliated with. Some doctors do better with older patients. Mom or Dad may feel more comfortable with a doctor who specializes in gerontology and is known for working well with the elderly. Finally, look into your parent's insurance restrictions and allowances. If your mom belongs to an HMO, contact the service representative for its "new patient" policies.

Make sure that there's good communication between your parent and the physician. Don't be surprised if Mom is very anxious about seeing her doctor and if her anxiety builds as the appointment gets closer. Once there, she may want to be done with the visit as quickly as possible: she may be too brief in describing her problems or concerns and be too quick to nod that she understands what the doctor is saying when, in fact, she doesn't. Or the situation may be reversed: the physician may be too hurried with your parent. Under the current managed-care system, physicians often don't have much time to spend with a patient.

You can do a couple of things to help. Encourage Dad to be honest with his doctor. Go over what he will say before the visit. You can also go to the doctor with your parent (having asked Mom's permission ahead of time). Before the visit, jot down the questions and concerns both of you have so you'll remember them. And take notes during the visit, too. If you have a lot to talk about, ask for extra time when setting up the appointment. The doctor may be willing to set up a back-to-back double appointment when requested.

If you have serious concerns about Mom, you can set up an appointment to see her doctor alone. This is much more respectful than having her in the room and then talking about her as if she weren't there. Also, it may be easier for you to talk about her confusion, her incontinence, and so on without her being there. This conversation could be a phone consultation. Remember: the laws of confidentiality will limit how much the doctor can say. He'll need to get your mom's permission to talk to you. Part of the intake information at her first visit will probably include a list of people your mother has approved to receive medical information. Be sure you're on the list. Even if her doctor can't give you information without her permission, you're free to give him an update. You will need to make sure that any extra time spent by the doctor is covered financially. Check with the doctor's staff to see if it is covered by Medicare or private insurance.

Be sure the doctor has been informed of your parent's wishes concerning end-of-life issues. Have all paperwork, such as the advance directive, living will, power of attorney for health care, and Do Not Resuscitate (DNR) order, completed and signed.

Remember that many diseases have a wide variety of symptoms. Even though your parent and a neighbor have the same problem, they may have very different symptoms. Or they may have the same symptoms but a different condition. Sometimes books at the library are out of date and the information presented in popular magazines is incomplete. Check your research.

Remember that by being an advocate for your mother, you're helping her doctor do a better job of providing care for her. You're making sure she doesn't fall through the cracks in a system that, at times, can seem impersonal and bloated with bureaucracy.

Remember, too, that if your parent isn't getting good care, you can demand it. And if that quality care still isn't provided, you both can choose a new doctor for your parent.

Dear God, thank you for all the men and women who have studied so long and so hard to learn about the human body.

Please help all physicians use their knowledge and skills with compassion. Amen.

Getting a Second Medical Opinion

There's nothing wrong with getting a second medical opinion. Sometimes it's exactly the right thing to do. If a doctor has given your mother or father a diagnosis that just doesn't seem right for whatever reason, getting that second opinion is important. A second examination may prove that the first diagnosis was wrong and a different treatment is needed. Then again, it may confirm what the first doctor said and make it easier for your parent and you to accept the hard truth you're hearing. (Be sure to verify that this second examination is covered by your parent's insurance.)

With that in mind, here are some suggestions:

Ask your mother why she thinks a second opinion is necessary. (If you think a second opinion is necessary, ask yourself why you think that.) Don't discount a vague "Something just doesn't feel right about it." Maybe Mom thinks the doctor didn't really listen to what she was explaining. Maybe the doctor was very abrupt in presenting a diagnosis. Maybe the diagnosis just seems pat and doesn't reflect all the symptoms Mom has. Maybe her condition is getting worse despite treatment for a particular problem.

Don't hesitate to ask for a second opinion because you're afraid of offending the first doctor. Maybe he or she is someone the family has been going to for years. Don't let that stop you. Any good physician has no problem with a patient seeing someone else to get a second opinion. A good doctor knows that some patients won't believe the diagnosis until they hear it more than once. Also, a good doctor always wants to be a better doctor. A good physician wants his or her patient to get the best care possible and also wants to know if he or she has misdiagnosed a problem.

Make sure you know why your parent is looking for a second opinion. Perhaps Dad doesn't believe any doctor unless the physician says the words he wants to hear. If he's chasing after a third, fourth, or fifth opinion simply to get the "right" diagnosis, it's a waste of time, energy, and money. Let him know that it's time to stop.

If you are concerned that the doctor is not listening to your parent or taking the time to explain things, set up another appointment with him or her. Make this one in the office, not in the examination room. Go with your mom or dad and explain what's going on and what concerns you and your parent have. Ask the doctor how he or she determined the diagnosis. This type of meeting could also be arranged with a nurse practitioner or a medical social worker, who may be able to take more time to explain what's happening and answer questions. If you and your parent still feel you need a second opinion, look into it.

Get information on the disease or condition that has been diagnosed. Many diseases (such as cancer, heart disease, stroke, and diabetes) have national organizations with local chapters. Contact them for up-to-date, accurate information. A national organization can sometimes suggest local physicians who specialize in treating that particular disease or condition. This is a great time to use the Internet for resources. Check the resources section in this book for a list.

Heavenly Father, help us understand what's happening. Show us how to find the answers we need and to accept your will. Amen.

When the Professionals and Your Parent Disagree

Mom doesn't want to move to a nursing home. Dad doesn't believe he needs someone in the house twenty-four hours a day if he's going to remain there. Mom is absolutely set against surgery. Dad would be crushed if someone took away his driver's license. But these are the steps that the professionals are recommending. What can you do?

The first reaction you may have to such professional recommendations is "This can't be true." This is a natural response. No child wants to hear the bad news that a parent's condition is deteriorating. It's easy to find excuses: "Mom has always been forgetful." "Dad never had good eyesight." "She was just tired." "He got confused with all those questions." It's tempting, too, to look at this professional, this outsider, as someone who is merely trying to drum up more business. Maybe more than anything else, it simply hurts to hear bad news. It hurts to have someone say a parent's health is getting worse and something big has to be done.

Regardless of how hard it is to get bad news about a parent, it is important to keep in mind that a health-care professional has the responsibility, the training, and the experience to see the overall picture—to assess a person's general well-being, and to determine if an older person is receiving the proper care or if that person is safe under his or her present living conditions. A professional assessment is based on a range of abilities—physical, mental, emotional, and social. Everyone has strengths and weaknesses within that range. Your parent's doctor isn't testing your parent to see if he or she passes or fails. The goal is to take note of the problem areas so that you can work toward a solution. Remember, too, that a competent professional looks at many, many seniors, whereas the average person often comes in contact with only a few older people.

If your family has questions about the accuracy of a doctor's assessment, by all means get a second opinion. If the concern is that the doctor is behaving like a salesman going after more business, know that Senior Information and Assistance can provide the names and numbers of professional assessors who are not associated with any nursing home, clinic, or other senior service.

Obviously, the news you don't want to hear can be even more devastating for your parent. It can immediately bring up tremendous fears and troubling questions. One way you can show you are on Mom's or Dad's side is to help answer those questions and address those fears. Together, you can get more information. You can explore what the realistic options are. You both can join a support group that welcomes an aging person and his or her family members.

Still, it's important to remember that resisting good professional advice can harm your parent. Very often, that advice—though painful to accept—can enhance the quality of your parent's remaining time on earth, and that is what every concerned caregiver wants.

> Holy Spirit, I feel caught in the middle. I respect the professional's opinion, but I also want to respect my parent's concerns. Please help me remember you're with me always. Amen.

At the Hospital

The sights, the sounds, the smells . . . a hospital seems like a different world to most of us who aren't in the medical field. It's a foreign place where we don't know the language, the rules, the customs. So when your father or mother must enter one, often it's not just a time of worry and fear, but also a time of confusion, both for your parent and for you.

These are some suggestions for making the experience easier:

Be sure that all paperwork regarding legal, financial, and end-of-life wishes is completed, signed, and filed with your parent's records.

Keep in mind that you're entitled to ask questions. If your parent has OK'd it with his or her doctor, it's perfectly all right for you to call your parent's physician, identify yourself, and find out what's happening now and what's being planned. In most cases, a physician will be very willing to discuss your parent's condition with you. Of course, this is only with your parent's permission.

If Mom is being seen by more than one doctor, you may need to plan a phone consultation with any specialists who are also treating her.

Once your father has been admitted to the hospital, introduce yourself to the staff on the floor where he has been assigned. (This can be done over the phone if you don't live near your parent.) Find out what the typical daily schedule is on that floor so you'll know the best times to call or visit.

Ask when your mother's doctor makes rounds. Usually this is done early in the morning and again in the evening. These are the best times to see her doctor and ask questions. The doctor may have a great deal of important information to share, so much that a patient of any age can feel overwhelmed. It helps to have two people hearing that information and asking questions.

If you or your parent thinks of questions when the doctor is not around, jot them down so you'll remember to ask. And jot down the doctor's answers, too. Sometimes it may seem as if there are so many health-care professionals seeing Mom or Dad that it's hard to remember who's who and who said what. Make a note of those things as well.

Ask about social services at the hospital and if a visiting chaplain or Eucharistic minister is available. Find out if the hospital has a chapel and visit it often. You'll find support there and the comfort you need.

Make use of the discharge planner. Often this person is contacted through the social services department. He or she is usually a medical social worker or a care manager who coordinates the discharge of patients. The discharge planner looks at what is happening now—based on information from doctors, nurses, occupational and physical therapists, and others—and what will happen when your parent goes back home or on to a nursing home or assisted-living facility.

The discharge planner is the one who lines up visiting nurses and therapists and has referral information about nonmedical assistance, such as housekeeping. Patients are discharged sooner now than they were in the past and may need special instructions for continuing care at home. The discharge planner can arrange for the physical or occupational therapist to teach you about the devices your parent may need. Watch for subtle, and not so subtle, pressure for you to accept more responsibility than you are able to handle.

He or she can also line up equipment for home use, often through Medicare. Don't be shy about asking for items for your parent; red tape and regulations can make it much more difficult and expensive to obtain that same equipment after your parent is back home.

Meet with the discharge planner early, before you receive word that your parent is going to be discharged. Often a patient is given less than twenty-four hours' notice of a discharge, and while it's going to be great to have Mom or Dad back home again so soon, this may not be enough time to get everything set up so that the homecoming is a safe and successful one.

Thank you, Father, for the many people who have dedicated their lives to the medical care of others. So many people have worked together to take care of my parent: to clean the room, prepare the meals, draw blood, do lab work, and provide personal care each day. Please bless them. Amen.

9

Physical Well-Being and Decline

We have been discussing the challenges of acute illnesses and life-threatening medical problems. But caring for an aging parent is largely a matter of managing chronic conditions and adjusting to the changes aging brings. In this chapter we will look at the most important of these challenges.

Vision Loss

Most of us, as the years go by, experience a gradual decline in our ability to see. Getting reading glasses or changing to bifocals is almost a middle-age rite of passage. But your aging parent's major vision loss may be due to illness, not just getting older. If Dad's eyesight is failing, it's critical that he have the problem checked by a physician. If the family has a history of diabetes, he should have his eyes examined more frequently.

Among the common complaints your parent may have are problems focusing on close objects (a condition known as presbyopia), floaters, dry eye, or excessive tears. Other illnesses and conditions that may affect your parent's vision are cataracts, glaucoma, macular degeneration, diabetes, and a variety of retinal disorders.

Even without suffering from an illness or low vision, your parent may not see as well as he or she did at a younger age. In older age, it's common for peripheral vision to diminish, for eyes to take longer to adjust in the dark, and for colors to fade and depth perception to decline. (These vision impairments make driving especially hazardous.)

Look for subtle signs. Maybe Mom has stopped doing her needlepoint or reading for pleasure. Maybe Dad is tripping over things. Maybe Mom looks more disheveled, because she can't see the stains on her blouse or the wrinkles in her dress. Maybe Dad has food in his refrigerator that is past its "use by" date, or he isn't following the directions printed on his medication.

These are things you can do to help your parent cope with diminished eyesight:

Be prepared to comfort and reassure your parent. Keep in mind that Mom may feel especially vulnerable if her eyesight is failing. She may isolate herself, and she will probably be very frightened at the thought of going blind.

Make sure Dad's house or apartment is well lit. Put in higher-wattage light bulbs (still within the safe and recommended range for the lamp or fixture, of course). Have multiple light sources shining from different directions—a single bright light makes dark shadows.

Light the top and the bottom of any staircases.

Make sure Mom has a night light. Leave the bathroom light or hall light on. Have a lamp within reach of the bed so that she can turn on the light before getting up. The "one touch" style of lamp is great for this.

Arrange the furniture in a pattern that makes it easy to get around. Once your parent is familiar with the furniture's pattern, don't rearrange it. Later you will have the challenge of removing clutter respectfully and with permission.

If Dad is still driving, encourage him to stop.

If Mom's place is going to be repainted, use contrasting colors to help her distinguish between doors and walls.

Write down important information, such as emergency phone numbers and addresses, in large, thick print and post it.

Get a telephone with an oversize keypad.

Get a good lighted magnifying glass.

Look for large-print books and magazines and audiobooks.

The next time you set up an appointment for your parent for a vision test, stay close by Mom or Dad. The dark room and testing can be intimidating, especially if your parent is also experiencing some hearing loss.

Be ready to provide the everyday support that can make such a difference. Offer Mom your arm as the two of you come to a curb. Read Dad the menu if the restaurant is dimly lit or the print is too small. Help your parent never lose sight of the fact that the two of you are facing this challenge together.

Most blessed Trinity, the gift of sight is so precious. Help us always be thankful for it. Even if our vision fails, help us see your love for us. Amen.

Hearing Loss

While hearing loss is not limited to older adults, most people think it is, and that might make your parent hesitate to admit the problem. After all, admitting hearing loss would be admitting being old. Then again, Mom may not realize she has a problem. And if you live nearby and see her often, you may not notice for a while, either. That's because often hearing loss develops gradually. Look out for subtle signs: Mom may naturally compensate by trying to see your face as you talk to her. Frequently, she may ask you to repeat what you've just said. She may turn the television volume up higher than she used to.

The change may be more obvious if you haven't seen your parent for a year or two. Then it may be apparent that Dad just doesn't seem to be catching a good deal of what's being said.

As your parent's hearing loss gets worse, he or she may hesitate to carry on a conversation for fear of answering inappropriately. Dad may actually be guessing some of the time at what's being said. Chatting with another person, or especially with a group of people, can be hard work, and so Dad may visit with others less often.

If you suspect your parent has hearing loss, make sure he or she is evaluated by a doctor. Usually, an evaluation is done by an audiologist, who can check hearing as well as speech. (This type of testing is more accurate than a simple beep test in a doctor's office.)

If a hearing aid is recommended, do your research. Hearing-aid technology has improved, and the quality of the aids is significantly better than it used to be. The price can range from one thousand to several thousand dollars. Look for a clinic that is willing to set up a payment plan and that offers the aid plus the follow-up appointments needed for adjusting the device. This can be critical to success.

Once your parent has the hearing aid, be sure it fits. Think of the fitting as the midpoint in this experience, not the final step. Remember, it will take time for your parent to become emotionally and physically used to having a hearing aid.

Here are some other steps you can take to make life easier for a parent with hearing loss:

Avoid shouting. This distorts your speech and makes you sound angry. Speak slowly and distinctly.

Try to make sure conversations are face-to-face. Don't call from another room and expect to be heard. Don't turn away or cover your mouth when speaking.

Get Mom's or Dad's attention first and then say what's important. Start with a "leader": "I was just thinking . . . it might be time to start fixing dinner." "Dad . . . have you taken your medicine today?" This gives your parent time to focus and concentrate on what's being said.

In a group setting, have one family member be the "summarizer"—someone sitting next to Dad who can tell him what's being said, but not word for word (for example, "Karen is talking about her new car"). Make the summarizer a rotating position so the older person won't come to depend on only one family member, who may not make it to all gatherings.

Cut down on background noise: the washer, dryer, dishwasher, television, fans, and so on. Also, it will be easier for your parent to hear the television if other background noises are eliminated.

Check to see if Mom's television has a closed-captioning feature. It may be a menu option or a button on the remote that came with the set. It may take a little fiddling to get the caption to appear at the bottom of the screen, and having it there may take a little getting used to, but it's well worth the time and effort.

Heavenly Father, thank you for the gift of hearing. Help us appreciate all the sounds we hear each day. And even if our hearing deteriorates, please be sure to keep whispering your loving comfort to us. Amen.

Dental Problems

Good oral hygiene remains a basic part of good health. In another of life's little ironies, you may find yourself being the one who reminds your parent to brush and floss daily. You can also be the one who arranges for those annual or, better yet, semiannual trips to the dentist.

With that in mind, here are some points to consider:

While it's tempting to believe "If it ain't broke, don't fix it," another maxim is more accurate when it comes to your parent's teeth: "An ounce of prevention is worth a pound of cure."

A mouth changes as years go by. The greatest danger for a youngster is tooth decay. For an older person, it's gum disease, which causes up to 70 percent of all tooth loss. Periodontal disease doesn't affect only the gums. It can also have an effect on the bones and tissues that help hold teeth in place. Older people can go to great lengths to hide a tooth or gum problem. Be on the lookout for warning signs: a change in eating habits (a switch to soft foods or an almost liquid diet), a change in chewing (obviously using only one side of the mouth or having difficulty tearing food with the front teeth), swelling in the jaw, reddening or bleeding of the gums, and foul breath.

If your parent hasn't been to a dentist in a long time, it can help to remind him or her that methods and equipment have improved a great deal since the 1950s and 1960s.

As with physicians, some dentists are better with older patients. Ask around. Check referral services to find out who works with the elderly. Choose a dentist your parent feels comfortable with and trusts.

Your parent should be involved in the decision making surrounding his or her dental problems. When there are options for treatment, help Mom or Dad in the decision making but don't step in and make decisions yourself.

A person who lives alone is less likely to cook nutritious meals. It's easier to snack instead. Remember: sucking on hard candy or sipping sugary soft drinks promotes cavities whether you're eight or eighty.

If your parent needs dentures or partial dentures, be aware that he or she may resist using them. It takes time to adjust to new teeth. Pay particular attention to the dentist's instructions regarding their use and maintenance so you can help your parent become comfortable wearing them.

Insurance won't cover dental work if dentures have been damaged. Don't try to fix partials or dentures yourself. Repair kits are available, but they may cause sores and irritate the tongue, gums, and cheeks. If your parent's dentures become loose, it may be because of a change in his or her gums or jawbone. Let a dentist check it out.

It is important for your parent's dentist to know if the family has a history of oral cancer. Its warning signs include white or velvety red patches that can't be rubbed away, persistent sores or swelling, repeated bleeding, and localized numbness or pain. Oral cancer is very treatable in its early stages.

Jesus, thank you for the professional individuals who provide dental care. Help them take care of my parent and do it with a gentle touch. Amen.

Poor Nutrition

Helping an aging parent develop and maintain a healthy, well-balanced diet can be a considerable challenge for an adult child. As a body ages, the digestive system is more prone to heartburn and constipation. Dental problems may make chewing painful. Some medications suppress a person's appetite or promote weight gain. Depression can bring on a change in appetite. Dad may simply not care about food. If Mom has memory loss, she may forget to eat or may think she *has* eaten. Finances may be tight. Some older people, after paying rent and utility bills, have little left over for buying food.

It can also be difficult to eat alone. It's so much easier to skip a meal or nibble on less nutritious foods when no one else is there.

And then, too, we each develop our eating habits over a lifetime. While we may know about the basic food groups or the food guide pyramid, that doesn't mean we always follow those guidelines. Changing lifelong habits is very difficult.

As the adult child of an aging parent, you can encourage your mother or father to eat well. This doesn't mean being pushy or disrespectful. It doesn't mean ignoring a parent's wishes. In fact, the more your mom or dad is involved in the process, the more likely it is to succeed.

A first step may be to talk to your parent's doctor and ask for the help of a nutritionist who can tell you what your parent specifically needs. Your parent may have to keep a daily journal of exactly what he or she eats. (The results can be surprising for your parent, but we would probably all be surprised if we kept track of what we ate each day.) A nutritionist will recommend an appropriate diet—low salt, low sugar, or low fat; high in fiber or calcium; and so forth. Encourage your parent to keep this diet. When the family gets together, make sure that foods on the diet are included in the menu. Don't serve your parent food he or she isn't supposed to have.

Check with the pharmacist to find out if any of your parent's medications would react negatively to particular foods (like milk, for example).

Be careful with vitamin pills. They aren't a catchall that makes up for poor eating habits. It's possible to take too many vitamins. And they're expensive.

Keep in mind that some older people find it easier to eat six smaller meals throughout the day rather than three regular-size ones.

Make food preparation as easy as possible for your parent. Freeze small portions that can be heated in the microwave. Make sure the food looks appealing.

Check out local community resources to see what kinds of meal delivery programs are available. Maybe your parent would like to go to a nutrition site at the local senior center and have a hot meal in the middle of the day. Help arrange transportation if needed.

Remember that no one likes to eat the same foods day after day. Encourage your parent to eat a variety of foods within the prescribed diet, and make sure your parent gets the items he or she prefers.

When grocery shopping for an aging parent, realize it's easy to fall into the trap of buying only ice cream or cookies or some other single food because "That's all she wants" or "That's all he'll eat." Like all of us, your parent would prefer to live on a single, favorite treat; like all of us, he or she needs nutritious food for good health.

Thank you, Lord, for a parent who always made sure there was healthy food on the table when I was growing up. Now it's my turn to do the same for my parent. Amen.

Problems with Mobility

We crawl and then we walk. We walk and then we run. We go from here to there without even thinking about it. Mobility is more than a symbol of freedom; it is an act of freedom. But while mobility helps give us independence, it doesn't always last a lifetime. When an accident or a disease chips away at a parent's mobility or takes a sudden swipe at it, it's hard on both parent and adult child. A parent may be forced to admit that he or she is getting old and there will be an end. An adult child can no longer deny what's happening to Mom or Dad.

Obviously, the best way for your parent to stay moving is to simply stay moving. The adage of "Use it or lose it" remains true here. It's so much harder to go through physical therapy and make a comeback than it is to remain in relatively good shape. But that's not always possible. An aging parent can be hobbled by any number of problems: an arthritic hip; a neurologically impaired foot; a leg, or two legs, that must be amputated because of complications brought on by diabetes; an entire side that is frozen by a stroke; and so on.

Here are some things to remember when caring for a parent who has problems with mobility:

Your parent may intensely resist mobility aids. Dad may deny any help is needed. He might "forget" a cane or walker and refuse to use a device in public. He's frightened, discouraged, and angry. Who wouldn't be? Coming face-to-face with a brace, a cane, a walker, crutches, or a wheelchair is hard.

You need to encourage and you need to support, but you are not helping if you step in and do it all. Let Mom complete the task, even if it takes her longer. Be patient and let her do as much as possible. Keep in mind that in this situation, as in so many, you may find yourself performing a balancing act: your mom needs your help, but she also needs to be in control. Finding the proper balance can be difficult.

It's hard to see someone you love struggle. Remember that many times a person has to work hard to gain new skills and new confidence.

Here are some ways to help a parent who can't get around like he or she used to:

When walking with your parent, be sure to slow your pace. Hurrying will only lead to falls and frustration.

Solicit the support of doctors, physical therapists, and other health-care professionals. Your parent might be more likely to listen to advice when it comes from more than one person.

Make sure your parent has the right equipment and that it's properly fitted. Mom or Dad must understand how to use the equipment, as well as the correct posture, rhythm, and speed to adopt when using it. A physical therapist can make this easier. Make sure your parent understands why the equipment is necessary.

Take the training along with your parent. That way you'll know which leg goes where and where the cane needs to be when you come to a curb. You'll know how to get a wheelchair down a ramp. You'll know how to help Mom or Dad get into and out of a car. You'll learn new skills together.

Give your parent time to adjust. The skills needed to use a device can't be learned in an afternoon. Mom or Dad may need time to practice at home before stepping back out into the world.

If your parent is recuperating after a loss in mobility, remember that things may never be the way they were before, but they can be much, much better than they are right now.

Some days Mom seems so fragile, my sweet Lord. Please help me when I see her slowly trying to get around. My heart feels like it is breaking. I need your comfort. Amen.

Wheelchairs, Walkers, and Canes

A wheelchair, walker, or cane can seem like a mixed blessing to the person who uses it. On the one hand, it offers security. On the other, it's a constant reminder of a disability.

Whether your parent needs to use a wheelchair, walker, or cane only temporarily following surgery or an accident or has to depend on one permanently, there are things you can do to help make the transition easier for both your parent and for you.

Get the piece of equipment that best suits Mom's need. These days the variety is incredible: a cane can have a four-footed base or be lightweight and adjustable; a walker can have small wheels at the ends of two of its legs or be easy to pick up and maneuver; and wheelchairs can be electric or manual. Find out from your mother's doctor or physical therapist what will work best for her, and ask her which style she would prefer.

Don't let cost make the decision for you. The most expensive option might not be what's right for your parent. The cheapest might not get the job done. See what equipment your parent's insurance will pay for. Check out what Medicare covers. Look into renting equipment or getting it on loan from the hospital or your local senior center. Renting or borrowing can make a lot of sense if the device is going to be used only temporarily, while your parent regains the ability to walk unassisted.

Make sure the equipment fits. Canes, walkers, and wheelchairs have to be the right size to offer the support a patient needs. The doctor or physical therapist can tell you if a particular device needs to be adjusted or if it simply can't be used in your parent's case.

Prepare the house for the new equipment. This might be as complicated as building a ramp or as simple as replacing a textured carpet with one that's easier to walk on. It might be necessary to move or remove some furniture to make more space for maneuvering.

Ease your parent into wheelchair use. If you're helping your parent in a wheelchair, tell him or her what you're going to do before you do it. "I'm going to turn you around so . . ." "I have to tip back the chair to . . ." This will help your parent build trust in you and your skills.

Keep in mind that both you and your parent need to learn how to properly use the equipment.

Go slowly. It's going to take time for your parent to get used to this new method of getting around. Often, sadness or a sense of loss comes with the realization that a wheelchair, walker, or cane is needed. And it can be frustrating, too. What used to be done so easily, without even thinking, now—for a time at least—takes hard work and concentration.

My dear Jesus, help us learn about all the equipment that my parent needs. Thank you for the dedicated individuals who design assistive devices. Amen.

Incontinence

The subject of incontinence is difficult to raise in many families. Often an older person believes that he or she is the only one who suffers from this difficult condition. But a lack of control over the bladder or bowels is more common than the general population realizes. Even so, incontinence may be extremely embarrassing for your parent. We're all taught from an early age that only very small children have accidents. Having accidents in adulthood, and wearing protective undergarments because of them, can feel humiliating.

These are some points to keep in mind:

Your parent may not admit to incontinence, but there are warning signs you can look out for. Dad might be isolating himself because he thinks it is too risky to venture out. Maybe Mom is remaining at home all the time now and her excuses just don't make sense. Maybe she no longer lets you help her with her laundry, or she doesn't allow you to change her bedding. Maybe there's an odor in the house that wasn't there in the past—an odor to which the person with incontinence has become so accustomed that he or she no longer notices it.

Dealing with the issue is not easy but needs to be done. The most critical step is making sure your parent is seen by a doctor. The reason for incontinence could be a serious, physiological condition or something relatively minor. A change in your parent's medication or the dosage of that medication could be causing the problem, or could stop it.

When your dad has an accident, take care to keep his embarrassment to a minimum. His needs shouldn't be met with finger pointing, snide remarks, or hurtful jokes, but with efficiency and respectful, compassionate care.

Gentle God, this is such a private and personal issue for my parent. I know the importance of dignity and pride. I want to always treat my parent with compassion and respect. Help me. Amen.

10

Mental Health

Mental Illness

More than two hundred disorders are classified as mental illnesses. Ranging from mild to severe, they're associated with a combination of genetic, biological, psychological, and environmental factors. Obviously, your parent's mental health is a very important part of his or her overall well-being. Just as you may need to intervene when a physical problem is negatively affecting your parent's daily activities, you may need to do the same when your parent seems to have a mental problem.

Mental illness can be difficult to deal with because it is often greatly feared and misunderstood. Far too frequently, mental illness not only goes undiagnosed and untreated, but also goes unmentioned. This is particularly true with older people. Seniors in need of mental health care often are underserved, don't get help, don't tell family members, lack good information on both causes and treatments, and view any mental illness as a stigma. Older people often view mental illness as a personal weakness, a character defect, a result of a poor upbringing, or a lack of self-discipline. Older Catholics might add "a sin" or "a lack of faith" to the list.

Appendicitis isn't the result of, or a punishment for, sin. Neither is chronic depression. You can't properly treat appendicitis through stoic determination. You can't treat depression that way, either. Whether the problem is physical or mental, most often the answer to one's prayers isn't an instantaneous miraculous cure. Rather, as the church teaches, grace works through nature. God uses the surgeon or therapist—and all that medicine has to offer—to bring about healing.

A family's strong tendency not to talk about mental illness or to cover it up with euphemisms or lies is one reason seniors can be under the false impression that "no one in our family has ever had mental problems" (or, in a senior's vocabulary, "no one in our family was crazy"). To this day, your mother or father may not know the real story of what happened to an aunt, an uncle, a parent, or a grandparent who suffered from a mental illness. "She had a little breakdown." "He went away for a while." "She had some troubles." "He died in an accident." It could well be that only a tight inner circle knew what happened. It could well be that even within that circle, the problem was misunderstood.

Today your mom may hear of more and more people being diagnosed with some form of mental illness and note that in *her* day that wasn't the case. She may strongly suspect there's simply something wrong with members of the middle and younger generations (most likely, a lack of self-discipline), and she's not about to fall prey to it!

Is there more mental illness today? There's no way of knowing for sure. Most likely, better diagnoses and treatments have made us all more aware of how common mental illness is. Then, too, there has been some chipping away at the stigma attached to being diagnosed with a mental problem and getting help for it. Perhaps a good analogy is the percentage of children today who rely on glasses or contact lenses to see properly. Certainly, at the beginning of the twentieth century far fewer kids wore glasses (and, of course, contact lenses were virtually unheard of). Did youngsters then have better vision? Or is screening better now and are more families able to buy glasses for their kids?

Mental illness can be hard to diagnose. Still, health-care professionals have outlined general warning signs and behaviors.

The following are some warning signs of mental illness:

- Confusion
- Poor concentration
- Memory loss
- Difficulty tracking conversations
- Ongoing sadness or irritability
- Anxiety, fear, or worry
- Isolation
- Anger
- Mood swings
- Poor hygiene or self-neglect
- Change in sleeping or eating habits
- Delusions or hallucinations
- Inability to cope
- Difficulty responding to questions
- Suicidal comments
- Denial of problems
- Multiple unexplained aches and pains or illnesses
- Use of alcohol or drugs

It's important to keep in mind, and to reassure your parent, that there are degrees of mental health, just as there are with physical health. Mom is not entirely physically healthy, but neither is she at death's door. Similarly, she can have some psychological distress without being "crazy."

It's also important to keep in mind, and to reassure your parent, that there are many treatments for mental illness. These include medication, psychotherapy, group therapy, and specific therapy (for example, cognitive-behavior and behavior modification). Whether used alone or in combination with others, each one has the goal of controlling symptoms.

The truth is that all of us, young and old, can do much to foster good mental health. Here's a basic list:

- Take time to pray each day and nurture your spiritual life.
- Join a support group.
- Get together with friends and have fun.
- Reduce stress and avoid overloading your schedule.
- Learn to recognize your negative thoughts and be positive.
- Identify problems and explore solutions and coping strategies.
- Look for something pleasant to do, and do it.
- Maintain your sense of purpose.
- Cherish family relationships.
- Exercise and eat healthy foods.
- Be patient with yourself.

My gentle Lord, calm our hearts and give us peace of mind. Make me aware of the warning signs that my parent may be distressed. Guide me. Amen.

Dementia and Alzheimer's Disease

It has become common to incorrectly use the term *Alzheimer's* to describe all kinds of dementia. *Dementia* is the loss of memory and the ability to think, to solve problems, and to use reason. It affects memory, intelligence, judgment, language, and behavior. There are a number of subcategories under this broad term, including Alzheimer's, multi-infarct dementia (which is stroke-related), senile dementia, and alcohol-related dementia. Historically, all the types of dementia were called "senility." An older person with some form of dementia "became senile."

Certainly your parent has heard of or known people who have "lost their minds" (to use another common expression) as they have aged. Even if Mom is seriously incapacitated because of physical problems, she may proudly and thankfully state, "At least I still have my mind."

Of course she is worried about Alzheimer's. The disease has become well known, and it—or any form of dementia—takes a horrible toll.

These are some points to consider:

Dementia impairs functioning. Some memory loss is common as we age. What's not normal is significant memory loss, but it can be hard to tell what's "significant." If Dad's memory loss impairs his daily activities, if it affects his independence, it is serious enough for concern. In the case of dementia following a stroke, the changes may be obvious and sudden. If brain cells are damaged by a series of small strokes, the changes may be difficult to notice because they're so gradual.

You may see changes in your parent's personality. Mom was once so prim and proper, but now four-letter words are part of her speech. Dad was always so gung ho, but now he just sits quietly.

Dementia will affect your parent's daily activities. Your parent may be confused about what time of day it is. If your parent is out and about, he or she may get lost even in a familiar place.

It's frightening. If the decline is gradual, your parent may be aware of it in its early stages and be very frightened. Dad knows something is wrong. He may feel frustrated, depressed, and angry and want to isolate himself.

A doctor can help. While there may not be a way to positively confirm Alzheimer's disease, your mother's doctor can eliminate other possibilities with a CT scan or an MRI. If she's suffering from memory loss for reasons other than dementia, it may be possible to stop and reverse what's happening. (Dementia, on the other hand, is a progressive decline.) The cause could be a new medication, a combination of the medications she's taking, or a change in her metabolism that's altered the side effects of a medication she has been taking for some time.

You shouldn't accept an on-the-spot diagnosis of Alzheimer's. Ask for additional testing. Ask for a second opinion. Ask for a psychiatric workup. Ask if there's a nearby university medical center conducting dementia assessments.

And if your parent is diagnosed with dementia, these are some suggestions for you:

Get support for yourself. Become educated. The road ahead will not be easy, but it may be less frightening or surprising if others are there to help you and if you know what, typically, dementia can bring. Remember: while dementia is progressive, it doesn't follow a set pattern or time schedule. Having gone through a particular stage doesn't mean your parent won't return to that problem or show those symptoms again.

Help your parent with modest memory loss. In the early stages, you can help Dad with his remembering by writing notes, setting up a calendar, leaving messages, and so on.

Remember that this is out of your parent's control. As the condition progresses, keep in mind that Mom can't control what is happening. She may need to be constantly pacing or to repeat the same question over and over. It doesn't do any good to say to her, "I just answered that." Instead, keep your response short and simple and then try to help her move on to another subject.

Be aware that your parent may exhibit what's known as confabulation. Dad may make things up to fit the circumstances. If he's lost his wallet, then "someone broke in the house last night and stole it." If he's been standing on the wrong corner waiting for a bus that never came, then "the bus company changed the route and didn't tell anyone."

Try to accept the facts. Mom may not remember all that you've been doing for her lately. And, in fact, she may tell others that you've neglected her. It can help to look at your parent's dementia the same way you would view any physical illness: if she had had a stroke and was no longer able to get out of bed, you wouldn't hold it against her that she didn't come to the dinner table. At the same time, it hurts when we do something for someone and we feel we're not appreciated. Remember, it isn't that Mom isn't grateful for what you've done; she simply doesn't remember it.

Realize that communication may be affected. Your parent may experience aphasia, the inability to come up with the right word at the right time. This will make expressive language difficult. If Mom has trouble with complicated questions ("What did you have for breakfast today?"), substitute a series that can be answered with yes or no. ("Did you eat breakfast today? Did you have toast? Did you have fruit?")

Don't jump to conclusions. If you live a distance from your father and he's been complaining about the treatment he's receiving from family members or professional caregivers, don't jump to any conclusions. Check it out. Maybe he needs help, or maybe he just doesn't remember all the good help he's getting.

Stay positive. If Mom doesn't remember the things you've been doing for her or the times you've visited recently, don't scold her about it or test her. Calmly mention the meal you shared a few days earlier or the television program you enjoyed together. There's no point in trying to get her to admit she was wrong, to admit that you're helping. Just state the fact and gently move on.

Look into arranging respite care for your parent. This could take place overnight, for several hours at home during the day, or for a full day at an adult day center.

Remember that dementia is progressive. Your parent will experience a loss of present skills and the ability to learn new things. He or she is going to become more and more dependent on you.

Do the best you can in providing care but accept the fact that your parent may reach a point where you're no longer able to be the primary caregiver. Your parent may need to move to a skilled-care facility.

Don't be surprised if you begin to grieve before your parent dies. One of the great heartaches of dementia is that Dad or Mom can slip away long before his or her body quits working.

Dear Lord, it's so hard to watch as Mom slips away. Even when she can no longer recognize me, help her recognize my love. Amen.

Depression and Suicide

If your parent is suffering from depression—and is not just "down in the dumps" for a while—he or she can't will it away. Your parent can't simply decide, "I'm not going to be depressed anymore." Research shows that much depression has a physiological basis. It is a form of mental illness that is treatable. With all your responsibilities, you yourself might be vulnerable to depression.

The commonly accepted signs of depression include the following:

- A persistently sad, anxious, or empty mood
- Feelings of hopelessness, pessimism, and apathy
- Feelings of worthlessness, helplessness, and guilt
- Frequent crying
- A loss of interest in doing things that were once pleasurable
- Disturbed sleep: insomnia, early waking, or oversleeping
- Disturbed eating: a loss of appetite, weight gain, or weight loss
- Decreased energy and constant fatigue
- Recurring aches and pains
- Restlessness and irritability
- Difficulty performing daily tasks, such as going to work
- Difficulty concentrating, remembering, or making decisions
- Neglect in personal appearance
- Thoughts of death or suicide

It may be easier for you to see the signs of depression in your parent than for your parent to see the signs in him- or herself. Most people with depression need counseling and/or medication. They need to become better educated about the cycle of depression and learn how to better cope with stress.

If Mom has four or more of the signs listed above and they persist for several weeks, you would be wise to consult with a health-care professional and share your concerns. Your parent should have a physical. Depression can be difficult to diagnose because other conditions have some of the same symptoms. For instance, Dad may be reacting to new medication or may have a physical condition that is causing the changes in his emotions.

Your parent may need mental health counseling, and it may be difficult to get him or her to agree to that. Your parent may not be comfortable with that kind of care, for the reasons we have already mentioned.

Mom may be prone to depression. It may be a part of her family medical history that no one realizes, or talks about. Your mother may also be more susceptible to depression if she feels she's not in control of things and if she sets unrealistic expectations for herself. Her depression could be triggered by the death of her spouse, the death of one of your siblings, or a diagnosis of a chronic and debilitating illness. She may feel numb after that and gradually slide into depression.

One of the most serious and telling symptoms of depression is having thoughts of suicide. Dad may talk about it but not use that word. This isn't a natural, coming-to-the-end-of-life thought like "I'm going to die. It may be soon." Instead, it is "I want out. I just can't take this anymore. I'm so tired; if I could just rest."

There is a very high risk of suicide among the elderly. Experts say the actual number of suicides among the senior generation is underreported. Unfortunately, the elderly who do try to kill themselves are usually successful.

This is important: you will *not* increase the risk of Mom committing suicide if you talk to her about it. Ask her if she's had suicidal thoughts or feelings. Find out if she has a "plan," a method, in mind. Her answers will give you a rough idea of how serious the problem is. If she talks about a gun that's in the house or about stockpiling her medications, that's serious. If she's wheelchair-bound and talks about jumping off a bridge to which she has no access, that might not be as serious.

Here are some suggestions for what you can do to deal with depression in your parent:

Become educated about depression. Know the signs of depression and the warning signs of suicide. Remember that depressed people can't control how they feel.

Get medical help. Get an assessment of a depressed parent. Make sure that Mom has a physical checkup to eliminate other possibilities for her behavior, and encourage her to get mental health care and the necessary medication.

Get support for yourself. It's hard to be around someone who has depression. It's not contagious, but at times it may feel that way.

Offer support. Be strong for a depressed parent. Assure Mom that with professional help these feelings will change. Remind her that you're in this with her. She doesn't have to have it all together right now. It's the two of you *together* facing this problem. Continually reassure her that, with help, this is a temporary condition. She won't be sure. She may feel as though it will last forever.

Have fun. Reintroduce pleasure into Dad's life—and yours.

Be alert to suicidal thoughts. Even if there is no immediate danger, talk to someone at the local crisis clinic or suicide prevention hotline. Explain what you're seeing with Dad and ask if you should be concerned. A professional can help you with whatever steps need to be taken.

Here are some final suggestions:

Encourage social activity. Get Mom or Dad involved in the parish or at a senior center. We all need time to socialize.

Continue to allow Mom or Dad as much control as possible in decision making in his or her daily life.

Learn about coping skills so that when the early warning signs appear, a strategy is in place and ready to be put to use.

Take a proactive approach and be positive.

Evaluate your parent's spiritual health. There is no better comfort and peace that we can offer to a parent than the awareness of the presence and support of our Loving Father. Explore what resources are available.

Continue to offer the compassionate care that helps your parent lead the richest and fullest life possible.

See the information sheet about depression in the back of this book.

Holy Spirit, give each of us the gift of hope. Without hope we feel so helpless. Be a light to us when all we see, when all we feel, is darkness. Bring your light and life into our daily lives. Amen.

Alcoholism

The Serenity Prayer

God, grant me the serenity to accept the things I cannot change, the courage to change the things I can, and the wisdom to know the difference. Living one day at a time, enjoying one moment at a time, accepting hardship as the pathway to peace; taking, as he did, this sinful world as it is, not as I would have it; trusting that he will make all things right if I surrender to his will; that I may be reasonably happy in this life, and supremely happy with him forever in the next. Amen.

—REINHOLD NIEBUHR

Alcoholism in a family is a touchy subject. Denial is one of the most common symptoms of the disease. To make matters worse, many older people think that alcoholism is simply a moral weakness and not a disease.

In fact, an older body has more difficulty processing alcohol. Maybe Dad has only been a social drinker, but as he advances in years, the same amount of alcohol packs more of a wallop and its effects last longer, because his tolerance level has dropped. A second factor is medication. Many older people take a variety of medications that shouldn't be combined with alcohol. An older person may also come to rely on the numbing effect of alcohol to deal with pain. While alcohol seems to dull both physical and emotional pain, it eventually compounds both.

Society has a better net for catching the younger alcoholic. The police stop him for drunk driving. The boss notices an employee's productivity is down at work. A husband or wife spots a spouse's problem and courageously speaks up. But an elderly person may not be driving anymore, is probably retired, and could be a widow or widower. The older person doesn't have to get up the next morning and face an employer. A widow doesn't have anyone else in the house or apartment to raise a question or an eyebrow as, day by day, the bottle is brought out earlier and earlier.

The temptation for adult children is to ignore the situation. It's bound to cause a fight, and maybe you're simply overreacting. After all, Dad doesn't have that much time left. Shouldn't his final years or months be happy ones? Drinking seems to be his only pleasure.

Experts on alcoholism answer those concerns this way: First, if you suspect a problem, there probably is one. It will only get worse. And second, your parent is *not* happy. An alcoholic who is drinking is not a happy person. Those final years or months will not be happy for your parent if the drinking continues. In fact, drinking may be shortening Mom's life. It's chipping away at her health and increasing the risk of accidents.

You need to keep an eye out for any warning signs of alcohol abuse: mood swings; general confusion; increasing isolation; bruises from bumping into furniture or falling; burns from falling asleep with a lit cigarette; a lot of empty bottles leaving the house; and "nesting," making one spot, usually a comfortable lounge chair, an entire world, with cigarettes, ashtray, TV remote, glass, and bottle within reach. Keep in mind that mood swings, confusion, and isolation can be caused by many things. But if you decide that your parent has a drinking problem, you need to get professional help. Tell a doctor, nurse, or social worker about your concerns. All too often, if a family member doesn't raise the issue, it remains buried.

Al-Anon is there to help your family. Alcoholics Anonymous, especially groups for older people, may help your parent.

It can be very difficult to bring up the subject of alcoholism with your parent. Do some research and learn about alcohol and aging. Be prepared to give accurate information to your parent, and have resource information ready. At this point in your relationship, there may not be a better way to show how much you love your parent.

> Dear Lord, you are truly the only real source of serenity. Help my family deal with this powerful addiction to alcohol. Help us as we struggle with this disease. We want to stop the destructive consequences. Please increase our faith in you. Amen.

Tobacco Use

The arguments for why a person should quit smoking are many. We've all heard them. We all know them. They're printed on every pack of cigarettes sold in America. Smoking increases one's risk of asthma, heart disease, chronic bronchitis, emphysema, general pulmonary disease, ulcers, stroke, and cancer. Secondhand smoke exposes those around the smoker—spouse, children, *grandchildren*—to a host of chemicals and carcinogens. Smoking is exorbitantly expensive, taking not only money from the family budget but also healthy years from the smoker's life. When one smokes, years of parenthood and grandparenthood—like a cigarette butt—are simply snuffed out.

Certainly the easiest way to quit is to never start in the first place. But years ago, when members of the senior generation began puffing away, smoking was considered glamorous and sophisticated, and the medical facts available now weren't known then.

Your parent may say he or she is too old to quit. But it's never too late. In the end, it doesn't matter *why* your parent stops smoking. It only matters that he or she does.

Here are some points to consider:

Withdrawal can be tough. Withdrawal begins within about twenty-four hours of quitting. The worst period is between twenty-four and forty-eight hours. Complete withdrawal may take three to four weeks. Many people have to try to quit several times before they quit for good. A good deterrent to relapsing is the thought of having to go through withdrawal again.

Smoking is both a chemical dependency and a lifestyle habit. It may be almost impossible for your mom or dad to imagine mornings without that cup of coffee and a cigarette. Or not having a cigarette after a good meal, while watching television, or while reading the newspaper. Smoking just goes with so many things your parent does, and doing those things without smoking doesn't seem right. And it is very hard.

There are many ways to quit. It doesn't matter what method your parent uses to quit. The important thing is to quit. Maybe Dad can do it cold turkey. Maybe Mom needs a doctor's help. Maybe he or she has to join a stop-smoking group. If your parent decides to gradually reduce the number of cigarettes he or she smokes, that's OK as long as the next step is to quit. Cutting down is only the beginning. Be sure to set a quit date.

How can you help your parent quit smoking? Here are some ways:

Plan to deal with cravings. Your parent needs to have an emergency plan for when he or she really, really wants to smoke. For instance, if your parent is thinking about lighting up, he or she could wait twenty minutes. Maybe Dad will walk out onto the front porch. Maybe Mom will read an anti-smoking pamphlet. Dad will get up and circle the dining room table five times. Mom will go wash her hands and face.

Encourage your parent to stay away from smokers for a while. While quitting, Dad should avoid friends who smoke. They can exert tremendous peer pressure. In fact, quitting smoking may cost him a friendship or two for a time. Mom needs to be around nonsmokers and ex-smokers whom she knows. They will welcome and encourage her. Every ex-smoker knows how hard it is to quit. Every ex-smoker knows it's worth it.

Plan a reward for your parent. Maybe Dad can buy himself something nice with the money he's saving by not spending it on tobacco. Maybe Mom wants to splurge on a trip for the two of you.

Encourage your parent to pray about this. And you pray for Mom or Dad, too. Pray that your parent will have strength and endurance and patience. Pray that he or she can succeed, because the battle your parent is waging isn't an easy one, but it's one that's so very important.

Here are some final points to keep in mind:

- Some people who are quitting smoking need to keep their hands and their mouths busy. They chew gum or suck on candy or fiddle with sunflower seeds. They destroy paper clips or fold paper airplanes.
- Dad shouldn't leave his smoking paraphernalia lying around: the favorite ashtray, the trusty lighter, the rack of pipes. They seem like old friends, but they're not! If he

can't give them away or throw them away, he should at least put them away.

- Smoking is a leading cause of house fires. And your aging parent is more likely to have an accident and be burned.

- Your parent should never smoke in the house if there is an oxygen tank there.

- Help Mom make a list of why she wants to quit. Encourage her to review it, and add to it, often.

- Dad needs to drink a lot of water. His body is flushing out its systems.

- Mom should keep some low-cal snacks on hand. If she's on a restricted diet, those snacks must be all right for her to eat.

Most Holy Spirit, I believe that the human body is truly a temple for you. I want to help my parent take better care of that body, that temple. Old habits and addictions are hard to break. Give us strength. Amen.

11

Emotional and Social Health

As a caregiver to an aging parent, you need to pay close attention to your parent's emotional and social health. Despite the losses that aging brings, your parent can and should remain engaged in fruitful, satisfying activities. You can do much to ensure that this happens.

The Need to Have Fun

When you're caught up in the worries and demands of taking care of a parent, it's easy to overlook how important it is for your mother or father to do something enjoyable. No matter how old we are, our emotional health depends a great deal on fun. Pleasurable activities are especially important when illness, depression, and grief dampen our spirits. Unfortunately, sometimes when we need those good times the most, they're the first things we eliminate.

Finding and suggesting something that will be enjoyable for your parent isn't always easy. It can take imagination, work—and diplomacy.

These are some suggestions:

Ask your parent what he or she would like to do for fun. It's important to ask, but realize that your question might be met with a less-than-enthusiastic response. When we're out of practice, having fun can seem like a foolish idea. Whatever idea you come up with, no matter how great it may be, it could take quite a bit of persuasion over an extended period before your father is willing to give it a shot.

Generate some ideas. What did Mom used to like to do? Travel? Collect? Play sports? Read? Listen to music? What was Mom's ideal vacation? What were her plans when she first retired? Obviously the time to do some of those things has passed. Mom won't be touring Europe. She may not be up to attending plays at the local college. The challenge, then, is to find another way for your Mom to continue to enjoy what has interested her.

Gently encourage and help. If Mom used to love to go to museums, find out what art books and videos are available at the library. Keep an eye out for television programs that are going to feature an artist whose work she especially admires. If it's going to be broadcast at an inconvenient time, tape it.

Do it together. Go through the book or watch the tape *with* your mother. This is especially important. The point is not for you to hand her a book or put in a DVD and then disappear. The point is for the two of you to talk about what you see. For that thirty minutes or hour, your mother once again can become an amateur art critic. She can enjoy a pastime that gave her so much pleasure when she was younger. And she can share that with you.

Be creative. If Dad loved to read murder mysteries, read one out loud to him for fifteen or twenty minutes several times throughout the day. If he was an avid sports fan, make a point of being there with him to watch some games on television. ("Go" to the Super Bowl together.) Make a friendly wager. If his diet will allow it, serve a halftime meal of hot dogs and beer. A little room decorated with sports paraphernalia will add to the experience.

Do it often. Put fun on the schedule. Finding something enjoyable you two can do together on a daily or weekly basis and then sticking to a schedule will give your parent something to look forward to.

Yes, it's corny, but don't let that get in the way of your fun. A lot of what ends up being fun can seem corny in the beginning. It might be silly, but it could also be just what you and your parent need to forget about those worries and demands for a time and simply enjoy each other's company.

> Dear God, when did having fun become so hard? It used to come naturally. But now, with doctors, appointments, tests, and pain, it's so easy to forget. Lord, teach us how to play. Amen.

The Danger of Isolation

Nesting is a common phenomenon of aging. It refers to burrowing in at home. The world shrinks to that one favorite chair in front of the television. Within reach are the TV remote, piles of old newspapers and magazines, snack food, and a coffee cup (and maybe a pack of cigarettes and a bottle of alcohol). Nesting is a sure sign that your parent has become too isolated.

We are social animals. We need to be around others. A parent who has become a hermit is in danger of developing a host of problems. Again, the maxim "Use it or lose it" is a helpful guide. A person who is mentally stimulated and challenged can think more clearly. A person who gets some physical exercise, who is out and about, feels better and sleeps more soundly at night. A person who is concerned about others, who feels he or she is making a contribution, is less self-absorbed. A person with basic social skills is going to pay attention to appearance and manners.

Of course, sometimes there are very good reasons for sticking close to home. We all have our downtimes. It could be that Mom has been sick. Maybe Dad is recovering from surgery. But for an aging parent, it's not hard for that recuperative period to lead to an unhealthy isolation. You realize that Mom used to belong to a parish guild or an altar society but now only attends Sunday Mass. She no longer takes the bus downtown for that once-a-month luncheon with friends. She only goes out to buy groceries, and she doesn't even want to do that.

Why does this happen? It might be that Mom's closest friends have died and it's not easy to make new ones. Maybe Dad is concerned that mentally he's not as quick as he used to be. He forgets names. He gets confused when he's out of the house. Maybe Mom is hiding the fact that she's having trouble walking. Or that she is getting dizzy sometimes, or having trouble controlling her bladder. Pride may be influencing the decision: "What will people think? I look terrible." Maybe your parent is simply afraid. The news is filled with stories of violent crimes, and your mother or father can feel vulnerable.

What can you do to help?

Bring up the subject of isolation. Ask Dad why he doesn't want to go out. Maybe there's a very simple explanation and solution.

Find out what community programs and activities are available. Visit a local senior center with your father. Better still, make a visit with Dad and take along a friend of his. Go on a tour. Have lunch there. Meet some of the other participants. Check the schedule and see what would be fun for your father and his friend to do. Your local Senior Information and Assistance program can help you find the nearest senior center.

Facilitate activities. Offer to drive Mom to an afternoon recital or a movie matinee and then pick her up. Find out about bus schedules, cab rates, and senior van pools. Encourage Dad to volunteer. Be on hand—as cohost and caterer—so Mom or Dad can have company over for lunch or coffee and cake.

Find out what's happening at the parish. Help Mom become more active there. Most likely a fellow parishioner is going to the presentation, party, or meal and would be happy to act as chauffeur.

Don't expect things to turn around overnight. Correcting the problem of isolation, like becoming isolated, is a gradual process.

Gentle Creator, you created us to be with others, to be part of a community. Help me find ways for my parent to feel the support and friendship of others. Amen.

Celebrating Birthdays and Anniversaries

Birthdays and anniversaries are wonderful opportunities for fun, but your parent may be approaching a birthday with mixed emotions. Your dad might have a great sense of accomplishment: "In spite of all that I have been through, I have survived. I have been richly blessed." But he might also have a sense of confusion, anxiety, or even dread:

"I never expected to live this long. I didn't plan to. I didn't want to. Why am I still here when my spouse and so many of my friends and relatives are gone?"

What can you do to help? These are some suggestions:

Let your parent take the lead. Maybe this year Dad would like the extended family to gather to celebrate his turning "the big Eight-O." Maybe Mom wants only a quiet lunch with you and your siblings. Ask.

Listen. Your parent may be feeling depressed as this emotionally charged day approaches. When Mom or Dad mutters, "I wish I had gone. It's time for me to go," don't immediately respond, "Don't say that!" This isn't a time to argue. Just tell your parent why you're glad he or she is still around. The greatest birthday gift of all might be for you to finally say out loud, "This is what you mean to me . . . This is what you mean to my children . . ."

Think about the right gift. It isn't always easy finding out what Mom or Dad wants for a birthday present. Your first several inquiries may be quickly shot down with "I want to be younger" or "I want my health back." In a sense, your parent is responding honestly. Often a good present isn't one that's bought. It may be something that gives the two of you time together. It could be arranging to go out to lunch once a month over the next year. Perhaps it's planning to come over with the kids to fix Mom's or Dad's favorite meal. It could be taking your parent to a "First Friday" or Sunday morning Mass at the old parish. It could be arranging to have a Eucharistic minister bring Holy Communion to Mom or Dad at home if your parent isn't able to leave the house. Gifts like these can mean so much more to an aging parent.

Plan parties with your parent in mind. Many older people tire easily. A four-hour blowout or an open house with dozens of guests might simply be too much. These days, with siblings often living in different parts of the country, it might be impossible to get the family together at the same time on the same day. The solution may be several smaller celebrations on different dates. Perhaps you can help your parent place calls to your siblings who can't be there. Or consider a "conference call party."

Assemble a birthday book. Family members can also put together a special "birthday book," either at the party or round-robin fashion if people can't make it to the celebration. Each person can jot down a few sentences on a particular topic; for example, "My funniest memory of Dad" or "A lesson Mom taught me that I'll never forget." Or you could arrange a "card shower," contacting relatives and friends and asking them to please send a greeting card to mark the occasion. Collect the messages and give them to your parent all at once.

Remember the dead. Party or not, sometimes on a birthday or anniversary it's good to pause and remember family members and close friends who have died, especially your parent's spouse. All too often the fear of saying the wrong thing or of upsetting a parent prevents an adult child from saying anything. Unfortunately, that silence can be interpreted as forgetfulness or, even worse, indifference. Keep in mind that the best birthday and anniversary celebrations often include tears as well as laughter.

Mark anniversaries of deaths. Families should note anniversaries of family members' deaths, especially the death of an aging parent's spouse. You might simply spend some time talking with your parent about the person who has died. Maybe Dad just wants a quiet lunch or dinner with you. Maybe Mom would like to attend a Mass said in memory of Dad. Maybe your parent would really appreciate being taken to the cemetery where his or her spouse is buried.

Dear Lord, we all have good memories, memories of times we have been together. Help us remember how much we love each other. Thank you for letting us be together today. Amen.

Grandparenthood

It might never have occurred to you that you're what could be called "bigenerational." You can feel equally at home with your parents and with your children. There really aren't many years that you have both your kids and your parents with you. Not surprisingly, this special time, this blessing, comes with particular responsibilities. As a member of the middle generation, you're being called on to be the bridge between your parents and your children. You are the one who can help them come to know one another better.

These days, that can be hard to do. It's not news that we live in a highly mobile society, and that many grandchildren and grandparents know each other only as visitors or as a voice over the phone.

Here are some suggestions for helping these two generations connect:

Give them time together. They should come to know each other, to love each other as much as you know and love them both. Give them time together so your parent can have a glimpse of the future, and your children can better appreciate the past and enjoy the lifelong gift of fond memories of a loving grandparent.

Teach your children to show respect for their elders. This may take some work. Offer suggested topics: "Ask Grandpa to tell you about his first car." It works the other way, too: "Mom, Mary would like to tell you about her project for the science fair." Remember that your kids are going to pick up and mimic your attitude. If you treat your parent with love, they'll do the same. And if you don't, they'll imitate that, too.

Explain things to your children. Explain your parent's medical condition or limitations (a restricted diet, hearing loss, or confusion, for example) in terms your children will understand. Remind your children to speak slowly and clearly when talking with Grandma. Let them know that just because Grandpa seems grumpy doesn't mean he's mad at them.

Involve your children in your parent's care. Let the children help your mother or father in an appropriate way, perhaps by vacuuming Grandma's room or reading the newspaper to Grandpa.

Dear St. Anne and St. Joachim, as grandparents of Jesus, help me establish a caring relationship between my parents and my children. I want my children to know and love my parents. Please help me do whatever I can to make that happen. Amen.

Writing Memoirs

Most of us tend to think that writing one's memoirs is something done only by those who have made a fortune, gained fame, or accomplished some remarkable or historic task. The truth is that everyone has a story to tell. Each person—an individual created and loved by God—has led a unique life, full of experiences, memories, and lessons. An older person who takes the time to write down some of those experiences, to share some of those memories and those lessons, gives a tremendous gift not only to his or her children, grandchildren, and even great-grandchildren, but also to him- or herself.

Your parent may have become more reflective with age. It's common for an older person to feel a need to review his or her life. While many may consider jotting down some of the highlights, most quickly dismiss the idea because they don't want to appear pretentious, and still others aren't really sure how to begin.

Here are some suggestions to share with your parent:

Just get started. This is the hardest part, but Dad doesn't have to start with the beginning of his life. He can begin by writing a little about something, some time, or someone who was important to him. He can start with one or two of the basic philosophies he has tried to follow or has found to be true. Suggest that he jot down a few memories of his father or mother, the home where he was raised, the day he met his spouse-to-be, his grandparents, and so on. After all, he may be the last family member who knows those things and can tell those stories.

Don't worry about grammar, punctuation, or spelling. This is an exercise done for love, not for a grade. You can always proofread and make corrections later. Ask Mom to imagine reading a letter written by her great-great-grandfather describing his life. Would she treasure it less, put it aside, or have a lower opinion of him if he had misspelled a word or failed to put a comma in the right place?

Choose the method and style that best suit you. If Dad likes to type, let him type. If he prefers a pen and a pad of paper, he should use those. If he feels more comfortable writing a paragraph or two on a variety of topics, he can do that. If he wants to use an outline form, that's fine, too. He can write a book, a collection of short stories, a handful of letters, a journal, or whatever works best for him.

The more you write, the more you will remember. One story, one memory, quickly leads to another, and soon there are many things to write about. Family members will appreciate having a record of who previously owned heirlooms—a ring, a pocket watch, a dish or bowl. Dad could write a little bit about each piece. Going through old family albums can spark many memories. As the two of you go through them, he can reminisce about the family and friends pictured.

You can go multi-media. If your parent prefers talking to writing, he or she can use a tape recorder or video camera to record memories. Sometimes it helps to have an interviewer. You can ask Mom some questions. This can be a very special time for both of you, precious time spent together. If Mom is worried about periods of silence on the tape, play some period music softly in the background. She can show her grandkids that today's music can't compete with the big band sound she enjoyed so much.

Remember that what you're creating is priceless. Dad's "life review" may help him take pride in the fact that through good times and bad, he has survived. Then, too, after Dad is gone, his words will bring consolation, encouragement, and happiness to his descendants. Dad may discover that some relationships with other people need to be resolved. Reminiscing can lead to an opportunity to forgive or to ask forgiveness.

In the end, writing one's memoirs often comes down to simply recording how you have been loved and how you have returned and passed along that love. It's focusing on what really matters, on what life is really all about.

Lord, I want to know my parent's life story and to share that story with the next generation. I promise to pass it on. Amen.

Leisure-Time Activities

Your parent's generation didn't just embrace the American work ethic; they embodied it. Year after year, decade after decade, they took great pride in giving an honest day's work for an honest day's wages. Then they retired. Abruptly, that precious and rare commodity known as free time filled their lives. What were they supposed to do? Some took awhile to adjust to their new state of life. Others acted like the proverbial kid set loose in the candy store.

Defining *leisure* isn't easy. One person's job is another's hobby. In general, leisure-time activities fall into several broad categories:

- Temporary shutdown: this is being a couch potato, which just about everyone enjoys from time to time, although obviously it's not good when it fills up an entire schedule
- Time alone: this might be reading or "people watching"
- Creative time alone: this would include activities such as knitting or carpentry projects
- Service: this is simply volunteer work
- Socializing: this is spending time with friends, family, and others for personal enjoyment

While a recent retiree may find a satisfying combination of the five for a while, that initial burst of enthusiasm doesn't always last. Then, too, as the years go by, declining health may mean adjustments have to be made.

Here are some recommendations for what you can do to encourage your aging parent to keep active:

Understand why Dad may be doing less. It could be that an illness has become the focus of his attention for a time, but as he begins to feel better, or to adjust to his new circumstances, his old hobbies will start to appeal to him again. If not, it's important to know that a lack of interest in the things that used to give him pleasure is one of the symptoms of clinical depression.

Keep in mind that sometimes Mom may hesitate to continue a favorite pastime because it's not going to be the same as it was before. Maybe she played cards with a group of friends for years, and now she's the only one who hasn't moved away or died. Playing with new people just isn't the same for her. After all, it wasn't the card game that mattered; it was the companionship. And even though your mother may want to make new friends, she hesitates. Won't they just move on or die, too? She may think, *I'm too old to make new friends.*

Ask your parent what he or she wants to do. Help Mom or Dad by asking, "What is it you've always wanted to do?" Encourage your parent to dream big.

Help your parent get whatever supplies, equipment, or instructions he or she may need. Check out what resources are available in the community. Some community colleges offer classes for seniors at little or no cost. Senior centers provide classes, activities, meals, and socials. Explore with your parent what type of volunteer work he or she might enjoy doing. The Retired Senior Volunteer Program (RSVP), an organization that helps seniors get involved in their communities, is listed in most phone books.

Be careful not to pack your parent's schedule from dawn to dusk. Remember: the point is to encourage, not to dictate or overwhelm.

Heavenly Father, my parent has earned the right to rest, to take some time off, to do something enjoyable and pleasant. Help me make this possible. Amen.

12

Spiritual Matters

Spiritual Health

If a tiny spark of God's love already burns within you, do not expose it to the wind, for it may get blown out. Keep the stove tightly shut so that it will not lose its heat and grow cold. In other words, avoid distractions as well as you can. Stay quiet with God. Do not spend your time in useless chatter. . . .

In meditation we find the strength to bring Christ to birth in ourselves and in other men.

—St. Charles Borromeo

It's not really possible for you to know your parent's spiritual health. Ultimately, none of us knows the state of another person's soul. That's between the person and God. Still, we can see indications of spiritual health, and we have ways to foster it. The Catholic Church exists to foster it! We can observe changes. If Dad always took a mile-long walk after dinner but now he doesn't, something could have changed physically. In the same way, if Mom never missed Sunday Mass but now her attendance is hit-or-miss, something may well have changed spiritually.

A good way to begin that "spiritual checkup" for your parent is to look at these changes. Keep in mind that the reason for the change may or may not have a spiritual basis. For instance, there's a difference between Mom being unable to go to church because she no longer drives or is having problems with incontinence and her not *wanting* to go to church as often as she did in the past because she's angry at God after the death of a loved one.

On the other hand, as we age we may pay more attention to spiritual matters. Mom may have moved from being basically lukewarm about spiritual matters to being intensely interested in them. This is not uncommon. Unlike physical or mental health, spiritual health can reach its peak in old age. Even as her mind and body falter, her soul can continue to grow in grace.

Are you unsure about your parent's spiritual health? As with other things, you can ask your parent about it: "Dad, would you like to go to Mass more often?" If he says yes, work at arranging that. (Perhaps you and your siblings can take turns driving him, or someone from the parish can provide a ride.) If he says no, this may be a good time to start a conversation about spirituality. Be willing to accept an answer of "None of your business!"

In general, does Dad seem at peace with this time of his life, or is he frightened, bitter, angry, or confused? Does he ever express a desire to improve the spiritual part of his life?

Here's a list of some central issues to consider:

If your parent cannot go to Mass, does a Eucharistic minister bring him or her Holy Communion on a regular basis? Does Mom have access to the other sacraments? Would she like Father to come to the house so she can go to confession and/or receive the anointing of the sick?

Parish involvement: Is Dad still involved in the parish to the extent that he's able? Does someone bring him the weekly bulletin? (It may be that you can download this from the parish's Web site and print it out for him.) Can he make it to a Knights of Columbus meeting or stay after Mass for a special Sunday morning pancake breakfast? Maybe he wants to be part of a prayer chain where parishioners pray for their fellow parishioners? Some seniors and others who are homebound find that this is a very satisfying way to continue to be a part of a parish.

Spiritual reading and media: Does Dad still get the diocesan newspaper and other religious periodicals he's enjoyed in the past? Would he like to have other books, such as a large-print prayer book or Bible? Would he like a daily devotional magazine (*My Daily Visitor,* for example) that focuses on the daily Mass readings or each day's feast? Would he enjoy listening to hymns on tape or CD? Would he like to listen to the local Catholic radio station or watch a Catholic television program?

Prayer: Would Mom like to find out more about a particular way of praying (charismatic prayer, for instance, or centering prayer)? Would she like to pray or read the Scriptures with you? Would she like to say the rosary? Does she have a rosary? Would she like to pray the stations of the cross? There are a number of versions of this traditional devotion, including some specifically for a person who is elderly, ill, or dying.

Pope John Paul II described prayer as central to your parent's spirituality. He stated:

Even in solitude and the loss of the closest ties of affection, the person of prayer is never completely alone since the merciful God is bending over him. Our thought goes to a well-known passage from the prophet Isaiah, who attributes to God sentiments of compassion and tenderness that are more than maternal: "Can a mother forget her infant, be without tenderness for the child of her womb? Even should she forget, I will never forget you" (Isaiah 49:15).

Let us remind all elderly persons, the sick, those neglected by everyone, to whom no one will ever show tenderness, of these words of the Psalmist and the prophet, so that they may feel the fatherly and motherly hand of the Lord silently and lovingly touch their suffering faces, perhaps furrowed with tears.

A final point: you can provide spiritual help to your parent even if these things don't appeal to you personally, even if your practice of Catholicism is very different from your parent's, even if you and your parent are of different faiths, even if you want nothing to do with any religion. It's not hypocritical to see to it that your parent receives the spiritual assistance that he or she is seeking, even if you don't see the need at all. At the very least, you are helping your parent find comfort and peace.

Gentle Spirit, come and be with my parent. Open his heart. Enlighten his soul. Invite and encourage my parent to turn to you to find peace and comfort. Amen.

Helping a Parent Find Forgiveness and Peace

An aging parent who is facing death may feel the need to make peace with a friend, with a relative, or with God.

Just as you help your aging parent eat right and get to doctors' appointments, you may also be called on to help Mom or Dad prepare spiritually for death. The task may seem overwhelming to both you and your parent. Neither of you may feel equipped for it. But helping your mother or father find peace can make such a difference for him or her—the dying parent—and for you, an adult child who will be left behind.

These are suggestions for helping your mom or dad heal old wounds by admitting mistakes, offering apologies, and accepting forgiveness:

Offer to pray. Mom may need a little help getting started. Try a traditional prayer of the church, such as the Act of Contrition. Or allow the Holy Spirit to guide you in an informal prayer. Silence and contemplation may allow her to more intimately speak and listen to an all-forgiving God.

Listen. Dad may need the opportunity to talk about serious matters that weigh heavily on his mind and burden his soul. It's not uncommon for a person facing death to review his or her life. Some things may need to be said out loud. Saying something out loud often puts it in a different, clearer light. It's easier to see how a mistake could have been made, how a falling out could have happened, how no one was entirely to blame or entirely without blame. Talking about such matters openly can make it easier to come to the realization that it's time to forgive others and oneself.

Facilitate reconciliation. Your mother may need to get in touch with someone. Maybe the other party wants to make peace, too. Let Mom know that you can help arrange a conversation between them. If the person with whom your dad wants to reconcile won't talk or has died, suggest that your father write a letter to that person, saying all the things he would say if they could sit down face-to-face. This letter will never be mailed, but writing it can be a way to say, "Please forgive me; I forgive you."

Do what's necessary. Sometimes a parent feels that talking or writing just isn't enough. Mom has to do something more. Maybe it's going to her parents' or spouse's grave and praying, crying, yelling, and apologizing there. Maybe it's compiling a list of regrets and then burning it. Your parent may need to cry a lot. Your parent may need to turn more to prayer. Do what's necessary to help her ask for and accept forgiveness.

Get some help. If there are issues that you can't help with, Mom or Dad might benefit from talking with a counselor. Hospice social workers have the skills to help a person sort through a life review.

Use the sacraments. Encourage and arrange for Mom or Dad to take advantage of the sacraments of reconciliation and the anointing of the sick. No matter how long your parent may have been away from the church, no matter what he or she may have done, an all-loving God is waiting with open arms to offer forgiveness and peace now, and to share his eternal joy at the time of death.

We all have made mistakes, Lord. Our hearts feel sad and our minds are concerned. Help my parent come to receive forgiveness. Help Mom deal with the issues that are bothering her and give her peace of heart and mind. Amen.

Welcome Back to the Church

People leave the Catholic Church for a variety of reasons. Some storm out. Others drift away. At the end of their lives, many want to return.

If your parent is considering a return to the church, you can help by talking to a local priest. How do you find him? Check the phone directory and call the parish in your area or your parent's area. Or contact the central office of your parent's diocese; you will be referred to the correct parish based on your parent's address. You may want to attend Mass there a few times and introduce yourself to the priest in person.

In most parishes, the days of visiting a priest by simply knocking on the rectory door have passed. The current shortage of priests means that parishes that used to have two, three, or even more priests assigned to them may now have only one. Many parishes do not even have a priest in residence. So don't be surprised if you get an answering service when you call sometime other than business hours (yes, business hours). Most likely you will be asked to leave your name and number and a brief message. Even during the day, you may need to leave a message with the parish office secretary.

This can feel very awkward, especially if you're not really sure why you're calling in the first place. It's enough to simply say, "My name is . . . and I'm interested [my parent is interested] in finding out about returning to the church." Or "I have [my parent has] some questions and would like to talk to a priest." You might also add what time of day you can be reached.

You can expect a friendly call from a priest who wants to help you. You *won't* get accusations designed to make you feel guilty, a scolding, the cold shoulder, or a sales pitch for a monetary contribution to the parish. If Mom is homebound or in a hospital or nursing home, the priest (or pastoral minister) will come visit her there. He'll answer her questions, and if it's been awhile since she's been an active Catholic, he may briefly explain what changes have taken place in the church and why they've happened.

Maybe Dad just wants to talk. That's fine. If he wants to go to confession, he'll be given the opportunity to do that and to receive holy communion and the anointing of the sick.

It's understandable if your parent is (or you are) nervous about this. But there's no need to be afraid. It may help to remember that the priest is there to help you and your parent. Certainly one of the great joys of his ministry is this very thing: welcoming back someone who has been away for a time, and helping that person better prepare for an eternal homecoming.

> May the dear Lord inspire the Catholic Church to be a welcoming community and to encourage all who are searching to come to the church to find his love. Amen.

The Gospel of Life

In 1995, Pope John Paul II wrote his encyclical *Evangelium Vitae* (*The Gospel of Life*), a stunningly beautiful document describing the true value of human life. He wrote:

> The elderly are not only to be considered the object of our concern, closeness, and service. They themselves have a valuable contribution to make to the Gospel of life. Thanks to the rich treasury of experiences they have acquired through the years, the elderly can and must be sources of wisdom and witnesses of hope and love.

To be a caregiver is to travel for a time with one who has gained insight into the mysteries of life and death.

Some parishes have established a special ministry designed for the elders in the parish community. Participants in the Ministry of Praise and Mercy are often homebound seniors who are no longer able to take an active part in the parish organizations. Their ministry is one of prayer for the parish community, for intentions of the Holy Father, for others who are suffering, and for caregivers.

Society too often and too easily promotes the lie that those who can't produce, who don't contribute as the majority does, have little or no worth. *The Gospel of Life* counters that the elderly, the ill, and the suffering serve a unique and precious role not only in society, but also in the church, the parish, and the family.

> My gentle Lord, remind us each day of the value you put on life. Help us protect all life and offer compassionate care to the elderly. Amen.

The Sacraments

The seven sacraments include three that your parent may be particularly interested in receiving at this time: *reconciliation* (also called penance or confession), in which, through the mercy and forgiveness of God, one is reconciled with God and also with the church; *the Eucharist* (also called Holy Communion), the reception of the true body and blood of Christ under the appearances of bread and wine; and *the anointing of the sick,* in which a priest prays over and anoints a baptized person who begins to be in danger of death because of illness or old age.

Penance and Reconciliation

> When it was evening on that day, the first day of the week, and the doors of the house where the disciples had met were locked for fear of the Jews, Jesus came and stood among them and said, "Peace be with you." . . . When he had said this, he breathed on them and said to them, "Receive the Holy Spirit. If you forgive the sins of any, they are forgiven them; if you retain the sins of any, they are retained."
>
> —JOHN 20:19, 22–23

The Catholic Church teaches that sin is "before all else an offense against God, a rupture of communion with him." The sacrament of reconciliation repairs the damage and has three essential parts: confession of one's sins, forgiveness of those sins, and reconciliation with God and the faith community.

In recent years this sacrament hasn't been used much, and that's sad. Even if your parent doesn't want to celebrate reconciliation, consider celebrating it yourself. It's a source of grace that can make a tremendous difference in your life, especially at this time in your role as a caregiver.

People hesitate to go to confession for many reasons: it has been a long time; they feel they've committed unforgivable sins; they are afraid they can't remember everything they need to confess; they don't want to tell their sins "outside the box," with the priest sitting in the same room with them. Many older people who have been away from the church for a long time are not sure *how* to go to confession these days. Some are afraid that they can't remember the Act of Contrition.

Your parent may not bring up the subject of going to confession but may appreciate it if you do. It's helpful to deal with the issues directly:

- If it's been a long time since your parent last celebrated this sacrament, then it's a great time to do it again. The priest isn't going to scold.
- No sin is unforgivable. Nothing Dad says is going to shock the priest.
- Mom doesn't need to remember every wrong she has done or worry about forgetting something. It's enough to say, for example, "There were times when I was angry and shouldn't have been."
- The priest, in Jesus' name, offers forgiveness and peace and God's grace. It can be wonderful to receive that face-to-face.
- Dad doesn't have to worry about how to go to confession. The priest will be happy to gently lead him through it.
- An act of contrition can be as simple as "I'm sorry." Your mother doesn't need to recite the exact prayer, word for word, that she learned as a child.

How does one prepare for the sacrament of reconciliation? Take some time to look at your life and review the choices you have made. Stand before God and look at what you have done—and what you have failed to do—from the viewpoint of a loving Father. What are the consequences of your actions, or your inaction?

St. Augustine suggested this form of preparation: "Return to your conscience, question it. . . . Turn inward, brethren, and in everything you do, see God as your witness."

Following the confession of one's sins, the penitent shows his or her contrition:

O my God, I am heartily sorry for having offended you, and I detest all my sins because of your just punishment, but most of all because they offend you, my God, who are all-good and deserving of all my love. I firmly resolve, with the help of your grace, to sin no more and to avoid the near occasions of sin. Amen.

The sacrament of reconciliation ends with the priest giving absolution:

God the Father of mercies, through the death and resurrection of his Son, has reconciled the world to himself and sent the Holy Spirit among us for the forgiveness of sins. Through the ministry of the church, may God give you pardon and peace, and I absolve you from your sins in the name of the Father, and of the Son, and of the Holy Spirit. Amen.

Loving Father, I'm sorry. Thank you for your comforting gift of forgiveness. Help me forgive those who have hurt me. Amen.

The Eucharist

I am the living bread that came down from heaven. Whoever eats of this bread will live forever; and the bread that I will give for the life of the world is my flesh. . . .

Those who eat my flesh and drink my blood have eternal
life, and I will raise them up on the last day; for my flesh is
true food and my blood is true drink. Those who eat my flesh
and drink my blood abide in me, and I in them.

—JOHN 6:51, 54–56

During Mass, the bread and wine are consecrated and become the
body and blood of Christ. When communion is brought to your parent at home or in a hospital, your parent is truly in the presence of
the Lord. This is an awesome gift. It is a time to pray, a time to settle
the heart, a time to listen to the gentle words of the Lord. He will
offer his comfort, the grace to accept the challenges of life, and the
strength to keep going day by day.

If you call the local parish and ask that your parent receive communion at home (or in the hospital or nursing home), it's likely that
a lay extraordinary minister of the Eucharist will be the one who
visits. The volunteer from the parish will bring whatever he or she
needs or will ask in advance if you can supply something (a candle,
for example). You will also be welcome to receive communion at that
time. The rules of fasting (no food or drink, except water, for one
hour before receiving) don't apply for your parent.

Typically, the prayers the Eucharistic minister says will seem
like an abridged version of the Mass. When the sacrament is administered at a home, there will first be a penitential rite, a scriptural
reading, prayers of the faithful, and an Our Father. Communion
(which will have already been consecrated at Mass) is followed by a
closing prayer. This may take five minutes or so. The service may be
simpler in a hospital or nursing home; there may only be a greeting,
an Our Father, communion, and a closing prayer. You or your parent

can choose a particular scriptural reading if you wish—Mom's or Dad's favorite, for instance, or one you or your parent find especially comforting. The exercise of selecting a reading is a good preparation for this sacrament.

Let the Eucharistic minister know if your parent has trouble swallowing. The minister can break off a tiny piece of a Host and give it to your mom or dad. Your parent may need a sip of water to swallow even a fragment of the Host. In the hospital, always check with a nurse first to make sure it's all right for your parent to have a little water. Obviously, turn off the radio or television during the communion service. And, if possible, let the phone calls go to voice mail.

With most parishes, it's possible to arrange for an extraordinary minister of the Eucharist to visit your parent on a regular basis. Don't worry about straightening up the house for this visitor or offering coffee or a snack. The Eucharistic minister knows this isn't a social call. Don't be concerned if this volunteer shows up at the same time that a visiting nurse or other health-care provider has to be there. The parish volunteer knows that these scheduling conflicts can come up unexpectedly and will simply wait until it's his or her turn, or the volunteer may offer to come back at a more convenient time.

My Lord and my God, thank you for being here with me. Amen.

The Anointing of the Sick

Are any among you sick? They should call for the elders of the church and have them pray over them, anointing them with oil in the name of the Lord. The prayer of faith will save the sick, and the Lord will raise them up; and anyone who has committed sins will be forgiven.

—JAMES 5:14–15

This sacrament is one of healing. The church community intercedes with God on behalf of the person who is seriously ill or frail because of old age. The community prays that God will provide the person with the strength to handle the pain and suffering and the courage to face the end of his or her life. The recipient is anointed with oil, and his or her sins are forgiven. This is the final preparation for one's death.

In the past, when the sacrament was known as extreme unction (final anointing), it was reserved for someone on his or her deathbed. One of the last things a family would do for a dying loved one was notify the local priest. He would hurry to the house or hospital and administer the "last rites." Since the Second Vatican Council (1962–65), the sacrament has become known as the anointing of the sick or sacrament of the sick. It can be administered to any Catholic over the age of seven who is seriously ill.

It's important to explain to your mother or father that *the recipient of the sacrament does not have to be near death.* Your calling the priest does *not* mean that your parent is dying. It does *not* mean your dad is in worse shape than he realizes or that you're keeping some information about your mom's medical condition from her. It's also important to know that the anointing of the sick isn't a "magical" sacrament designed to cure illness. Yes, sometimes a person does get well, but the purpose of the sacrament is to give the person grace and to forgive his or her sins.

In administering the sacrament, the priest will anoint your parent's forehead and hands with blessed oil (usually olive oil) and say some prayers. You, and others, are welcome to be present. A person can receive this sacrament more than once. If you aren't sure if it would be appropriate for your parent to be anointed, ask your local priest.

The pleas of gravely ill persons who sometimes ask for death are not to be understood as implying a true desire for euthanasia; in fact, it is almost always a case of an anguished plea for help and love. What a sick person needs, besides medical care, is love, the human and supernatural warmth with which the sick person can and ought to be surrounded by those close to him or her, parents and children, doctors and nurses.

—Declaration on Euthanasia

God the creator, bless my parent's head and hands. Bring comfort and peace. Amen.

13

Your Parent's Safety

Older people become more vulnerable to accidents as they age. There are dangers in the home. There are even more dangers out in the community. As a caregiver, you need to look through your parent's house with safety in mind and carefully monitor your parent's personal safety.

Home Safety

Your parent is probably not used to disposables. People who lived through the Depression and World War II were taught to make do with what was on hand until it was completely worn out. Because of that upbringing, many elderly people "make do" with a hodgepodge of ancient extension cords. They "use up" old prescriptions even though the doctor has taken them off the medication. They "wear out" items like space heaters and fans to the point that they are in danger of getting a shock or starting a fire. They emphasize self-sacrifice and thrift to such an extent that their safety is jeopardized, and that can be a serious, even deadly, mistake.

In the same way that a couple with small children must baby-proof their home, you must make your aging parent's house safe for him or her. How can you do that? Here are some suggestions:

Look first for obvious dangers. Are electrical outlets overloaded? Are smoke detectors installed and in good working order? Make sure there's a bath mat in the bathtub; that doors are not blocked by furniture; that drapes, furniture, or other flammable items are not near electric baseboard heaters.

Install safety bars. All stairs, inside and out, need sturdy handrails and need to be well lit. Make sure the bathroom has a grab bar. Don't rely on a towel rack for this. Grab bars are designed—and installed—to bear the weight of an adult. Medical supply stores offer dozens of similar safety items—from bathtub benches to raised toilet seats—that can make a home safer for your parent.

Look at kitchen safety. Try to avoid the need for a step stool. Move bulky and heavy items to lower cupboards, because it can be difficult for your parent to reach up and lift things down. If items taken from lower cupboards are dropped, they will land directly on the floor, not on Mom or Dad. If bending is a problem for your parent, dishes and cookware may need to stay out on the counter.

Make sure the house is equipped with adequate lighting. In particular, put a night-light in Mom's bedroom or make sure she can easily reach a lamp—perhaps a "one touch" lamp—from bed.

Get rid of clutter. Furniture buried in mounds of junk mail and floors stacked with old newspapers and magazines can make it difficult for anyone to get around, especially someone using a cane or walker.

Review and organize medications. Make sure medicine bottles are clearly labeled in print large enough for Mom to read. (The same applies for household cleaners.) If she has trouble remembering what medicine to take when, use a seven-day medication dispenser (available at drugstores). Help Dad throw out prescribed medications that he no longer needs or that have passed their expiration dates. Some seniors just *hate* to throw away a "perfectly good" expired prescription because it costs so much. You can remind your dad that outdated medicine loses its effectiveness and that older medicines, combined with his current prescriptions and conditions, could cause serious side effects. Avoid an accident by putting these medications away.

List needed phone numbers. These should include your work and home numbers, the doctor's office number, and the general emergency number, 911. Write them in large print that can be read without glasses, and post them by each telephone. Program those numbers into any speed dial systems. Write down your parent's address and phone number and keep it by his or her phones. In a crisis, anyone can have trouble remembering that information.

Issue safety reminders. For instance: Don't smoke in bed or just before nap time in your favorite chair. Don't wear the bathrobe with the floppy sleeves when cooking something on the stove. Don't use the stairs for storage. Most of your suggestions won't be new to your parent. Mom may seem a little annoyed as she answers, "I know, I know." Don't let that discourage you. It's probably the same answer you gave her years ago when she was teaching you valuable lessons.

Consider an emergency response system. With an emergency response system, Mom or Dad can get help by pushing the call button on a necklace or bracelet or the system's base. Your parent can speak on the system's speakerphone to a system attendant. If your parent pushes the button but is unable to speak or is too far from the base to be heard, the attendant summons aid. Ask your parent's doctor about companies offering the service. Find out if the response is local or if the system is monitored in another part of the country.

And if the call button is pushed, do staff operators then call you or call the police in your parent's area? Also, be aware that some of these companies may emphasize their vast array of products (they may vigorously push entire home alarm systems) but fall short when it comes to service.

Consider a reassurance phone call. Again, ask your parent's doctor about this. With this system—often administrated by the local hospital—someone calls your parent at the same time every day to make sure he or she is all right. If there's no answer, the person informs the people on your parent's contact list.

For more information, see the checklist section in the back of this book.

> Dear God, I can't be with my parent every minute. Help me make her home a safe and comfortable place. Make me aware of anything that will harm her, and give us your protection. Amen.

Personal Safety

Older people are often the victims of crime. A mugger is looking for the easiest target that will yield the best results. Often it's a vulnerable older person. What can your parent do to protect him- or herself? Here are some suggestions you can share with Mom or Dad:

Pay attention in public. Mom should walk purposefully, appear strong and uninviting, and be alert for dangers. Remind Mom that crime is happening day and night now. She needs to be alert whenever she goes out.

Take prudent precautions. Mom shouldn't be out in public wearing a lot of expensive jewelry. A woman should *not* have her purse strap draped around her neck. That doesn't stop today's thief; it only increases the likelihood that the victim will be hurt as well as robbed. Go shopping with your parent and observe. Does Mom leave her purse unattended in the shopping cart? Does Dad flash the cash in his wallet when he's at the checkout stand? We all need reminders when it comes to personal safety. We all slip into what could be dangerous habits. Tell your parent what a would-be robber would see. If your parent is still receiving pension or Social Security checks through the mail, arrange for direct deposit at the bank.

Be cautious even in familiar areas. Help your parent understand that the neighborhood may have changed since the family first moved there. It may no longer be safe to walk to the grocery store or to church. Offer to give or to arrange a ride.

Take advantage of security. Encourage your parent to use security escorts when walking to the parking lot at the hospital or doctor's office, the mall, and other places.

Don't be a hero. If someone demands a wallet or grabs for a purse, Mom or Dad should just let it go. Its contents aren't worth being injured for. For an aging parent, a punch or push could easily lead to broken bones, or worse.

Take care in the car. If Dad still drives, make sure his car is well maintained. That decreases the odds that it will break down at a time or place that isn't safe. Also, be sure he keeps all the doors locked. It's a great idea for an older driver to carry a cell phone (and a very bad idea for him or her to be on the phone while driving).

Watch out for scams. Keep an eye out for "friends" that suddenly appear in your parent's life. Some people befriend an elderly person to take money from him or her. Remind Mom not to give out any personal information over the phone, even if she thinks she knows the caller. The elderly are favorite targets for phone fraud.

Identity theft is rampant, and anyone can be fooled. Your state attorney general's office can offer tips on how to help your parent avoid getting stung. It's also a good idea to watch out for packages arriving at your parent's house. Your parent may be shopping online, by mail, or from phone solicitation and may have given out financial information.

Get help from the neighbors. If there is a Block Watch program in the neighborhood, chat with the coordinator and tell him or her that your parent lives alone. Ask that person to keep an eye out for your parent. Get tips from him or her on making your parent's community and home safer. You could also ask a trusted neighbor to keep an eye on Dad's house.

Be positive. Don't let fear keep Mom or Dad—or you—from enjoying life. The solution isn't to become isolated; it is to use caution and common sense.

> Guardian angels, watch over my parent when I can't. Give your protection and guidance. Amen.

In Case of an Emergency or a Disaster

It's important that you have a plan in place to keep your parent safe, warm, and well fed in the case of any kind of emergency (storm, flood, earthquake, heat wave, power outage, terrorist threat, or some other disaster). Here are some steps you can take:

Prepare. Get current emergency information from your local Red Cross or Federal Emergency Management Agency (FEMA) office. Being prepared is the best first step to surviving a disaster. If at all possible, arrange for help *before* the disaster hits. If you're not going to be able to travel from your part of town to your parent's, arrange to have a neighbor, a member of the parish, or a volunteer do some grocery shopping for Mom. Even if she doesn't need anything from the store, ask that person to stop in and make sure your mother is doing all right.

Have emergency supplies ready. These would include a flashlight with fresh batteries, a transistor radio, a nonelectric clock, a hand-operated or battery-powered can opener, water, nutritious food that doesn't need to be cooked, and a supply of critical medication. Make sure these supplies are stored in a place that is easily accessible. (For the most current information on this, check the latest suggested list from the Red Cross or FEMA.)

Encourage Mom to stay indoors if a disaster has made being outside dangerous. Even if she plans on walking only a short way, she might fall, and falls lead to broken bones. It's better for her to suffer a little cabin fever for a few days than spend weeks or months laid up in bed.

Stay in touch. Even the most independent person can feel a little uncomfortable knowing that, for days on end, he or she won't be able to get out and no one else can get in. If the phone systems are working, try to call your parent at least once a day. A simple daily telephone call can work wonders in providing needed reassurance. (This is another reason to be sure to have a list of important numbers—family, friends, neighbors, doctor, parish and community resources—posted by your parent's phone.)

Make medical preparations. If Dad is taking medication, be sure he has enough on hand to last through any emergency. Remember that even though he might not be able to get out, others may be able to come to him. Check with his pharmacy for suggestions in cases like this. If Mom is on some type of life-support system, such as oxygen, contact her doctor and the local electric company ahead of time to see what they recommend. (You may have to provide a small backup generator.)

Stay warm. If the furnace has gone out but the electricity is still on, make sure Mom or Dad does not try to heat the house with an appliance, such as an oven with the door wide open. Your father will stay warmer in a home or an apartment without heat by wearing layers of clothing (underwear, pants, light shirt, heavy shirt, sweater, jacket, heavy coat, hat, gloves) rather than one bulky winter coat. If the fireplace is to be used, be sure the chimney is clean and the screen is in place. Remind Mom not to try heating a room with a barbecue, a hibachi, or any type of grill that emits carbon monoxide.

Here are some things not to do in an emergency:

- Do not overload an electrical outlet or extension cord with an electric heater.
- Do not have anything near an electric space heater (and don't sit too close, either).
- Do not use candles for heating or for light.
- Do not shovel snow or worry about cleaning up debris. Someone will take care of that later.

And here are some things to remember:

- Food in the refrigerator and freezer might keep for several days if the doors aren't opened frequently or for any long period of time.
- Remind your parent that it's all right to call 911 if he or she isn't able to stay warm or fix meals and no one else is available to help.
- Remember that if you lose contact with your parent, you can also call 911 and ask a police or community service

officer to do a well-person check on Mom or Dad. Better still, you can ask that your parent be placed on a check-list of people in the community to be contacted if a storm strikes. Sometimes officials want to know who might need help in an emergency so assistance can be planned.

Jesus, whatever may happen, please be with my parent. There is no need to fear when you are near us. Please comfort people who have died or been injured in this emergency. I want to trust in you. Give me more faith. Amen.

14

Is It Time for Your Parent to Move?

Your parent is finding it increasingly difficult to live at home, so what comes next? It may be time to set up, or to increase, outside help in your parent's home. Or it may be time to look at other housing possibilities. Some families think that one's home and a nursing home are the only options when it comes to deciding where an aging parent can live. The truth is that those are simply the two extremes on a broad spectrum of choices. Within that range are a host of options that can be examined and evaluated.

Housing Options

The first step is to ask your parent what he or she would like. Does Mom want to stay in the family home? Would Dad prefer to move to an apartment? Sometimes a parent feels that keeping up the house is just getting to be too costly and demanding. It would be a relief to no longer have that responsibility, but your parent is afraid that the next and maybe only step is a nursing home. Here are more choices.

In-Home Care

If your parent wants to stay put but needs more help, a number of services are available in most communities. Nurses, physical therapists, occupational therapists, and other health-care professionals can come to your parent's home and provide any needed health-related assistance.

You can also arrange for your parent to receive home care—which may involve having a person come in to do the shopping, laundry, cooking, cleaning, and the like—as well as personal care, such as assistance with bathing or dressing. Many seniors are able to stay in their own homes with only a minimum of assistance, perhaps as few as three or four hours a week. Or you may need someone to be with your parent during the night. This type of help is now available in many communities.

Adult Family Home

Licensed by the state, this is a private home that provides a family setting for the elderly person and assistance with particular tasks, such as bathing and managing medication.

Retirement Community

Retirement communities are designed for and restricted to seniors. They have planned social activities but not services. The community may be private condominiums, apartments, or mobile homes.

Retirement Home

This facility has a range of housing options and services—from a private apartment with limited services such as meals and housekeeping to assisted living with more significant care available. Your parent might enter at one level and, as it becomes necessary, begin to get more and more help. The cost increases as more services are added.

If the retirement home is based on a rental agreement, there is no entry fee and the tenant pays a monthly rent. In other cases the tenant actually buys into the facility with a large sum and then pays a monthly fee. Prices, methods of payments, and services can vary. Don't be afraid to ask a lot of questions when visiting these facilities. Be sure to find out if any of the expenses will be covered by Medicare or Medicaid.

And don't be afraid to raise this topic with an aging parent who is still living at home and doing well. Helping Mom or Dad investigate what options are available in the community before he or she needs help can go a long way toward alleviating anxiety and misconceptions.

For more information, see the checklist section in the back of this book.

Oh sweet Trinity, sometimes I'm not sure what to do. Thank you for so many options. Help me find the best place for my parent to live. Amen.

Choosing a Nursing Home

In a perfect world, your parent would never have to go to a nursing home. In a near-perfect world, both of you would have already explored nursing home options and made decisions before the need arises. In the real world, you may be doing the investigating and choosing alone right before Mom or Dad is discharged from the hospital.

Here are some suggestions for making that choice less difficult:

Do your research first. Find a few facilities to visit. Don't rely on secondhand information. Viewing places online is not as good as seeing them in person. Take a sibling or friend along to help you more clearly evaluate the home. The more eyes the better.

Don't be shy when asking about costs. A nursing home admissions director may quote a figure, but you need to find out what is included in that number, what costs extra, and what that additional cost will be. Ask what's covered by Medicare, Medicaid, insurance, and private pay. Ask if your parent's bed will be held if he or she has to be temporarily hospitalized.

Find out how a patient's care plan is written. Is it personalized, or does a general plan apply to almost everyone? Find out who monitors the care plan. Ask what happens to that plan if your parent's health improves or gets worse. Can you be involved in the planning? How often is the plan reviewed and evaluated?

Inquire about medical care. Ask if one doctor is assigned to the nursing home, if there are several doctors, or if a patient continues to use his or her own physician.

Verify the certification and licenses for the facility. Request a copy of the most recent audits by your state Department of Health. Be sure any "deficiencies" have been corrected. You can also get this type of information online. Ask for a copy of the nursing home's bill of rights for its clients.

Observe the facility carefully. Walk through. Look around, inside and out. Is it clean and well maintained? Are the halls stacked with various kinds of equipment because there isn't enough storage space? Are there any unpleasant smells? Look at the patients. Do they appear well attended? Are they clean, appropriately dressed, and well groomed? Look at the rehabilitation unit. Most nursing homes have a room for physical and occupational therapy. Is the equipment falling apart? Is it being used at all?

Walk through again. A good plan is to walk through, talk to the admissions director, and then walk through again about an hour later. You should be able to tell if there has been some activity. Are the patients still in the same place? No patient should be in a hallway "waiting for lunch" for an hour.

Eat the food. Many places will be happy to invite you to stay for a meal. Ask to be served whatever the residents are being served. Is it nutritious? Does it look and taste appetizing?

Ask about security. Is it a twenty-four-hour secured facility? Who is allowed to come and go? Security should protect the patients not just from someone wandering in from the outside, but also from theft by fellow patients and staff. Find out who is responsible for monitoring this, to whom one reports a problem, and what the procedure is when something is missing.

Find out how room assignments are made. Obviously rooms will be all-male or all-female, but are matches done according to compatibility, or does the next person through the door simply get the next vacant bed? What's the procedure if problems arise between roommates?

Find out if there is a continuum of service? If your parent's health gets better or worse, will he or she need to move?

Ask about moving day. Will someone be available to help on moving day? Who helps with the transition when Mom or Dad first settles in? Depression is typical and certainly understandable. Is there a social worker available to help?

Think about it. Don't sign a contract during that first visit. Go home and think about it. Take notes during your visits to several homes so you can remember what you saw and where you saw it.

One final note: If your parent does end up moving to a nursing home, make sure you get to know the staff. And make sure they know you. The more contact you have with them, the better care your parent will receive.

For more information, see the checklist section in the back of this book.

Holy Father, I need to be a good observer and a wise planner. Help me be both. Open my eyes to everything around me and guide my parent and me as we make this critical decision. Amen.

Should Mom or Dad Move In?

Trust in the LORD with all your heart,
 and do not rely on your own insight.
In all your ways acknowledge him,
 and he will make straight your paths.

      —PROVERB 3:5–6

If you're considering having your mother or father move into your family home, remember that adjusting to such an arrangement takes a commitment by your parent, by you, and by your family. Often the emotions you each feel before such a move—worry, stress, guilt, anger, jealousy, and so on—aren't eliminated by the new arrangement; unfortunately, they're intensified. Any discussion about this new living arrangement needs to begin with two key questions: First, have other possibilities been considered? And second, is this something *both* generations want?

Sometimes the move just isn't right, for a variety of reasons. Dad is a late riser and you have a houseful of young children who are up at the crack of dawn every day. Your house is already too small and simply couldn't accommodate one more person. You were recently promoted at work, and right now your new duties leave you little time for anything else. You and your parent may just get along better with a little more space—physical and emotional—between you, and living under the same roof will bring up old issues and attitudes that neither person wants.

It's better for both of you to be honest from the beginning. The hurt from hearing "This won't work" is less painful than the hurt of living in a situation that could possibly tear the family apart.

Talk with your mom before the need arises for any move. How does she feel about the idea? She may appreciate your bringing it up but not want to move. Maybe she likes the idea of being with other seniors in a community setting. Maybe moving in with you, even though she loves you dearly, would be her last choice, not her first. Or maybe this discussion would be very comforting to her.

You need to ask yourself: Why do I want to do this? Is it because I have to? Is it because I'll feel so guilty if I don't? Is it because my parent or siblings or other family members are in some way forcing me to do it? Or do *I* want to do this? Is it an opportunity for my children to get to know my parent better? Is it a chance for me, in some way, to give something back to my mother or father? Is it an opportunity for us to spend time together, time that is passing so quickly?

Be clear about this. When the daily grind begins to take its toll—and having anyone of any age move into a household can stir things up—you need to have that basic reason to fall back on. Yes, things are hard, but you know why you agreed to do this. You know why this is good not just for your parent but for you.

Lord, I'm asking my parent to move into not just my house, but also my home. Give us patience as we make our plans. Help us explore all possibilities and give us the wisdom to choose the best option. Amen.

When Mom or Dad Moves In

Having your parent come live with you may be the right move, but that doesn't mean it will be easy for either generation. Being aware of each other's feelings and concerns can help make the transition a smooth one. Here are some points to consider:

This is hard for your parent. Your father is grieving not just because he has lost his family home or apartment, but also because he has lost his way of life. He may have had to say good-bye to his friends, neighborhood, and parish. Then, too, the change has more than chipped away at his sense of independence and control. He doesn't have a home anymore. He must accept the fact that he's living in his son's or daughter's home.

This is hard for you. It's hard to watch a parent's health deteriorate. It's hard to see the family home—the home of your childhood—up for sale. It's hard to give up some of your privacy, and ask your spouse and children to do the same, by having someone move in with you.

You must be honest with each other. Both of you—parent and adult child—feel as if you must tiptoe around the other person, holding in any emotion that might be considered negative. But if this new arrangement is going to work, then, like all strong and healthy relationships, it must be based on a loving and respectful honesty and openness. You're on a two-way street of communication, willing to accept and give helpful criticism as well as praise.

Your parent needs to be given as much control of his or her life as possible. Things that might seem trivial to you can be important to your mother. Ask her if she would like to move in at the beginning of the month or on the fifteenth. Let her decide how to decorate her room. What color would she like it painted? What material and pattern would she like for the curtains? What furniture and other household items would she bring with her? Putting her favorite chair in your living room or family room can mean a lot!

Your parent's memories deserve respect. Reducing a houseful of belongings, collected over a lifetime, to an amount that will fit into a single room can be a very difficult task. Be respectful as you help Mom sort out the items. Old newspapers, trinkets, and bric-a-brac might be priceless to her. Treat every item as if it were a treasure. If giving it away is too painful for your mom, you may need to find more storage space.

Your parent has the right to choose. Let your parent decide what she will take with her to your house, what she will toss, what she will give to charity, what she will give to family members. Keep in mind that Mom may want to distribute a good deal of her possessions while she is still alive. She's not being morbid; she just wants to enjoy seeing each person inherit his or her special gift.

Maybe your parent would like to be given some household duties. Dad may feel less like a burden and more like a contributing member of the family if he takes his turn drying the dishes or oversees a homework session one evening a week. But don't expect a built-in babysitter. You have to think, *If Dad can't live alone, can he safely watch my kids?*

You may observe emotional changes in your parent. Your dad needs more than food and shelter; he needs your emotional support. Even if he was strong and optimistic when he lived on his own, the dramatic change in his life and the host of emotions that comes with that change can easily lead to depression. You need to be available. You are making a real-time commitment with this arrangement.

Having your parent move into your family home can be a tremendous blessing if each family member remembers that a home is more than just a house, and a family is more than just a group of people living together.

Each member is entitled to a loving and caring environment. That's the task facing all of you: how can you make that happen—together?

> OK, God, we've made the decision. Thank you for your guidance in making these plans. Now help us make this work for everyone. Teach us patience and respect for each other. Amen.

Saying Good-Bye to the Family Home

No matter where your parent moves, many families find themselves saying good-bye to the family home. It's a special time in the life of a family. It's a time to remember what has been and what is passing away. There will be no more Thanksgiving meals in that dining room, with the parents and grandparents sitting elbow to elbow at the table with its extra leaves, and the kids giggling at their own, fun table. There will be no more placing the Christmas tree (a big one when Mom gets to pick it, a small one when it's Dad's turn) in that corner.

Sometimes the move can be bittersweet. Mom is leaving—and that's difficult—but she's moving into a lovely smaller home or apartment. She's bought a condominium. She's going to a retirement community that better suits her needs now. She's heading for a warmer climate.

Sometimes sorrow can dominate the move. Dad isn't able to take care of the house anymore. Taxes, insurance, and maintenance on the house take too big a bite from a fixed income. The neighborhood has changed; it's no longer safe. Mom has passed away and Dad really isn't able to live alone. For the widow or widower, saying good-bye to the family home can feel like having to say good-bye again to that loving spouse. This was their house, from the time they first saw it on the market until long after the paperwork for the mortgage was burned. They were partners here. It's very sad to leave.

If your family is getting ready to say good-bye to the family home, here are a few things you can do:

Let your parent choose what comes with him or her and what goes. What is junk to you may have a lot of sentimental value to Mom.

Lend a hand. Dad may need your help sorting and packing; moving takes a lot of work, and there's always a lot of worry involved. (And you may finally have to do something with those boxes of your stuff you've been storing in his basement or attic.)

Preserve the memories. Take some pictures of the inside and the outside of the house. Of course the family has taken hundreds of snapshots there for years and years, but maybe not of each bedroom, the family room, the basement. This house is part of your family's history. Better still, walk around with a video camera. Let the family join you for a running commentary: "Here's where we kept track of how tall each child was." "This is the window that was broken twice in the same week by the same baseball." "Dad built this bedroom onto the back of the house after Susan was born."

Come together for one last meal to say good-bye. Sometimes families make it a final Thanksgiving, Christmas, or Easter dinner, or a meal for a parent's birthday. It's an opportunity to share memories, to laugh and to cry.

Don't forget that a house is only a structure. It's the people and the love they've shared that have made this place so special. Those people, that love, aren't being left behind; they're simply moving to a new address. Remember, the home didn't make the family; the family made the home. And the family is still here.

> Thank you, my dearest Jesus, for all the precious memories. There have been so many happy times and some sad ones. You have been so good to my family. Continue to watch over us. Amen.

Finding Help for Your Parent

You've reached the point where you know your parent needs more help than you alone can provide. What do you do now?

Whether you live nearby or in another state, a good first step is to call Senior Information and Assistance in the area where your parent lives, which is listed in the phone book; go online to Eldercare.gov; or call Eldercare Locator, at (1-800) 677-1116. All you need is your parent's ZIP code, and you will be able to find social service programs in the area. You can request a list of private and public social service programs, including case managers, for the region in which your parent lives.

Available services typically include home health care (visiting nurse, bath aide), home care (housekeeping, laundry, grocery shopping), housing, legal and financial assistance, transportation, and nutrition programs, such as Meals on Wheels. Take note of every service that is available. Perhaps six months or a year from now your parent will have an additional need, and you'll have a better idea of how it can be met.

Keep in mind that financial help is available. Some programs are not limited to low-income individuals, and your parent may be eligible to receive low- or no-cost services, so be sure to ask. Don't shy away from a program because, at first glance, it seems too expensive. It may in fact use a sliding fee scale.

Social service providers can be considered a formal support network for your parent, but don't forget the informal network. This includes other family members as well as your parent's friends, neighbors, and fellow parishioners. Sometimes those most pleased to help are the ones who have an elderly family member in another part of the country who is benefiting from his or her own informal network. They know how much that help has meant not only to their relative, but also to them.

Just a quick warning: be sure to carefully check out any private services. Not everyone is honest.

Lord, I know there are many good people ready and willing to help. Give me patience during this search. Thanks for the support of family and friends and all who work with the elderly. Amen.

Hiring a Case Manager

Are you having trouble keeping track of everything that's happening? Are you afraid you may drop one of the many balls you are trying to juggle? Consider hiring a case manager to help you out.

Typically, a geriatric case manager, sometimes called a care manager, is a social worker or a registered nurse who has been trained to work with elderly clients. This person can assess your parent's needs and design an individualized care plan. He knows resources in your area and the eligibility criteria for programs and will be able to assist you and your parent with accessing whatever services you may need.

If you're a long-distance caregiver, this person will continue to monitor your parent's condition on a regular basis and report to you any changes or concerns.

If you and your parent live in the same area but the demands of your job or your family make it difficult, if not impossible, for you to help as much as you would like to at this time, or if you simply don't know where to start to look for the variety of services your parent needs, hiring a case manager might be the solution.

Some social service agencies offer case management as part of their programs. You can also look into hiring a private case manager. There will be a cost. There may be a fee for the initial assessment and/or family consultations. Fees vary widely. It pays to shop around. The most expensive is not necessarily the one that will best fit your parent's needs. And, of course, the most reasonable might not work either.

If you decide to hire a private case manager, do your research. Find several individuals and check out what each has to offer. See if he or she is affiliated with a national organization that monitors case managers. (See the resources list in the back of this book for more information on the National Association of Professional Geriatric Care Managers.) What about the case manager's education and other credentials? Request a list of references. Does he or she have a social work or a medical focus? Will he or she be in contact with you on a regular basis, or are you supposed to check in with him or her?

And, of course, bring your aging parent in on the process as much as possible. Let Mom or Dad meet this person. If they clash, it's probably not going to work with that individual.

Keep in mind that a case manager will not clean your parent's house, drive Dad to the doctor, or give Mom a bath, but he or she will set up services to ensure those things get done.

If your parent's condition worsens, services can be added (even to the point of placement in a nursing home). If it improves, those services can be modified or dropped.

A good case manager can be your eyes and ears. This person can make sure your mother or father is receiving the care that's needed and put your mind more at ease, too.

> Sweet Lord in heaven, thank you for the people who work so hard taking care of others. Help me find the right one for my parent. It's hard for me to trust someone else working with my parent. So I turn it all over to you. Amen.

When Mom or Dad Doesn't Want Help

There may be times when Mom simply says no. When Dad wants *nothing* to do with what you're proposing. You may have come up with what you think is a great solution to whatever problem or need your parent is facing, but your mother or father doesn't see it that way. And so Dad digs in his heels or Mom gets that look in her eyes, and you know it's going to take a lot of work on your part to get your parent to budge on this one.

What can you do to avoid that kind of confrontation?

Prepare for a crisis. It helps to talk about concerns early and often. It's much easier to hold what-if discussions before a crisis arises. "What if you need some help around the house?" "What if you can't safely drive anymore?" What could your parent do, what could you do, what could someone else do to help out? What are other people you both know doing in those situations, or not doing? The more comfortable your Dad is discussing what-ifs, the easier it will be for him to tell you when he needs the help.

Give some options. If there's already a need, don't present your choice as "the solution." Try to give Mom or Dad a number of possibilities. Let your parent decide. If your parent isn't mentally competent, get professional help to assist you in planning and making necessary decisions.

Go with the minimum service first. Maybe Mom doesn't want someone in her home several days a week, but she'll agree to a person coming in for two hours once a week to help with the cleaning or laundry. As she and the in-home worker get to know each other, the idea of increasing those hours and the workload may not be nearly as threatening to her.

Preserve independence. Your goal is not to take over your parent's life but to assist him or her in getting what's needed. That can be done without trampling on Mom's or Dad's right to choose. It can be done while continuing to show great love—and respect—for your parent.

Jesus, help me be gentle but firm. When assistance is needed, we have to be willing to ask for it, and we need to humbly accept. Please help me always be respectful and offer compassionate care. Amen.

15

Finances and Other Paperwork

Finances are a big concern for most older people and their caregivers. Here are some suggestions for help in this area. Bear in mind that what is said here is no substitute for professional legal and financial advice.

Financial Management

Handing over management of the finances might be as difficult for Mom or Dad as giving up the car keys. Often an older person sees this as an assault on his or her independence. It's easy to understand why they can be resistant. Still, it may be that Mom or Dad needs your help even if he or she doesn't realize it, or, at times, it isn't wanted or appreciated. Then again, maybe Dad knows he needs the help but hates to admit it and doesn't want to ask.

Your parent is probably anxious about his or her finances. Mom is afraid that eventually all her money is going to be used up and she'll find herself destitute. She's saving that money for her "old age." She may have reason to be concerned. Find out how much is coming in and going out. Income can be from a variety of sources: Social Security, pension, insurance, savings, investments, and so on. Estimated expenses need to be realistic, to reflect inflation and the added costs that are likely to crop up as your parent gets older. People are living longer after retirement than they ever anticipated. Your parent's best financial planning may not have taken this into account.

Discussing finances with an aging parent is never easy. It's not unusual for siblings to have different opinions on how best to proceed. It's important to avoid turning the task into a turf war; instead, concentrate on doing what's best for your parent and respecting his or her wishes.

These are some suggestions:

Look at your parent's financial records. You need to know where these are kept. This is especially important if your parent has dementia. A person with dementia may put items in very unusual and often quite surprising places. If you're handling the finances, keep extremely good records. Write everything down. It would be a good idea to have a sibling review the paperwork with you along the way. Sometimes a parent who is confused or forgetful may accuse an adult child of stealing or mishandling money.

Get professional help. Consider having a certified financial planner handle this chore right from the beginning. This may be easier for both you and your parent. A professional financial planner can be the one to review your parent's financial status, including all available assets, and make suggestions for best management of the finances. He will be up to date on current trends and the laws in your parent's state.

Do some research. If you decide to handle the finances yourself, you'll need a good money-management plan for your parent's resources. Check the information posted on the AARP Web site, www.aarp.org. Your parent may be eligible for a number of federal and state services—such as respite care and Meals on Wheels—regardless of his or her income. Look at the National Council on Aging's "Benefits Check Up" at www.benefitscheckup.org.

Consider durable power of attorney. Discuss with your parent the possibility of giving you durable power of attorney for finances. This is a document that gives a person chosen by your parent the power to make financial decisions for him or her. Be sure the word *durable* is included in this document. This will allow the power of attorney to remain in effect even if your parent becomes incapacitated and no longer able to express his or her wishes. It can go into effect immediately after signing or at a date in the future when there is an issue of competency. This document will also give you access to your parent's bank accounts so that you will be able to manage money and write checks. Durable power of attorney is a very critical role. If your parent is not comfortable with you doing this, suggest that he or she designate someone else.

Heavenly Father, help me be a wise steward with Dad's money. He worked so hard all his life. Thank you for the example he set for me. I take this responsibility seriously. Please help me do a good job. Amen.

Health Care and End-of-Life Decisions

End-of-life decisions may be very difficult to discuss with your parent, because the topic is so packed with emotion. At the same time, talking about this can make things much easier for both your parent and you during the final days of your parent's life, when these decisions are needed. When talking with Mom, stress the fact that you want to respect and fulfill her wishes, and so you need to know what her decisions are. If Dad doesn't want to discuss these things with you, ask him to talk about them with a trusted person who can be his representative.

Remember, too, that your assistance can make these decisions and preparations easier for your parent. Your mother or father needs not only basic legal and medical information, but your respectful care and support as well.

Here are some terms you may come across:

The Patient Self-Determination Act: This is a federal law that guarantees your parent the right to confidentiality and the right to make his or her own health-care decisions. Any health-care provider (doctor, hospital, nursing home, home-care service, and so on) that receives Medicare or Medicaid funds will give this information to your parent.

Informed consent (or informed refusal): No one can force your parent to undergo a certain medical treatment without his or her approval. Before your parent makes any decision, a health-care provider must give him or her information regarding the diagnosis, the nature and purpose of the treatment, any risks or consequences of the treatment, the probability that the treatment will be successful, any feasible alternative treatments, and prognosis if your parent chooses not to receive the treatment.

Health-care advance directive: This document is a combination of two documents, a living will and a health-care durable power of attorney. These are instructions your parent gives in the event that he or she is not able to make medical decisions. It covers his or her wishes regarding life-sustaining measures and palliative care, or pain management. It can include what your parent wants and doesn't want. Regulations regarding advance directives vary from state to state. If your parent spends part of the year in one state and part in another, set up directives in both states.

Living will: This part of the advance directive is a document stating your parent's wishes regarding life-sustaining treatment at the final stages of his or her life. It takes effect in the event that your parent is no longer able to make medical decisions. It needs to be dated and signed in the presence of two witnesses. A witness cannot be the health-care provider or someone who will benefit in some way from your parent's death. A living will can be amended at any time, and the directives it contains can be very specific.

If your parent's doctor is not comfortable respecting your parent's wishes, he or she must refer your parent to another doctor who agrees to carry out the wishes stated in this document.

Health-care power of attorney (health-care agent): The second part of the advance directive is a document that gives a person chosen by your parent the power to make decisions for him or her regarding medical treatment and other health-care issues. It takes effect when Mom loses the ability (temporarily or permanently) to make her own decisions because of illness or injury.

Do Not Resuscitate order: This document instructs health-care providers not to attempt cardiopulmonary resuscitation if your parent has cardiac or respiratory arrest. This document must be signed by a physician. One copy will be kept with your parent's medical records. Another copy will be on file if your parent is admitted to a health-care facility. There should also be a copy available at your parent's home, in case of an emergency. An EMT will need to see this document.

> Lord, help me get through the maze of legal terms and choices that we face. Be sure my parent knows I want to respect the life you have given to him or her. Help me protect my parent's life. We now put the time of our death into your loving hands. Amen.

Personal Affairs

There are a few other terms you should be familiar with:

Will: This is a legal document outlining your parent's wishes concerning the distribution of his or her assets after death. When writing a will, it is a good idea to consult with a lawyer. The law differs from state to state. A lawyer will know the state's laws and current regulations and will be able to assist with concerns about probate, inheritance taxes, joint ownership, and right of survivorship.

Mentally incapacitated: This can be a temporary or permanent condition leaving someone unable to make choices or make his or her choices known. A judge or court—not a doctor or family member—must declare your parent mentally incapacitated, in which case a legal guardian can be assigned. This could be a family member, friend, or court-appointed advocate.

If your parent is declared mentally incapacitated, there is a priority system regarding who can make decisions for him or her. In descending order, they are legal guardian, person with durable power of attorney, spouse, adult children, parent, and siblings.

Here are some additional points to keep in mind about paperwork:

- If your parent has already completed any of this paperwork, be sure you know where the documents are located.
- Get professional help.
- Do some research in advance of any discussions. Contact an expert such as the American Bar Association, the local Area Agency on Aging, or an elder-law attorney. More information is available by calling Senior Information and Assistance. Ask about free or low-cost assistance.
- It's possible for your parent to give durable power of attorney in different areas to different children. For example, you may have this responsibility for medical issues, and your sibling may have it for financial decisions.
- Keep in mind that power of attorney is a very critical role. You may be willing to assume this role, or it might be better, because of conflict or family dynamics, if your parent designates someone else.
- Regulations regarding advance directives and other legal documents vary from state to state. If you spend part of the year in one state and part in another, set up directives in both.

For more information, see the checklist section in the back of this book.

My God, I want to be prepared. Help me accept my responsibilities, and be my guide along the way. Amen.

16

Some Special Problems

Helping Your Parent Give Up the Car Keys

We are a nation of drivers. In the United States, getting one's driver's license is a giant step on the road to adulthood. Having to give up one's driver's license is also a rite of passage. It's seen as a giant step on the road to one's final days. It isn't easy on families when an adult child must tell an aging parent that it's no longer safe for him or her to drive. It's a sad time for both.

If an older person has some general confusion, a distraction can be a minor irritant in everyday home life but dangerous or even fatal while driving. Again and again, you must ask: Is it safe for my parent to keep driving? Is he in danger of harming himself or someone else?

It's the lucky family that has an older parent who realizes and can admit his or her physical limitations, who understands the danger to him- or herself and others, who voluntarily says, "I can no longer drive." Unfortunately, sometimes those who have become least capable, those at the highest risk, can be the ones who not only refuse to admit any problems but also refuse to even discuss the possibility with a concerned adult child. And they may try to convince you and themselves with self-imposed restrictions. "I don't go out on the freeway," "I don't go down that busy street," "I don't go out at night" might offer only a false sense of security.

These are some suggestions if you're concerned about your parent's driving:

Look ahead. Talk with Mom about your concerns with her driving before the situation is critical. Let her know that when she is no longer able to drive, you will be available to help her get around or to arrange rides. Watch the news reports with your parent. Unfortunately, reports on accidents involving older drivers are not uncommon. This can be the catalyst for a conversation.

Prepare. The goal is not to *take away* the keys, but rather to help your parent decide to stop driving. Do your research and gather information about older drivers. AARP and most insurance companies have materials on this. With that information in hand, your parent may realize that your suggestions and concerns are valid. It becomes his or her decision, and resistance doesn't play a part.

Be calm. Don't swoop in one day and confiscate the car keys. This almost guarantees anger, resentment, and a nearly total lack of cooperation on the part of your parent. Prepare what you're going to say. Stick to the facts (accidents, close calls, rising insurance rates, failing eyesight, and so on). Don't get caught up in your parent's anger and begin firing back. If Dad has given you power of attorney, refer to that when discussing this issue, not as a threat but as a reminder that he trusts your judgment. If someone else has power of attorney, ask that person to help you with the discussion.

Get help. Enlist the help of your parent's doctor to explain why this action is necessary. Check with the Department of Motor Vehicles in your state. Ask what the procedure is for reporting your concerns. As drivers become older and older, many states have implemented plans to address this issue. (Also, ask about getting a photo ID that is not a driver's license.)

Make a plan. Perhaps most important of all, keep in mind that you cannot take away the car keys without actually providing some backup. You need to help your parent figure out how he or she is going to get around now. When can you drive? When can your siblings? When can your spouse or children? Can someone in your parish help out? What about neighbors or friends? Are taxis or buses a possibility? Call the local Senior Information and Assistance number to find out about special low-cost van rides for the elderly.

Realize that this is hard. Recognize that your love, respect, and concern can ease your parent's sense of loss but can't eliminate it.

For more information, see the checklist section in the back of this book.

Holy Spirit, this is such a difficult time for my parent. So many things are changing, and the losses are adding up. Help me give good counsel, support, and respect to my parent. Amen.

Long-Distance Caregiving: Talking on the Phone

Long-distance caregiver is a term used to describe an increasing number of adult children who live in one part of the country but are trying to monitor the health and well-being of an aging parent in another. Most sons and daughters who do this experience worry, frustration, and guilt. How do you know if Mom is eating right? Why didn't she tell you she was going in for that test? Why did you take this job so far away? How many voice-mail messages do you have to leave before her doctor calls you back? What's going on there? The urge is to hop on a plane and go find out. The reality in most cases is that commitments to one's spouse, children, and job, not to mention the expense of airfare, make that impossible.

Here is a list of steps to take when caregiving from a distance:

Make contact information accessible. Make sure your name, address, and phone number are posted by your parent's phone with a note asking that you be contacted if there is a problem. Be certain that your parent's doctor—as well as any home-care workers (visiting nurse, housekeeper, physical therapist, and so on)—has the same information.

Involve neighbors and friends. Give your name, address, and phone number to the neighbor or friend who is already in regular contact with your parent, and get his or her number, too. Ask if you can give him or her a call if you can't reach your parent. Maybe you can arrange to check in with this person once in a while just to see how Mom is doing.

Plan in advance. If your parent is going to be released from a hospital or nursing home, ask to speak to the discharge planner as soon as possible. This is the staff member who figures out what services your parent will need and how frequently he or she will need them. Don't wait until the day your parent is going home. Sometimes there's not much notice of discharge day, so do some planning in advance.

Contact local resources. If you're looking for health care or social services in your parent's area, call the telephone directory in his or her area code and ask for Senior Information and Assistance, or call the toll-free Eldercare Locator number: (1-800) 677-1116. You can also visit their Web site at www.eldercare.gov/Eldercare/Public/Home.asp. Most areas have case management services. Through a state-subsidized or private program, a case manager can coordinate the team of health- and home-care professionals who will be working with your parent.

When you talk to your parent on the phone, make sure to do the following:

Pay attention. Is something new going on? For example, is Mom talking about friends dying? Is she suddenly concerned about a particular ache or pain? Don't discount comments because you've "heard it all before." Listen to the message between the lines. Is she afraid of being alone? Is she worried that she may have a new medical problem?

Talk to both parents. If both parents are still living, spend time talking to each alone. Ask Mom how she's doing and how Dad is doing. Ask Dad the same.

Call frequently and regularly. Agree on a time that's good for both of you: "I'll call you on Monday evening" or "I'll call Thursday morning." Mark it on your calendar so you don't forget. A week probably passes very quickly for you. That may not be true for your parent, who really looks forward to hearing from you and will worry about you if you fail to call.

Make a list. Suggest that your parent jot down a few notes between calls to get ready for the next one. You do the same. This way neither of you will forget something important that needs to be discussed or a bit of news that will be fun to share.

> Dear God, I really hate being so far away from my parent. But I know you're always close by, always watching and protecting. Increase my faith and trust in your will. Give me patience for the challenges we face. Amen.

Long-Distance Caregiving: Visiting Home

The telephone can be an invaluable tool for monitoring your parent's well-being, but it works best when coupled with visits to Mom or Dad. Those visits can go a long way toward making sure your parent's needs are met and helping calm your worries, too. Here are some things you can do when visiting your mom or dad:

Plan ahead. Maybe you want to call Dad's doctor and others working with him and arrange meetings with them to discuss how he's doing. If possible, include your father in any meetings. Waiting until you are at Dad's house to begin setting up meetings means trying to make arrangements on short notice and spending time on the phone that could be better spent with him.

Be prepared for medical questions. When you do meet the doctor, have your list of questions and concerns ready, based on what Mom has said—and not said—during your telephone conversations, on what you have observed during this visit with her, and on the most current assessment. How have your parent's health and living conditions changed since the last time you were home? What needs have become more prominent? Are there new ones?

Don't panic. You may encounter what seem like drastic changes, including a great deal of deterioration. Because you haven't witnessed those changes on a day-to-day or week-by-week basis, the difference between now and six months ago may seem more startling to you than to your parent or a sibling who has been around more frequently. Their failure to mention these changes to you does not mean they have been hiding them from you; they simply may not see them. You each have a unique perspective; all are helpful when trying to make an accurate evaluation.

Don't charge into town with all the answers. You will often meet with stiff resistance, not just from Dad but from your siblings who live closer and also have been playing a role in taking care of him. Ask how you can help and offer suggestions. Work *with* your father and siblings.

Think small. Prioritize the needs. Begin with suggestions that are least threatening and that allow your parent the greatest amount of independence. Maybe this is the visit to set up some sort of housekeeping. Next time you may arrange for assistance with finances. But begin that process now by raising the issue with your parent. You are not going to fix all the problems in one visit. Give yourself time. Becoming agitated with yourself, your parent, or your siblings will only get in the way.

Remember that your role as long-distance caregiver is something new not just to you but to society as well. In days gone by, most members of the extended family lived close to one another, and those who did move far away returned infrequently, if at all. Automobiles, interstate highways, jets, cell phones, and the Internet have made our world smaller and made the role of long-distance caregiver possible.

> Please, sweet Jesus, help me find a way to get back home for a visit. And help me be ready for what I may find there. I want to trust in you completely. Help me increase my faith. Amen.

Keeping Secrets, Telling Lies

It's a bad idea to keep it a secret from immediate family members that your mother or father is facing a terminal illness. Not always telling Mom or Dad the whole truth is a mistake, too. Sooner or later, that secret is going to be revealed. When that happens, a loving relationship based on trust is damaged. People are hurt more than they would have been if everyone had simply been honest from the beginning.

The temptation to keep secrets can be powerful. If Dad is terribly frightened by the words *cancer* and *malignant*, it's easy to want to gloss over what the doctor has said. Why not just refer to his condition as "stomach problems" and keep his spirits up by telling him he'll soon be back on his feet and good as new? But your father is an adult. He has the right to hear the truth, even if it's a harsh truth, and he has the right to make his own decisions. He will be asked to sign a consent form for any treatments he receives. To make good decisions, he needs to know all the facts.

Telling little lies also sells a parent short. Mom didn't reach old age without going through hard times and squarely facing difficulties that couldn't be avoided. Often a parent, even one who is frail, is much tougher and wiser than an adult child realizes.

If both your parents are still living, there may also be times when one of them says to you, "Don't tell your mother" or "Don't tell your father." But a spouse knows when there's a serious problem, and hearing "Everything's fine" can make him or her worry even more, because obviously everything *isn't* fine. Obviously something is very wrong. It's usually far better for your parents to talk about the situation openly and candidly.

There may also be times when a parent wants to keep some of his or her children in the dark. "Don't tell your brother. He has enough to worry about with his job." "Don't tell your sister. It will only upset her." Of course bad news will add to his worry! Of course it will upset her! Some things in life are very upsetting, and it is very upsetting to be excluded from a family circle. After the fact, your sibling may think, *Why wasn't I told? Did Dad like my sibling more than he liked me? Did Mom have such a low opinion of my ability to cope? Was it my sibling who shut me out?*

Keeping such secrets also robs a person of the time to prepare for what's going to happen. Everyone needs time to come to terms mentally, emotionally, and spiritually with the idea that a mother or father is going to die.

Getting the secret out into the open means more than simply stating it out loud. It means being there for your parents, for your siblings, as they too acknowledge the harsh reality that must be faced. It means supporting, encouraging, consoling, and loving one another. Maybe it means all of you coming together, one final time, as a family.

What about keeping secrets when it's *not* a life-and-death situation? Lying can seem like such a good idea at the time. For example, Mom has made it clear she will not pay for extra medical help at home. If her health insurance doesn't cover a visiting nurse, then she will do without. But you're the one handling her bills now. You know she has plenty of money. She's just being stubborn. So you go ahead and hire a nurse and tell Mom that the insurance company has a new policy. No harm done, right?

That's not so. When you start lying to your parent or begin withholding information from him or her, harm *is* being done. When the truth comes out, and it always seems to at the worst possible moment, it can take a long time before trust is reestablished. "Why didn't you tell me?" is the natural question. "What else have you been lying about?" comes next. "What else are you *going* to lie about?" follows.

You may truly have your parent's best interests at heart. You don't want to upset Dad. You don't want Mom to know, because she won't agree with the decision. But, again, your parent has a right to know. Mom needs to know if she is going to make informed choices. Dad needs to know if he is going to be able to prepare for what's coming.

When you're tempted to lie, imagine someone keeping similar personal and vital information from you just so you won't worry. You would be furious—and rightly so.

Imagine that you suddenly find out that you need a very serious operation very soon, but your loved ones have known for a year that this was a possibility and didn't tell you. Yes, you would have worried for a year if you had known, but you would have also had time to prepare yourself for this. Worse, how can you trust your loved ones now when they didn't even respect you enough to tell you the truth then?

Telling the truth is another way to show your love for your parent. Love makes many demands, and one of them is honesty. Love never tricks a person. Love never uses a person's resources without that person's knowledge. Love never says, "I know what's best for you, and so you have no say in this." The truth can be cold and cruel and terrifying. When we tell that truth or when we hear it, we need the warmth, the caring, and the comfort only a loved one can give.

> Holy Spirit, I know I should not tell a lie. But sometimes it seems like a good idea. Help me tell the truth about very difficult subjects. Show me the way. Amen.

Dealing with Your Parent's Racial and Ethnic Prejudices

It's not uncommon for an aging parent to use a derogatory term to describe someone's race or ethnic background. It's embarrassing to you and disrespectful to the people providing care for your mom or dad. Sometimes Dad isn't deliberately trying to offend anyone, but his prejudices stand out more starkly now as society continues to try to move beyond a time of ignorance and hate.

With that in mind, here are some things you can do to help your parent and the person who comes to assist him or her:

Talk with Dad about the person who is helping him. Emphasize the nurse's, therapist's, or worker's training and experience. If you're bringing in someone to assist with home care, don't just spring that person on your father and hope for the best.

Remind your parent and the care provider that it may take a lot of patience on both sides. A professional caregiver may speak

English as a second language and have a strong accent. It might take your mother a while before she can easily understand what he or she is saying.

Don't let your parent off the hook. Challenge prejudice, especially if your parent slips up when your children are around. Grandparents can have a profound influence on the youngest generation, an influence that can be negative as well as positive. Remember that none of us is ever too old to learn. None of us is ever too old to become a better—a more loving—person.

Jesus, we were all created as equal. Help us, your brothers and sisters, love one another. Amen.

Euthanasia and the "Right to Die"

As the "right to die" movement continues to push forward in the political arena, with arguments centering on quality of life and the right to choose, society is in grave danger of closing its eyes to the value of human life. Your parent may be influenced by this talk. It's frightening to think your mom might come to believe that her life means so little that the world—or your family—would be better off without her. But that's one of the messages the movement is sending. The messages are coupled with the natural human fear of pain—fear of being in pain; fear of seeing a loved one in pain.

In 1995, the Pontifical Council for Pastoral Assistance published the "Charter for Health Care Workers." It is the "synthesis of the Church's position on all that pertains to the affirmation, in the field of health care, of the primary and absolute value of life: of all life and the life of every human being." Here is a particularly pointed quote:

The sick person who feels surrounded by a loving human and Christian presence does not give way to depression and anguish as would be the case if one were left to suffer and die alone and wanting to be done with life. This is why *euthanasia is a defeat* for the one who proposes it, decides it, and carries it out. Far from being an act of mercy to the patient, euthanasia is a gesture of individual and social self-pity and an escape from an unbearable situation.

These are some points to keep in mind:

There is a time to die. Advances in medical technology have made it possible to manipulate that natural timing, but just because something can be done doesn't necessarily mean it should be done. Pope John Paul II offered a good example of that in his final years and in his death. (For more information concerning euthanasia, see the *Catechism of the Catholic Church*, 2276–79.)

You can educate yourself. Finding out what your parent wants is important. So is talking to a priest or Catholic chaplain about your family's particular concerns and questions.

Pain can be controlled. Despite what the backers of the right-to-die movement say, pain can be controlled in most cases. Advances continue to be made in the area of pain management. If Dad is in pain, talk to his doctor about it.

Hospice is an option. It is a tremendous service. Take advantage of it.

The final months, weeks, or days of your parent's life may be very difficult, but they also may be very rewarding. Your mother may need that time to better prepare to die. You may need that time to say good-bye, to prepare to be a survivor, the one left behind. To miss out on those months, weeks, or days—to cut them short—would be a tragedy.

> Almighty God, protect all life from conception to natural death. Help each of us see the true value of life as you see it. Guide us, as a society, to stop the campaign of fear and embrace your loving will for us. Amen.

Taking Care of a Crabby or Formerly Abusive Parent

It's hard to be patient when you're taking care of a parent who's crabby, and it can be extremely difficult to care for a parent who physically, emotionally, or sexually abused you when you were younger.

Let's look at the crabby parent first. It could be that Dad has always been grumpy. When you reached adulthood, you had a real sense of relief because you could move out and be on your own. But now he needs your help. He doesn't necessarily want it and may, in fact, resent it, but he needs it. Each time you approach his front door you feel as if you're entering the lion's den. You hope you'll be lucky enough to come out unscathed.

Sometimes a parent who has been pleasant for most of his or her life suddenly turns grumpy. That isn't surprising, and, most likely, it's temporary. Mom's change in disposition may be triggered by the other things happening to her. It's easy to snap at the people around you, even those you love the most, when you don't feel well.

But if that change in personality continues to stretch on, you need to talk it over with your parent's doctor. It could be related to a medical, a mental, or an emotional problem that can be addressed. It could be the side effect of a new medication, one that leaves your mother feeling anxious. Or it could be that a prescription Mom has been taking for a long time is causing this new and different reaction because her body chemistry is changing.

Whether your parent has been a lifelong crab or is only being nasty temporarily, it's important for you to remember that this is a situation that presents a high risk of abuse. It's possible for an adult child to lose control and harm a parent. Obviously, that's never right. Neither is an aging parent hitting an adult child. Sometimes it may be necessary for you to make sure you are at least an arm's length away from Mom or Dad. You have to keep yourself safe. If this situation arises, contact your parent's doctor and get professional help as soon as possible.

Here are some suggestions for dealing with a difficult parent:

Always respect your parent. Even when the going is rough, keep in mind the basic guidelines and principles in chapter 2. Mom should be respected. She should always be given compassionate care.

Talk about it. During a calm period, sit down with Dad and tell him what he's doing that bothers you. Be specific. It could be that your father isn't even aware that something is upsetting you.

If the situation becomes volatile, get away completely. Get out of the house, calm down, and try to analyze the situation more objectively. If Mom is pushing your buttons—and nobody can push our buttons like family—try to control your reaction. Change the subject. Move on.

Consider stepping aside. If Dad fights you every step of the way, maybe you can't be his primary caregiver. Look into getting someone else to do the cleaning, the laundry, the personal care, and so on. Research your resources.

Get support. Talk with others who understand what you're going through. A support group can be a wonderful release. A long lunch with a good friend can do wonders. You need to remember to take care of yourself, not just for your own sake but for the sake of your parent.

Pray. Of course, the best support for you, one that's always available, is God. He's there, always ready to comfort you, to guide you, and to love you completely. Turn it all over to God. Prayer can go a long way in helping you through this challenge.

If your parent abused you when you were younger, a caregiving role is probably extremely difficult, if not impossible. Perhaps you simply can't be the one to take care of Dad. There's no reason to get down on yourself if you're not able to help him. There's no reason to offer an explanation to others who ask why, except to say, "I'm not able to do that." You do not have to be the frontline caregiver. You can be the one who arranges for your parent to get help from other people.

If you do assume a caregiving role, get the support you need. Counseling can help. Ignoring memories and feelings—and the many physical, mental, and emotional complications they can trigger and aggravate—doesn't make them go away.

It may be clear now that you're never going to be able to resolve this situation with your parent, but you may be able to come to terms with it yourself. That may mean you have, at best, a neutral attitude toward Dad. You love him as you would a stranger. You're civil to him, but there is no parent-child relationship or bond there. Your situation is a part of the unfairness that can touch an innocent person's life.

The ideal is to find forgiveness for those who have hurt us. However, some things seem to be unforgivable. Some damage has no quick fix. This is a time for prayer, an opportunity to receive the spiritual support of your Catholic faith: the sacraments, your parish community, daily Mass, and your parish priest, for example. All are readily available.

> Most holy Trinity, give me patience! And stay near. I'll need more soon. Amen.

Refereeing Fights between Mom and Dad

If both your parents need your help with caregiving, you may face the added challenge of handling friction in your parents' relationship. An aging couple may not get along for many reasons, and their so-called golden years of marriage may seem to be anything but that. The sad truth is that divorce is not unheard of among couples whose children have grown up and moved away. While a youngster can do little, if anything, to stop a fight between his or her parents, an adult child may feel an obligation to step forward. Here are some points to consider if you find yourself in that position:

They are two different people. Parents are not a single unit. Your mother and father are two individuals who may be at two different points in their lives. Each is dealing with his or her own losses, concerns about what is happening, worries about health, and so on.

The dynamics of the relationship are changing. One parent may be becoming more dependent on the other, a development each finds frustrating and frightening. Maybe Dad was always the strong provider and guardian. Now Mom must assume those roles. Maybe Mom did the cooking, the cleaning, the shopping, the laundry. She balanced the checkbook and sent out the Christmas cards. Now Dad is learning those jobs. This change of roles is hard on any two people of any age.

There's a history here. Maybe Mom and Dad's relationship has always been confrontational. Some couples bicker throughout their married lives.

A personality change could be a symptom of a health problem. Alzheimer's disease, a stroke, or another medical condition may change Mom or Dad from meek and mild to combative and aggressive. Talk to your family doctor about this.

A woman's role in society has changed. In years past, a woman was a housewife who took care of the children, managed the family home, and followed her husband's lead. Times have changed. An old-fashioned husband may have difficulty when his wife begins to change, too.

Your parent may be suppressing anger to keep the peace. Subconsciously, one parent may not want to disagree in any way with his or her spouse for fear that his or her last words to a spouse will be words of anger. Instead, Mom will swallow her words, and the anger will build up inside her until one day it explodes over something minor.

What can you do if your parents are having more battles?

Consider what the fight is about. How important is the issue? Is it a question that needs to be resolved, or is it just everyday friction? Is it something they need to handle themselves—for example, which soap opera to watch while they're eating lunch? (Can one program be watched and the other taped? Would it be easier if they ate that meal separately, with one parent claiming "the big television" for a week, while the other uses the smaller set that's in the bedroom or kitchen?) Or is the issue something big that needs your attention, too? Perhaps Dad wants to move to an apartment and Mom doesn't want to sell the house.

Try to avoid taking sides. Talk to each parent separately and alone. Listen to that person's point of view. If you hear both sides, you may be able to better understand each point of view. If the fight seems to be unequal and one parent really needs help, provide it. For example, it's no longer safe for Mom to drive, but Dad can't get her to give up the car keys. Or Mom is in danger of becoming ill herself, because taking care of Dad is so taxing and he refuses to allow her to spend money on outside help.

Remember that the arbitrator's role is always a delicate one, especially when all the parties are in the same family.

> I hate hearing them fight, Jesus. Please give me the strength and wisdom to be a good diplomat, to ease tensions and calm nerves, to help us remember our love for each other, and to always protect that gift. Amen.

17

Dying and Death

Preparing for Death

I'm like a tired and harassed traveler who reaches the end of
his journey and falls over. Yes, but I'll be falling into God's
arms!

—St. Thérèse of Lisieux

The summons usually begins with a phone call or an e-mail. A
brother reaches you at work. A sister leaves a message on your voice
mail. Mom is very sick. Dad is dying. Come home. As fast as you
can. Now. There is no easy way of letting go, no gentle way of saying
good-bye to a parent, not even when our faith tells us that death is
not the end.

If you live some distance from your parent, you don't want to
think about the day that call will come, but you know someday it
will. And you may hope it will come because it would be worse if the

call comes after Mom or Dad dies, leaving you no last opportunity to say, "I love you. I want to thank you. I'll miss you."

Death has been surrounded by folklore and traditions throughout human history. Every culture has rituals for and beliefs about preparing for death, death itself, and life after death. What's it *really* like to die? We don't know. How do you prepare for that moment? How do you help your parent prepare? What can you do to prepare for that time? There's no way to take away the pain, but these are some suggestions that may make that period less confusing:

Examine your own beliefs and let your parent talk about his if he wants to. Maybe the two of you believe different things about heaven and God. If your father is afraid, offer him comfort. If you're the one who's uncertain, trust your dad. This isn't the time to have a theological argument. Help him be at peace with what's happening.

Read about death and the dying process. Learn about what typically happens, step by step, as a person dies. The more you know, the better prepared you will be.

Make preparations if you don't live where your parent does. If Dad is seriously ill, or his health is steadily declining, think about what needs to be done in order for you to get to him on short notice. Who can cover for you at work? What arrangements need to be made for your spouse and kids?

Ask Mom where she would like to die. At home? At the hospital? With family at her bedside? With friends nearby? Maybe she doesn't like hospital room mob scenes and wants the opportunity to see each of her children privately when she's near death. You may need to ask her more than once where she wants to die, because as time goes by and she gets closer to death, her answer may change.

Figure out your role. Try to get a mental picture, based on your parent's preferences, of what his or her death will be like and what your role will be. If it is at home, are you leading prayers? If it is at the hospital, are you at the bedside? In the chapel?

Take care of necessary funeral details ahead of time. As the time of death approaches, you will want to focus on the immediate needs of your family.

Don't wait until the last minute to say good-bye to each other. Say the words, or the equivalent. It can be tremendously difficult for family members and a dying loved one to get those words out. But after your parent has died, it will mean a great deal to you and other family members if you were able to do this.

Help Dad prepare spiritually. Pray together. Would he like to receive the sacraments of the Eucharist, reconciliation, and the anointing of the sick, if possible?

Don't open old wounds. A parent's final days are not a good time to rehash old family arguments. If you need to resolve something between yourself and a parent or sibling, do it before this time comes, when emotions won't be running as high. Perhaps you need to resolve a family issue by yourself, on your own or with the help of a counselor or therapist.

Let people be themselves. Remember that when an aging parent is dying, family members will show their grief in different ways. Each may need to cope with it in a different way. One may want to be quiet and alone, spending time in the hospital chapel. Another may keep busy handling details that need attending. One may chatter nonstop. Another may always be demanding the latest update on a parent's condition from the medical staff. Let each person do what works best for him or her, and you do what works best for you.

Talk about how precious life is. Just because someone is bedridden doesn't mean that person's life has no value. Maybe this is a special time for Mom to pray. Maybe it is a time to reminisce with family and friends and say good-bye. Maybe it is all of those and, above all, a time to prepare for the life that comes after this life.

Your parent's death is an extremely difficult time for you, but it can also be a very rich time. Up until now you've been given the chance to show your mom how much you love her. Now you are being given the gift of being with her as she dies. You're being given the opportunity to exchange good-byes. You're being given the blessing of being there as your responsibility for her care ends and her heavenly Father calls her home. You'll be there with her as our heavenly parent reaches out to gently lead her to eternal peace, to eternal joy, to eternal life.

> Thank you, my Father, for the people who are helping my parent as the end of his or her life is approaching. Richly reward them for what they do for families like mine. Bless each of them, and give peace to their own families, too. Amen.

Talking to Your Children about Death

It's difficult, if not impossible, to explain death in words that children will understand when we don't even really understand it ourselves.

Still, it's important to take the time to talk to your children. These are some points to keep in mind:

It's easier to talk to your children about death before your parent is near death. And it is easier to talk about death in general, or the death of someone who isn't too close to the family, than to talk about the death of a loved one. You might prepare your child by bringing up the subject after an elderly parishioner or neighbor has died.

You can use books to prepare your child. Local Catholic bookstores will have age-appropriate books for children about death. Examples include *Your Grieving Child* by Bill Dodds (Our Sunday Visitor) and *Water Bugs and Dragonflies* by Doris Stickney (Pilgrim Press).

You're upset, too. It isn't just your parent's approaching death that can be upsetting to your child; it's seeing you so upset as well. Don't gloss over or hide your feelings, but be aware that your child is picking up on them.

Your child may take the death of your parent very personally. "I'm not going to see *my* grandma ever again."

A child's sense of security can be rattled. If Grandpa can die, that means Dad can die. If Dad can die, that means I can die.

It's important to choose your words carefully. In some ways, talking to your child about death is like explaining "the birds and the bees." You use words and concepts that someone at his or her age level will more easily understand. At the same time, it helps to remember that different children have different personalities and points of view. One child is more intellectual. Another is more easily frightened. Another is more sensitive. Use an approach that fits each child best. It's also best to talk to each child individually before bringing up the subject with all your children as a group.

Talking about death as "falling asleep" or using similar analogies can be confusing for a child. Phrases like those can make it difficult for some children to sleep, because they're afraid that if they do, they too will die. Also, if they see Grandma napping, they may become frightened that she has died. "God wanted Grandpa with him in heaven"—another common explanation—can make God seem pretty selfish, if not downright mean.

This can be a good time to talk about spiritual beliefs. Talk about bodies and souls. Yes, we won't see Grandma again here on earth, but where she's going is a much better place. Where she's going she'll be happy forever, and someday we'll all be there, together again.

Help me find the right words, Holy Spirit. Give me wisdom and understanding so that I can answer any questions that come up. Help me do this right. Amen.

Words That Sting, Words That Comfort

If your parent is seriously ill, you may soon discover that the reactions of others, and your own emotions, can take surprising twists and turns. It's hard to think about what is happening to your parent; it may be harder to have to say those words out loud. "Mom has had a stroke." "Dad was diagnosed with cancer." "It's at the stage where nothing else can be done." "The doctor said it's only a matter of months . . . of weeks . . . of days."

If your parent is seriously ill, you'll have to speak about the situation repeatedly. That's when questions from some of your peers may hurt. "How old is your dad?" "Did your mom smoke?" "Had he been sick for a while?" "Did she take good care of herself?" Though it's never explicitly said, the meaning seems clear: Thank God it's your parent who's sick and not mine. Mine is younger. Mine never smoked. Mine is healthy. Mine exercises and eats right.

These people don't mean to be rude, but sometimes their words sting. Theirs is a natural reaction, not unlike what combat veterans recall feeling when they learned a comrade had been killed in battle.

They felt a sense of relief, of gratefulness that—for now, anyway—they had been spared.

When your loved one is ill or dying, some people don't know what to say or are afraid they'll say the "wrong" thing. They don't say anything at all to acknowledge your parent's illness or death. They try to avoid you altogether.

Don't be surprised if you feel a strange burst of resentment toward older people who are still healthy. It's not that you wish them ill. It's not that you wish anyone ill. But why is someone your parent's age or older doing so well when your aging parent is failing so rapidly? And how can everyone else behave so normally, continue with business as usual, when your mother, or your father, is so close to death?

Seek support from people of your generation who know what you're going through. These are people whose parent or loved one has been ill or has died. They have survived those thoughtless, stinging questions. These friends and coworkers can offer unmatched compassion. They can share an amazing grace. They clearly know the power of the simple "I'm so sorry to hear that. I'll keep you and your parent and your family in my prayers."

Lord, make me more aware of you and your gentle kindness. Teach me to give comfort to others and to accept kind words in the spirit intended. Amen.

Hospice

Hospice offers tremendous support for both the terminally ill patient and the caregiver. First established by Dr. Cicely Saunders in Great Britain in 1967, hospice is a concept that has spread to countless communities. It is endorsed by medical professionals and covered by

Medicare and many insurance policies. Typically, hospice provides service for a person who is terminally ill and has less than six months to live. The hospice team includes the patient, the caregiver, the doctor, nurses, aides, respite volunteers, a social worker, and a spiritual counselor. Hospice care manages the symptoms of a disease or illness (controlling pain, for example) but doesn't aggressively treat a condition. Hospice also plays a role in protecting the rights of a dying patient.

A patient can receive hospice care at home with a family's or caregiver's support or in a hospice setting, which is usually associated with a medical facility. Hospice is designed to help a patient stay in a familiar or at least more homelike environment that can offer more personalized care. In a hospice setting, a patient has more control over his or her dying. That's not to say that this is a form of assisted suicide—which hospice opposes—rather, the patient is actively involved in making decisions. Hospice stresses providing the patient with full and accurate information about his or her condition. The patient is involved in decisions about what measures to take to prolong life.

The hospice goal is to make a person as comfortable as possible at the end of his or her life and to help that person prepare for death. With the help of the hospice team, a patient is encouraged to tell his or her life story and to take the opportunity to explore the meaning of death. After the patient has died, bereavement counseling is available for the caregiver. Obituaries in the daily newspaper that refer to a person dying peacefully while "surrounded by family" are describing the hospice ideal.

Information about hospice is available from your parent's doctor, from the hospital, and online. (There us a list of resources in the back of this book.) Be careful about relying on information given in the news on end-of-life issues; these reports can be frequently misleading about one's choices when approaching death. It is amazing how well some groups disguise their true intentions. Look for "hospice" or "palliative care" when doing your research. Hospice services are in accordance with the teaching of the Catholic Church.

Hospice has been an incredible experience for many families, but that doesn't mean your parent—or you—should feel obligated to choose it. For some families, hospice simply may not be a good fit. That doesn't mean you aren't doing things "right." Right is whatever works best for your parent and you. But it's good to keep in mind that hospice workers—much to their credit—are known for their ability to help each family develop a plan that fits its unique situation.

> We need to prepare for death, my gentle Lord. We can't do that without you. Be with us. Help the whole family feel your gentle arms around us. Thank you for your comfort. Amen.

Sorting Out, Moving On, Remembering

It's a strange feeling to no longer be a caregiver. The death of a parent brings with it a lot of grief, but it also brings a sense of relief. Maybe strangest of all, it gives you so much time. So much time to do . . . what?

This hasn't been easy. You're to be congratulated. Taking care of a parent until he or she dies is a tremendous accomplishment. Take pride in the areas where you did well, and don't get down on yourself about things you wish you had done differently. Don't get caught in the traps of "What if . . ." and "I should have . . ." and "Why didn't I . . ."

It's time to sort things out: not just your parent's belongings and the necessary paperwork, but also your own feelings. You've said good-bye to two people—the parent who was ill and the healthy person your parent used to be. Both slipped away.

It's good not to make any major changes at this time. And there's no reason to rush through cleaning out your parent's belongings, either. Try to respect your parent's wishes about getting mementos to the friends and relatives Mom or Dad wanted them to go to. See to it that this or that item is donated to the charity your parent requested. As you're sorting these things out, you may just want to sit there for a while, surrounded by and holding close the items that belonged to your mother or father. In this setting, it may be easier for you to pray for your parent. You might even pray *to* your parent.

It's going to take time for you to sort out all the feelings and emotions you've experienced as a caregiver and are experiencing as a survivor. And as time goes by, those emotions will change. There will come a time—and there's no need to rush this—when you'll want to move on. You may want to find a way, a personal ritual, to say good-bye. There's no right way of doing this. And not doing it isn't wrong.

Moving on takes time. Just as you probably didn't become a full-blown caregiver overnight, you won't instantly move on to your "new" life or return to your pre-caregiver life. Now you have to learn how to rebuild your personal life without the role that dominated it for so long. Now you may go back to jogging, gardening, and attending soccer games. You can return to the little, ordinary joys that were a part of your life before you became a caregiver. You may find new ways to experience that kind of simple joy—the joy of being alive.

In a sense, your life now has two holes. One is in your heart. You miss your mother or father, and no one can replace your parent. The other is in your calendar. You have so much time, so much *free* time.

That commodity that was so precious and so rare just a little while ago now fills your schedule.

A part of sorting out and moving on is remembering. Some of your memories might be related to your role as caregiver. You recall a good time, even a happy time, during that difficult period. Maybe it was when Mom talked about her death and wasn't afraid. Maybe when Dad made some small joke and you were both so tired it seemed like the funniest line ever said, and the two of you laughed until tears streamed down your faces.

Certainly, you will remember the time before your mother or father was ill: your childhood, birthdays and anniversaries, family events and milestones.

It can help to remember your parent's words of wisdom, his or her personal creed or philosophy. Maybe Mom or Dad never even put it into words. Maybe it's something you want to think about for a time to help you get through the difficult period following your parent's death. In any case, it's something you want to imitate in some way. It can also help to remember the times when your parent comforted you—those times when he or she helped you when you were hurting or unsure or restless, when you were discouraged or sad or frightened.

It can help if you sit down, take a deep breath, and smile, remembering—acknowledging—that as a caregiver you did the same for your mother or father.

And now your parent is at peace.

Most gracious Lord, I've reached the end. It's over now. Thanks for your help. Amen.

18

The Church and Dying

Funerals, Memorial Services, and Cremation

Years ago, Catholic funeral Masses talked of "wrath" and "mourning," and the priest was robed in black vestments. Now, while acknowledging the sorrow survivors feel, Catholic funeral Masses emphasize Christ's resurrection from the dead and the celebrant wears white. Now funerals speak of eternal life, of "angels leading you into paradise."

Here are some steps you can take when planning a parent's funeral:

Make some basic decisions. Will you have a funeral Mass, a memorial Mass, or a service only at the funeral home? Will there be an open or a closed casket; a traditional embalming and burial or a cremation? Where will your parent be buried (if he or she doesn't already have a plot)?

Ask your parent what he or she wants. Some people have no problem talking about their own funerals. Others are never able to do that. Let your parent take the lead, and offer Mom or Dad the opportunity to share her or his preferences about this. Mom may find great comfort in planning her own service. This can be a chance for her to offer a final good-bye to her friends and family. It can give her the opportunity to share, with the scriptural readings and songs she chooses, what she has come to believe about life, death, and resurrection.

Remember that funerals are for the living. Dad may see planning his funeral as a way of making his death easier for you and his other loved ones. And, being ever frugal, he may even have an eye on the bottom line as he picks out a reasonably priced casket and headstone. He may not realize that a funeral isn't just for the deceased, but also for the survivors. It's an opportunity for family and friends to gather and support one another in their sorrow while remembering their loved one with joy. It can be an important—some say vital—step in the grieving process.

Consult your parish. The local priest can give you up-to-date information on choosing between a funeral Mass and a memorial service; between a rosary and a prayer service the night before the funeral; between burial and cremation. He can help you decide about other details, too (memorial cards and pallbearers, for example).

A special note about cremation and why the church now allows it: For centuries the church banned cremation, and about a hundred years ago the church officially said cremation was forbidden because it was seen as an anti-Christian symbol. It was seen—and sometimes meant—as a slap in the face to those who believe in the resurrection of human bodies at the end of time. (The anti-Christian position held that there was no way God could raise a body from the dead if its remains had been reduced to ashes and scattered to the four winds.) The ban was loosened in the 1960s, by which time the symbolism had faded. Later, cremation was approved, as long as it is not chosen as an anti-Christian statement or to show contempt for the church.

It has become more common in recent years for adult children to forgo a funeral for a parent who hasn't made his or her wishes known. In that confusing time immediately after Mom's or Dad's death, it can be hard to come up with an answer to "Why should we have a funeral?" It can be harder still to imagine having to plan such an event and then attend it (or, even more daunting, play a role in it). Wouldn't it be easier for all concerned to have a quiet, immediate-family-only service at the cemetery? Wouldn't it be simpler to pick up the cremated remains from the funeral home, take them home, and make no immediate decision at all?

The fact is that since the church's very beginning, a burial service has been important. In part, this is because of the church's Jewish roots. Jesus was reverently buried according to Jewish custom. The remains of the earliest martyrs were (illegally) gathered by fellow Christians and secretly buried. These sites became places where community members gathered to pray and were later established as shrines. Those shrines were built and rebuilt into churches and great basilicas. (For example, as you may know, St. Peter's Basilica in Rome is built over the first pope's grave.)

But how do the practices of the first century apply to the twenty-first? How is what the church did then still of value for us now? In a 1999 pastoral statement titled "The Need to Promote the Consistent Use of Catholic Funeral Rites," Bishop Michael A. Saltarelli of the Diocese of Wilmington, Delaware, wrote:

The Church celebrates the funeral rites:

> To offer worship, praise, and thanksgiving to God for the gift of a life which has now been returned to God
>
> To affirm the Church's belief in the sacredness of the human body and the resurrection of the dead
>
> To commend the dead to God's merciful love and to plead for the forgiveness of their sins
>
> To bring hope and consolation to the living
>
> To renew our awareness of God's mercy and judgment and to meet the human need to turn always to God in times of crisis
>
> To support the Church's emphasis on the indispensable role of the wider community in the dying and death of a Christian
>
> To affirm and express the union of the Church on earth with the Church in heaven in the one great communion of saints

The celebration of the Catholic funeral rites promotes a healthy grieving process that can lead to deep levels of personal conversion and spiritual growth. In contrast, the avoidance of these funeral rites may short-circuit grief and healing.

Our Catholic tradition urges the Church today to face death with honest rituals that preserve its Christian and human values. Since, in rising to new life, Christ won victory over death for his followers, faith impels the Church to celebrate that victory in its funeral liturgies.

You may have noticed the use of the plural there: *liturgies.* The Order of Christian Funerals has three major liturgical celebrations and times of prayer.

The Vigil

The Order of Christian Funerals notes that the vigil is the first gathering of family and friends with the faith community immediately following the death of a loved one. It's the first opportunity for the mourners to experience God's comforting word through Scripture reading and communal prayer within the context of the Christian community.

If you have already been through this liturgy after the death of someone close to you, you know how much it means to a grieving family to have others come to share a hug, a prayer, a tear, and even a laugh. In modern times when schedules can be so busy, the vigil gives people who can't attend the funeral the opportunity to not only pay their respects to the one who has died but also offer comfort and support to those left behind.

The broad term *vigil* can include the visitation, the wake, and what might be called the vigil itself. Typically, the formal vigil prayer occurs within the visitation. The family can help design and take part in this service in a number of ways if they choose to do so. (For example, there can be Scripture readings, prayers, music, and the sharing of stories or memories.) This liturgy often includes the recitation of the rosary, so it may be referred to as the rosary.

In times past, this was held in the home of the deceased. Family members and friends stayed by the deathbed, got the body ready for burial, and then maintained a vigil through the night (a "wake") until the funeral. In the last hundred years, it has become customary for funeral homes to ready the body for burial and keep the body there. The visitation (hours during which others can pay their respects and offer support to the family) and the vigil service are sometimes held at the funeral home. In other cases, the body is transported to the church where the funeral is to be held and the service takes place there. Typically, the visitation and vigil service are held the day or evening before the funeral.

> For the repose of the soul of my parent.
> Hail Mary, full of grace, the Lord is with you. Blessed are you among women, and blessed is the fruit of your womb, Jesus. Holy Mary, Mother of God, pray for us sinners, now and at the hour of our death. Amen.

The Mass of Christian Burial

The funeral Mass includes the reception of the body at the church, the Liturgy of the Word, the Liturgy of the Eucharist, and the final commendation and farewell. Because the funeral is a rite of the Roman Catholic Church, the parish is responsible for coordinating the aspects of the liturgical preparation, including the readings, music, and ministries, such as the reader at Mass and the extraordinary ministers of the Eucharist.

At this Mass the community of believers comes together to reaffirm that life is changed, not ended. Symbols of the Resurrection (such as holy water, the pall [a long cloth placed on the coffin during Mass], the Easter Candle, incense, and white vestments) are used as reminders that the risen Christ is present, bringing the promise of baptism (from death to life) to fulfillment.

Typically, the community gathers at the parish church to commend to God one of its deceased members. That is because it's here that the Christian life begins in baptism and is nourished in the Eucharist. Once in a while, under unique circumstances and with permission from a local church authority, the funeral Mass is celebrated in a cemetery chapel.

As with the vigil, family members are encouraged to recommend Scripture readings and appropriate musical selections and to be involved in various ministries: pallbearer, singer, musician, placer of the funeral pall on the casket, reader, gift bearer, Eucharistic minister, greeter, and server. Someone can also offer a few memories of the deceased after Holy Communion. This is when family and friends can share a few details of a loved one's life and his or her influence on others. (The priest's homily, given immediately after the reading of the Gospel, is not a eulogy. Rather, it focuses on eternal life and resurrection.)

Eternal Rest

Eternal rest grant unto them, O Lord, and let perpetual light shine upon them. May their souls and all the souls of the faithful departed, through the mercy of God, rest in peace. Amen.

The Committal Rite

The Order of Christian Funerals explains that when the community commits the body to its resting place, it expresses the hope that the deceased awaits the glory of the resurrection with all those who have gone before marked with the sign of faith. This rite is an expression of the church's belief in the communion of saints. It acknowledges a change in the relationship with the deceased because of a physical separation but emphasizes that the relationship continues in the Spirit who raised Jesus from the dead.

In some places, it has become customary for only the deceased and his or her family to go to the cemetery for the rite of committal. (Sometimes the body is buried with no one there but the cemetery workers.) It's true that weather can play a role in this, but the practice of the other mourners staying at the reception following the funeral as the immediate family dashes to the cemetery for the burial is far from ideal. As the last rite of the public liturgy of the church, the committal of the body is for all.

At the committal, short Scripture passages and intercessions are read, music can be played or sung, and what could be called clear signs of leave-taking are displayed. Since loved ones can no longer see or touch the deceased, they may direct gestures toward the urn or casket. These might include, for example, a bow, a touch, a tracing of the sign of the cross, the placing of a flower, or a kiss. A family or couple may choose to do this as one. Then, too—and this is important—cultural and ethnic traditions and customs in keeping with Catholic belief need to be respected and given expression. Flowers, printed mementos, and other keepsakes can serve as reminders of the committal and the deceased.

A final point: Don't assume that if your deceased family member was not a practicing Catholic, he or she cannot have a Mass of Christian Burial. Contact the local parish or diocesan Catholic Cemeteries office for more information.

> Holy angels, lead my parent into paradise. Escort this soul into the arms of our loving Father. Amen.

The Communion of Saints

The Catholic Church's teaching on the communion of saints can be very consoling as your parent nears death and after he or she has died. You can pray for, and to, your departed parent. You can ask for your mother's or father's help. The teaching says that love is more powerful than the grave. It says that the relationship you two share doesn't have to end. Your love goes beyond death.

The *communion of saints* doesn't refer only to those holy men and women who have been canonized, who have been declared saints. Rather, it includes the faithful who are still on earth, the souls who have gone to heaven (and the angels there), and the departed who are in purgatory. The traditional terms for the three different groups is the church militant (the faithful on earth), the church triumphant (the souls in heaven), and the church suffering (the souls in purgatory).

Purgatory may seem like an old-fashioned or outdated concept. It isn't talked about much these days, and the way it was presented in the past tended to be confusing or childish. We need to think of purgatory as a state of being in which we're sorry for our sins. Perhaps we see clearly the ramifications of our selfishness and begin to understand the far-reaching effects of all our sins.

Is purgatory painful? Yes, if admitting mistakes and realizing how we've hurt others causes us pain. And since this is painful on earth, why wouldn't it be painful where we're becoming better at loving and are getting rid of our attachment to what isn't good? Again, on earth any personal growth or change is typically accompanied by fear and anxiety. And while being in purgatory has been compared to a precious metal being purified in a fire, that doesn't mean purgatory has fire as we know it.

How long does a soul stay in purgatory? We don't know, although with God, a day can be as a thousand years, and a thousand years a day (2 Peter 3:8). Time really is relative. It passes quickly when we're having fun and seems to stand still when we're in pain, whether physical or emotional.

In a general audience in 1999, Pope John Paul II noted:

> For those who find themselves in a condition of being open to God, but still imperfectly, the journey towards full beatitude [heaven] requires a purification, which the faith of the Church illustrates in the doctrine of "Purgatory." . . . Those who live in this state of purification after death are not separated from God but are immersed in the love of Christ. Neither are they separated from the saints in heaven—who already enjoy the fullness of eternal life—nor from us on earth—who continue on our pilgrim journey to the Father's house. We all remain united in the Mystical Body of Christ, and we can therefore offer up prayers and good works on behalf of our brothers and sisters in Purgatory.

What does this teaching mean for you and your parent? It means that as Dad says good-bye to you and his family on earth, loved ones in heaven are preparing to greet him and to welcome him home with the angels. It means that Mom, trusting in God's mercy, may spend time after her death further getting ready to enter her heavenly reward. And as she does, you can continue to pray for her. You can continue to help her.

It means that now in heaven (or purgatory), your parent still loves you. Your parent can ask God to bless you, to watch over you, to give you strength and comfort. Your parent can ask God to help you find your way. Your parent can ask God to lead you toward that incredible day when, once again, you and your parent will be together. Together forever.

Saints in heaven, welcome my parent. Saints in heaven, guide my parent home. Saints in heaven, pray for us. Amen.

Part Three
Appendixes

✝

Appendix I:
Resources for Caregivers

This section lists many of the organizations that can help caregivers find the resources they need to do their jobs well. Because Web sites are constantly changing, you may want to check my Web site, www .youragingparent.com, for updated resource information.

The resources are arranged in the following categories: Caregiver, Catholic, Critical Issues, Death and Dying, Disability, Diversity, Government, Grandparents, Housing, Legal, Mental Health, National Organizations, Resource Information, and Support.

Caregiver

Caregiving.com
www.caregiving.com

Caring to Help Others (online caregiver training manual)
www.caringtohelpothers.com

Catholic Caregivers
An online caregiver community and resources for parishes and dioceses
www.catholiccaregivers.com

Children of Aging Parents

www.caps4caregivers.org

(1-800) 227-7294

ElderCare Online

www.ec-online.net

Family Caregiver Alliance

www.caregiver.org

(1-800) 445-8106

Friends of St. John the Caregiver

Catholic organization promoting care for the caregiver

www.FSJC.org

National Alliance for Caregiving

www.caregiving.org

National Family Caregivers Association

www.nfcacares.org

(1-800) 896-3650

Your Aging Parent

Spirituality, information, and resources for Catholic caregivers

www.youragingparent.com

Catholic

Caregiver Assistance Network of Catholic Social Services of Southwestern Ohio

www.cssdoorway.org/caregiver.html

(513) 241-7745

Catholic Caregivers

An online caregiver community and resources for parishes and dioceses

www.catholiccaregivers.com

Catholic Charities USA

www.catholiccharitiesusa.org

(703) 549-1390

Catholic Health Association of the United States

www.chausa.org

National headquarters: (314) 427-2500

Washington office: (202) 296-3993

Catholic Information Network

www.cin.org

Catholic Medical Association

www.cathmed.org

(781) 455-0259

Catholic News Service

www.catholicnews.com

(202) 541-3250

Catholic Online

www.catholic.org

(661) 869-1000

Creighton University Online Ministries

www.creighton.edu/CollaborativeMinistry/online.html

Online retreat

www.creighton.edu/CollaborativeMinistry/cmo-retreat.html

Friends of St. John the Caregiver

Catholic organization promoting care for the caregiver

www.FSJC.org

Knights of Columbus

www.kofc.org

(203) 752-4000

National Association of Catholic Chaplains

www.nacc.org

(414) 483-4898

National Catholic Bioethics Center

www.ncbcenter.org

(215) 877-2660

The mission of this autonomous entity, formerly the Pope John XXIII Medical-Moral Research and Education Center, is to safeguard the dignity of the human person through research, education, publishing, and consultation in the medical and life sciences.

National Pastoral Life Center

www.nplc.org

(212) 431-7825

New Advent Catholic Supersite

www.newadvent.org

Pontifical Council for Health Pastoral Care

www.healthpastoral.org

The council is in charge of coordinating the activities of the different dicasteries of the Roman Curia as they relate to the health-care sector and its problems. It spreads, explains, and defends the teachings of the church on health issues and favors the church's involvement in health-care practice.

Sacred Space

www.sacredspace.ie

This daily prayer site is produced by the Irish Jesuits.

Universalis Publishing: Liturgy of the Hours

www.universalis.com/-700/today.htm

U.S. Conference of Catholic Bishops

www.nccbuscc.org

Catechism

www.nccbuscc.org/catechism/text/index.htm

Death and Dying
www.usccb.org/prolife/publicat/deathdyi.htm
Issues in Care for the Dying
www.usccb.org/bishops/directives.shtml#partfive
(202) 541-3000

Vatican
www.vatican.va/phome_en.htm

Your Aging Parent
Spirituality, information, and resources for Catholic caregivers
www.youragingparent.com

Critical Issues

American Medical Association: Older Driver Safety
www.ama-assn.org/ama/pub/category/8925.html
(1-800) 621-8335

National Center on Elder Abuse
www.elderabusecenter.org
(202) 898-2586

National Clearinghouse for Alcohol and Drug Information
www.health.org
(1-800) 729-6686
Español: (1-877) 767-8432

National Highway Traffic Safety Administration:
Older Road Users
www.nhtsa.dot.gov/people/injury/olddrive
(1-888) 327-4236

National Senior Citizens Law Center
www.nsclc.org
Washington: (202) 289-6976
Los Angeles: (213) 639-0930
Oakland: (510) 663-1055

National Strategy for Suicide Prevention:
Suicide among the Elderly
www.mentalhealth.org/suicideprevention/elderly.asp
(1-800) 789-2647

Substance Abuse and Mental Health Services Administration
www.samhsa.gov
(1-877) 696-6775

Death and Dying

Aging with Dignity
www.agingwithdignity.org
(1-888) 5-WISHES (594-7437)

Americans for Better Care of the Dying
www.abcd-caring.org
(703) 647-8505

Caring Connections
www.caringinfo.org
(1-800) 658-8898

Hospice Net
www.hospicenet.org

**Supportive Care of the Dying:
A Coalition for Compassionate Care**
www.careofdying.org
(503) 215-5053

Disability

ABLEDATA
www.abledata.com
(1-800) 227-0216

DisabilityInfo.gov
www.disabilityinfo.gov

**Untangling the Web: Where Can I Go to Get
Information about Disabilities?**
www.icdi.wvu.edu/Others.htm

Diversity

Indian Health Service: Elder Care Initiative
www.ihs.gov/MedicalPrograms/ElderCare/index.asp
(413) 584-0790

National Asian Pacific Center on Aging

www.napca.org

(1-800) 33-NAPCA (336-2722)

National Caucus and Center on Black Aged

www.ncba-aged.org

(202) 637-8400

National Hispanic Council on Aging

www.nhcoa.org

(202) 429-0787

National Indian Council on Aging

www.nicoa.org

(505) 292-2001

National Resource Center on Native American Aging

www.med.und.nodak.edu/depts/rural/nrcnaa

(701) 777-3848

Government

Administration on Aging

www.aoa.gov

Elders and Families

www.aoa.gov/eldfam/eldfam.asp

(202) 619-0724

Agency for Healthcare Research and Quality
www.ahrq.gov
(301) 427-1364

AgingStats.gov
www.agingstats.gov

Centers for Disease Control and Prevention
www.cdc.gov
(1-800) 311-3435

Centers for Medicare and Medicaid Services
www.cms.hhs.gov
Medicaid overview
www.cms.hhs.gov/medicaid/CONSUMER.ASP
(1-877) 267-2323

Federal Emergency Management Agency
www.fema.gov
(202) 566-1600

Federal Trade Commission: Consumer Information
www.ftc.gov/ftc/consumer.htm
Aging Parents and Adult Children Together
www.ftc.gov/bcp/conline/pubs/services/apact/index.html
(1-877) FTC-HELP (382-4357)

FedWorld.gov
www.fedworld.gov
Voice mail: (703) 605-6000

FirstGov for Seniors
www.seniors.gov
(1-800) FED-INFO (333-4636)

Healthfinder
www.healthfinder.gov

Health.gov
www.health.gov

**Health Resources and Services Administration:
Division of Facilities Compliance and Recovery**
www.hrsa.gov/osp/dfcr

Healthy People
www.healthypeople.gov

Library of Congress: THOMAS: Legislative Information
http://thomas.loc.gov
(202) 707-5000

**Medicare: The Official U.S. Government Site
for People with Medicare**
www.medicare.gov
(1-800) MEDICARE

National Cemetery Administration
www.cem.va.gov

National Institute of Mental Health

www.nimh.nih.gov

(1-866) 615-6464

National Institute on Aging

www.nih.gov/nia/

Resource Directory for Older People

www.nia.nih.gov/healthinformation/resourcedirectory.htm

(1-800) 222-2225

National Institute on Drug Abuse

www.nida.nih.gov

(301) 443-1124

National Institutes of Health

www.nih.gov

(301) 496-4000

National Library of Medicine

www.nlm.nih.gov

(1-888) FIND-NLM (346-3656)

National Mental Health Information Center

www.mentalhealth.org

(1-800) 789-2647

SeniorHealth.gov

www.nihseniorhealth.gov

Social Security Online

www.ssa.gov

(1-800) 772-1213

U.S. Consumer Product Safety Commission: Older Consumers Safety

www.cpsc.gov/cpscpub/pubs/older.html

(301) 504-6816

U.S. Department of Health and Human Services

www.dhhs.gov

Aging

www.dhhs.gov/aging

(1-877) 696-6775

U.S. Department of Veterans Affairs

www.va.gov

Veterans Health Administration

www1.va.gov/health_benefits/

VA Benefits: (1-800) 827-1000

U.S. Environmental Protection Agency: Aging Initiative

www.epa.gov/aging/index.htm

(202) 564-2188

U.S. Food and Drug Administration

www.fda.gov

(1-888) INFO-FDA (463-6332)

U.S. Senate Special Committee on Aging
http://aging.senate.gov
(202) 224-5364

Grandparents

Consumer Product Safety Commission: A Grandparents' Guide for Family Nurturing and Safety
www.cpsc.gov/cpscpub/pubs/grand/704.html
(301) 504-7923

Foundation for Grandparenting
www.grandparenting.org

Generations United
www.gu.org
(202) 289-3979

Housing

Consumer Consortium on Assisted Living
www.ccal.org
(703) 533-3225

Myziva.net: The Complete Nursing Home Guide
www.myziva.net
(1-866) 469-9482

Legal

American Bar Association

www.abanet.org

Consumers' Guide to Legal Help: Finding Free Help

www.abanet.org/legalservices/findlegalhelp/faq_freehelp.cfm

Facts about Law and the Elderly

www.abanet.org/media/factbooks/eldtoc.html

Commission on Law and Aging

www.abanet.org/aging/

(1-800) 285-2221

**National Handbook on Laws and Programs Affecting
Senior Citizens**

www.neln.org/ababook.pdf

National Senior Citizens Law Center

www.nsclc.org

Washington: (202) 289-6976

Los Angeles: (213) 639-0930

Oakland: (510) 663-1055

Mental Health

American Association for Geriatric Psychiatry

www.aagpgpa.org

(301) 654-7850

American Association of Suicidology
www.suicidology.org
(202) 237-2280

American Psychological Association Office on Aging
www.apa.org/pi/aging
(202) 336-6135

Anxiety Disorders Association of America
www.adaa.org
(240) 485-1001

Geriatric Mental Health Foundation
www.gmhfonline.org/gmhf/
(301) 654-7850

National Alliance on Mental Illness
www.nami.org
(1-800) 950-NAMI (6264)

National Mental Health Association
www.nmha.org
(1-800) 969-NMHA (6642)

National Mental Health Consumers' Self-Help Clearinghouse
www.mhselfhelp.org
(1-800) 553-4539

National Organizations

Alcoholics Anonymous
www.alcoholics-anonymous.org
(212) 870-3400

Alzheimer's Association
www.alz.org
(1-800) 272-3900

American Cancer Society
www.cancer.org
(1-800) ACS-2345

American Council of the Blind: Resources for Older Individuals Who Are Blind or Visually Impaired
www.acb.org/resources/older.html
(1-800) 424-8666

American Diabetes Association
www.diabetes.org
(1-800) DIABETES (342-2383)

American Foundation for the Blind: Seniors
www.afb.org/Section.asp?SectionID=35
(1-800) AFB-LINE (232-5463)

American Heart Association
www.americanheart.org
(1-800) AHA-USA-1 (242-8721)

American Hospice Foundation
www.americanhospice.org
(202) 223-0204

American Liver Foundation
www.liverfoundation.org
(1-800) GO-Liver (465-4837)
(1-888) 4HEP-USA (443-7872)

American Lung Association
www.lungusa.org
(1-800) LUNGUSA (548-8252)

American Pain Foundation
www.painfoundation.org
(1-888) 615-PAIN (7246)

American Parkinson Disease Association
www.apdaparkinson.org
National office: (1-800) 223-2732
West Coast office: (1-800) 908-2732

American Red Cross
www.redcross.org
(202) 303-4498

American Stroke Association
www.strokeassociation.org
(1-888) 4-STROKE (478-7653)

Amyotrophic Lateral Sclerosis Association

www.alsa.org

(1-800) 782-4747

Arthritis Daily

www.arthritisdaily.com

Arthritis Foundation

www.arthritis.org

(1-800) 568-4045

Depression and Bipolar Support Alliance

www.dbsalliance.org

(1-800) 826-3632

Epilepsy Foundation

www.epilepsyfoundation.org

(1-800) 332-1000

Hospice Association of America

www.nahc.org/HAA/

(202) 546-4759

Hospice Foundation of America

www.hospicefoundation.org

(1-800) 854-3402

Huntington's Disease Society of America

www.hdsa.org

(1-800) 345-HDSA (4372)

Leukemia and Lymphoma Society

www.leukemia-lymphoma.org

(1-800) 955-4572

Lupus Foundation of America

www.lupus.org

(202) 349-1155

National Cancer Institute

www.cancer.gov

(1-800) 4-CANCER (422-6237)

National Hospice and Palliative Care Organization

www.nhpco.org

(703) 837-1500; (1-800) 658-8898

**National Institute of Arthritis and Musculoskeletal
and Skin Diseases**

www.niams.nih.gov

(1-877) 22-NIAMS

National Multiple Sclerosis Society

www.nationalmssociety.org

(1-800) FIGHT-MS (344-4867)

National Osteoporosis Foundation

www.nof.org

(202) 223-2226

National Parkinson Foundation
www.parkinson.org
(1-800) 327-4545

National Stroke Association
www.stroke.org
(1-800) STROKES (787-6537)

Osteoporosis and Related Bone Diseases—
National Resource Center
www.osteo.org
(1-800) 624-BONE

Resource Information

AARP
www.aarp.org
AgeLine Database
www.aarp.org/ageline
AgeSource Worldwide
www.aarp.org/research/agesource/
Legal Hotlines
www.legalhotlines.org
(1-888) OUR-AARP (687-2277)

Alzheimer's Disease Education and Referral Center
www.alzheimers.org
(1-800) 438-4380

Alzhome: The Key to Keeping Your Loved One at Home
www.bsu.edu/web/nursing/alzhome
(765) 285-1471

Alzinfo.org: The Alzheimer's Information Site
www.alzinfo.org
(1-800) ALZINFO

ALZwell Caregiver Support
www.alzwell.com

American Federation for Aging Research
www.infoaging.org
(212) 703-9977

Food Research and Action Center:
Food Stamps for the Elderly Resource Center
www.frac.org/html/news/fsp/fselderlycenter.htm
(202) 986-2200

Health and Age
www.healthandage.com
Aging and Its Implications (online primer)
www.healthandage.com/html/res/primer/index.htm

Health Compass
www.healthcompass.org
(212) 703-9977

Hospice Education Institute
www.hospiceworld.org
Hospicelink: (1-800) 331-1620
(207) 255-8800

Hospice Web
www.hospiceweb.com

Internet Public Library: Health and Medical Sciences
www.ipl.org/div/subject/browse/hea00.00.00/

Mayo Clinic Senior Health Center
www.mayoclinic.com/health/senior-health/HA99999

Medline Plus
www.nlm.nih.gov/medlineplus

National Association of Area Agencies on Aging
www.n4a.org
(202) 872-0888

**National Institute on Aging: Long Term Care:
Choosing the Right Place**
www.niapublications.org/agepages/longterm.asp
(301) 496-1752

OncoLink
www.oncolink.com

Support

BenefitsCheckUp (A service of the National Council on the Aging)
www.benefitscheckup.org

Eldercare Locator
www.eldercare.gov
(1-800) 677-1116

Lifeline
www.lifelinesys.com
(1-800) 380-3111

National Association of Professional Geriatric Care Managers
www.caremanager.org
(520) 881-8008

National Respite Locator Service
www.respitelocator.org
(1-800) 473-1727, ext. 222

Visiting Nurse Associations of America
www.vnaa.org
(617) 737-3200

Well Spouse Association
www.wellspouse.org
(1-800) 838-0879

Suggested Reading

Ball, Ann. *The Catholic Book of the Dead*. Huntington, IN: Our Sunday Visitor, 1995.

Beerman, Susan, and Judith Rappaport-Musson. *Eldercare 911: The Caregiver's Complete Handbook for Making Decisions*. Amherst, NY: Prometheus Books, 2002.

Breitung, Joan C. *The Elder Care Sourcebook*. Chicago: Contemporary Books, 2002.

Carr, Sasha, and Sandra Choron. *The Caregiver's Essential Handbook*. Chicago: Contemporary Books, 2003.

Catechism of the Catholic Church. 2nd ed. Washington, DC: United States Catholic Conference, 1997.

Chiffolo, Anthony F., ed. *John Paul II: In My Own Words*. New York: Gramercy Books, 2002.

Chilson, Richard W. *Meditation*. Notre Dame, IN: Sorin Books, 2004.

Delehanty, Hugh, and Elinor Ginzler. *Caring for Your Parents: The Complete AARP Guide*. New York: Sterling Publishing, 2005.

Dodds, Bill. *Your Grieving Child*. Huntington, IN: Our Sunday Visitor, 2001.

Foley, Leonard, ed. *Every Day and All Day: Catholic Prayer.* Revised by Patti Normile. Cincinnati, OH: St. Anthony Messenger Press, 1997.

Friesen, Lynette. *After Goodbye: A Daughter's Story of Grief and Promise.* Notre Dame, IN: Sorin Books, 2005.

Gausseron, Nicole. *Believe That I Am Here.* The Notebooks of Nicole Gausseron, book 1. Chicago: Loyola Press, 2003.

————. *I Am with You Always.* The Notebooks of Nicole Gausseron, book 3. Chicago: Loyola Press, 2004.

————. *Walk with Me.* The Notebooks of Nicole Gausseron, book 2. Chicago: Loyola Press, 2004.

Ingram, Kristen Johnson. *Wine at the End of the Feast: Embracing Spiritual Change as We Age.* Chicago: Loyola Press, 2003.

John Paul II. *Go in Peace: A Gift of Enduring Love.* Edited by Joseph Durepos. Chicago: Loyola Press, 2003.

————. *Lessons for Living.* Edited by Joseph Durepos. Chicago: Loyola Press, 2004.

Koch, Carl J. *Journalkeeping.* Notre Dame, IN: Sorin Books, 2004.

Loverde, Joy. *The Complete Eldercare Planner: Where to Start, Which Questions to Ask, and How to Find Help.* 2nd. ed. New York: Three Rivers Press, 2000.

McDonnell, Rea, and Rachel Callahan. *Harvest Us Home: Good News as We Age.* Cincinnati, OH: St. Anthony Messenger Press, 2000.

McLeod, Beth Witrogen. *Caregiving: The Spiritual Journey of Love, Loss, and Renewal.* New York: John Wiley and Sons, 1999.

Mintz, Suzanne Geffen. *Love, Honor, and Value: A Family Caregiver Speaks Out about the Choices and Challenges of Caregiving.* Sterling, VA: Capital Books, 2002.

Morris, Virginia. *How to Care for Aging Parents.* Rev. ed. New York: Workman Publishing, 2004.

The New Revised Standard Version Bible: Catholic Edition. Nashville, TN: Catholic Bible Press, 1993.

Perry, Angela, ed. *The American Medical Association Guide to Home Caregiving.* New York: John Wiley and Sons, 2001.

Pontifical Council for Pastoral Assistance to Health Care Workers. *Charter for Health Care Workers.* Boston: St. Paul Books, 1995.

Rhodes, Linda. *Should Mom Be Left Alone? Should Dad Be Driving? Your Q & A Companion for Caregiving.* New York: New American Library, 2005.

Socias, James, ed. *Handbook of Prayers.* Princeton, NJ: Scepter Publishers, 1995.

Spencer, Glenn M., Jr. *Blessed Are Those Who Mourn: Comforting Catholics in Their Time of Grief.* Huntington, IN: Our Sunday Visitor, 1999.

Strom, Kay Marshall. *A Caregiver's Survival Guide: How to Stay Healthy When Your Loved One Is Sick.* Downers Grove, IL: InterVarsity Press, 2000.

Williams, Gene B., Patie Kay, and David Williams. *The Baby Boomer's Guide to Caring for Your Aging Parent.* Lanham, MD: Taylor, 2005.

Appendix II:
Assessment Guides,
Checklists, and Reminders

This section provides checklists and guides to help you organize some of the more challenging and complicated tasks you will face as a caregiver. Go to www.youragingparent.com for versions of these lists formatted for printing.

This is what you will find in this section:

Tips for the Caregiver
Caregiving Stress: Warning Signs
An Assessment Checklist
Home Safety Checklist
Depression Checklist
Driving Skills Checklist
Legal and Financial Paperwork Checklist
Elder Abuse Checklist
Evaluating Housing Options
Evaluation of Assisted-Living Facility
Evaluation of Nursing Home

Tips for the Caregiver

- Be aware of the presence of God and nourish your spiritual life.
- Plan ahead. Don't wait for a crisis.
- Don't panic.
- Be creative. If your first solution doesn't work, find a new one and try again.
- Get reliable information about your parent's illness and be aware of any emotional issues.
- Learn about your role as a caregiver and improve your skills.
- Practice new coping strategies for the particular challenges you face in caring for your parent.
- Find your family's strengths and work together.
- Accept offers of informal support from your family, friends, and parish community.
- Respect yourself and set limits.
- Take care of yourself with rest, good nutrition, exercise, and some time off.
- Access the formal support of social services in your community.

Follow the advice of St. Francis of Assisi: "Start by doing what's necessary, then what's possible, and suddenly you are doing the impossible."

Caregiving Stress: Warning Signs

Caring for an aging parent is such demanding work that stress can become a major factor in coping with the situation. The symptoms you may experience are similar to the symptoms of depression.

Here are some warning signs that stress is taking its toll:

- You feel angry or irritable and just want to deny the whole situation is even happening.
- You feel as if you don't have the time or energy to "waste" on pleasant activities, and you become more isolated.
- You find it hard to concentrate because you are constantly thinking about your parent's needs and what you have to do.
- You feel more and more depressed.
- Even though you are exhausted, you have problems sleeping.
- You start to develop health problems of your own.

You may feel stress for any number of reasons:

- There are multiple demands on your time and energy, but you feel as if you should be doing more.
- Some tasks and responsibilities are in direct conflict with others, and you're worried that you can't do it all.
- It seems that everyone has high expectations of you.
- You don't have the knowledge you need of aging issues and of your parent's illness, so sometimes you don't know what to do.
- You feel you can't meet the needs of your parent.
- You have limited access to the support you need and limited money to cover the costs of care.

- You feel "stuck" or "trapped" in the role of caregiving and don't know if you can do it for much longer.
- You're embarrassed when you take your parent to appointments or out for dinner.
- You and your parent and siblings don't agree on everything.
- You feel "put upon" because of lack of support.
- You feel as if your life has been taken from you.
- There is a general lack of communication—with your parent, with your parent's doctor, with your siblings.
- Your family and friends express negative attitudes about your role as a caregiver.
- It is hard to watch a parent's gradual but progressive decline.
- There are problems in other parts of your life.
- You miss your own life, your friends, your privacy.

An Assessment Checklist

There are a few basics to keep in mind when making an assessment. First, remember that what you want to accomplish—to gather information so that you can really see the whole picture—isn't something that can be done in one sitting.

To make an assessment, use the following lists of abilities and activities and:

1. Talk with your parent about each item. This is getting information from your parent's point of view and gives you a chance to form your own thoughts.

2. Later, on your own, review the information you have gathered and make a new list of the particular needs you identified with your parent.

3. Go over the list of specific items and determine your parent's degree of impairment by choosing the statement that best matches his or her ability in regard to each item:

   • My parent can do this but needs a little help, takes longer, or requires some verbal or physical assistance.

   • My parent cannot do essential parts of this and needs verbal and physical assistance.

   • My parent cannot do this and needs someone to do it for him or her.

4. Again, sit down with your parent and, item by item, plan how a need will be met and who can help your mother or father meet it.

The Overall Picture

Begin an assessment with a look at the overall picture.

Physical:
❑ Sleeping problems

❑ Weight gain or loss

❑ Smoking or drinking

❑ Problems with mobility

❑ Current medications

❑ Parent's concerns about his or her own physical health

Mental:
❑ Short-term and long-term memory loss

❑ Confusion

❑ Poor judgment

❑ Inability to have a conversation

❑ Mood swings

❑ Recent losses

❑ Grief

❑ Parent's concerns about his or her own mental health

Emotional and social:
❑ Isolation

❑ Contact with family

❑ Contact with friends

❑ Leisure-time activities

❑ Negative view of life

❑ Parent's concerns about his or her own emotional and social health

Spiritual:

❑ Parish involvement

❑ Mass attendance

❑ Reception of the sacraments

❑ Awareness of spiritual life

❑ Feeling of peace

❑ Parent's concerns about his or her own spiritual health

Activities of Daily Living

Review the following lists and determine if your parent can or cannot do the activities described.

Eating:

❑ Chew and swallow hot and cold food

❑ Swallow hot and cold beverages

❑ Cut food into digestible pieces

❑ Use eating utensils

Bathing:

❑ Get in and out of the shower or bathtub

❑ Turn on and off the faucet

❑ Regulate water temperature

❑ Wash body parts

❑ Dry the body

❑ Care for any special needs due to illness

Grooming:

❑ Take care of personal appearance

❑ Shave

❑ Wash and brush hair

❑ Brush teeth and/or clean dentures

Dressing:

❑ Choose clothes appropriate for the weather and the day's activities

❑ Put on underwear, clothes, shoes, prostheses, or assistive devices

❑ Use buttons and zippers

Mobility:

❑ Move from lying down to sitting

❑ Move from sitting to standing

❑ Reach a cane, walker, wheelchair

❑ Move into position to use the toilet

❑ Move into a wheelchair

❑ Move out of a wheelchair

Incontinence:

❑ Move fast enough to get to the bathroom

❑ Need reminders

Instrumental Activities of Daily Living

Managing money:

❑ Handle money and pay bills

❑ Use cash for simple transactions

❑ Handle paperwork

❑ Write checks or money orders

Using the telephone:

❑ Place a call

❑ Answer the phone

❑ Understand and share information on the phone

Preparing meals:
❑ Prepare hot and cold food
❑ Open containers
❑ Use the stove, oven, microwave, toaster oven
❑ Clean up after meals and put away food
❑ Wash, dry, and put away dishes

Doing laundry:
❑ Sort clothes
❑ Carry laundry
❑ Load the washer and dryer
❑ Unload the washer and dryer
❑ Put away clean clothes
❑ Use coins if needed for machines

Doing housework:
❑ Sweep
❑ Clean the floor
❑ Vacuum
❑ Dust
❑ Clean up spills
❑ Clean the sink, toilet, bathtub
❑ Maintain a safe and clean environment

Doing activities outside the home:
❑ Get to the bank
❑ Get to the post office
❑ Get to the store
❑ Get to the Laundromat

- ❏ Use stairs
- ❏ Use entrances and exits in houses or buildings
- ❏ Use transportation in all types of weather
- ❏ Get transportation
- ❏ Give directions to and from home
- ❏ Use proper personal safety when in public

Managing health:
- ❏ Understand directions from a doctor, nurse, therapist
- ❏ Use medical equipment
- ❏ Manage simple dressings
- ❏ Monitor blood pressure, pulse, temperature
- ❏ Manage medications

Being alone:
- ❏ Able to be left alone
- ❏ Recognize and react to emergencies
- ❏ Able to evacuate or tell someone that help is needed
- ❏ Exercise judgment regarding personal health and safety
- ❏ Often alone and isolated

Home Safety Checklist

Kitchen:

- ❏ Items are kept in lower cabinets.
- ❏ A sturdy step stool is available.
- ❏ There is a place to set groceries.
- ❏ The stove and oven are turned off.
- ❏ Enough storage is available to avoid clutter.
- ❏ Towels, dishcloths, and curtains are not near the stove.
- ❏ Oven mitts (not towels used as pot holders) are available.
- ❏ Water temperature in the water heater is set below 120 degrees Fahrenheit.
- ❏ Electric wiring is grounded where there's water.
- ❏ Appliances are unplugged when not in use.
- ❏ Leftover food is properly stored and eaten or disposed of before it spoils.

Does your parent:

- ❏ Wear appropriate clothes when cooking?
- ❏ Always remain in the kitchen when cooking?
- ❏ Wipe up spills immediately?

Bathroom:

- ❏ Grab bars (not just a towel rack) are installed in the bathroom.
- ❏ A grab bar is installed beside the toilet.
- ❏ Soap is within reach.
- ❏ The bathtub has a bath mat.
- ❏ A chair is in the tub.
- ❏ The toilet has a raised seat.
- ❏ There is nonslip flooring or a rug for when the floor is wet.

❑ There is a handheld showerhead.

❑ Water temperature in the water heater is set below 120 degrees Fahrenheit.

❑ The door does not have a lock.

❑ Appliances are unplugged when not in use.

❑ Electric wiring is grounded where there's water.

Bedroom:

❑ A lamp is accessible from the bed and easy to switch on or off.

❑ Night lights are in the bedroom, the hall, and the bathroom.

❑ A flashlight is by the bed.

❑ Hot pads and electric blankets are in good condition.

Does your parent:

❑ Use a hot pad and/or an electric blanket in a safe manner?

Security:

❑ Doors, including the garage door and the door leading from the garage into the house, are locked.

❑ Windows and sliding doors are locked.

❑ There is a peephole in the door and a screen/security door.

❑ An emergency alarm system is installed.

❑ Addresses and phone numbers are by the phone and written in large print.

❑ Phone is cordless to reduce risk of falls.

❑ Locks have dead bolts (but not a two-key system, which makes it harder to get out).

❑ If there are bars on the windows, they have a quick-release latch.

Does your parent:
- ❏ Come home alone to an empty house?

Outside:
- ❏ Walks and driveway are free of wet leaves, snow, ice, and cracks in concrete.
- ❏ Door has a mat for wiping wet feet.
- ❏ Garden tools are put away.
- ❏ Bushes are cut back from the walks and windows.
- ❏ Outdoor lights have motion detectors.
- ❏ Handrails are installed.
- ❏ A ramp is installed, if needed.
- ❏ Front door is well lit.

Lighting:
- ❏ Lighting shines from several angles to avoid shadows.
- ❏ Tops and bottoms of stairs are well lit.
- ❏ Front door is well lit.
- ❏ A light switch is by the front door.
- ❏ Daylight comes in through windows.
- ❏ Correct wattage bulbs are installed in lamps and fixtures.

Stairs:
- ❏ All stairs have handrails.
- ❏ Handrails line the full length of the stairway.
- ❏ Handrails are a different color than the wall.
- ❏ Stairs are in good condition.
- ❏ There are no rugs at the tops or bottoms of stairs.
- ❏ There are no frayed rugs or runners on stairs.

❑ Color-contrast paint strips are used on the edges of steps if a parent has trouble with vision.

Does your parent:

❑ Use stairs for storage?

Living room and floor plan:

❑ Rugs have nonslip backs.

❑ Rugs are free of curled edges that would cause tripping.

❑ Hallways are at least four feet wide.

❑ Halls are free of furniture, boxes, storage, and other clutter.

❑ Walkways from room to room, bedroom to bathroom are clear.

❑ Cords for phones, lamps, appliances are secured and out of walkways.

❑ Chairs have arms for support.

❑ Furniture is sturdy.

❑ Furniture is spaced four feet apart.

❑ Depth of carpet nap is not a hindrance if a parent has trouble with mobility.

❑ No items are stacked in walkways.

❑ Space heaters are placed at least three feet from flammable items.

❑ Extension cords and outlets are not overloaded.

❑ All cords, outlets, and switches are in good repair.

Fire safety:

❑ Smoke alarms are installed on each floor and in or by the bedroom.

❑ Smoke alarms are tested on a regular basis.

❑ Smoke alarms are adapted if a parent is hearing impaired.

- ❏ Fire extinguisher is easily accessible.
- ❏ Fire escape plan is established.
- ❏ Escape routes are clear of clutter.
- ❏ Fireplace has a screen.
- ❏ Carbon monoxide detector is installed, if needed.

Does your parent:
- ❏ Smoke?
- ❏ Follow rules for safety when smoking?

Special situations:
- ❏ House is childproofed if young children are coming to visit.
- ❏ Area where medication is taken is well lit.
- ❏ Precautions are taken if pets are in the house.
- ❏ Precautions are taken if firearms are in the house.

Depression Checklist

Has your parent (or have you) had any of these symptoms for more than two weeks:

- ❑ A persistently sad, anxious, or empty mood
- ❑ Feelings of hopelessness, pessimism, and apathy
- ❑ Feelings of worthlessness, helplessness, and guilt
- ❑ Frequent crying
- ❑ A loss of interest in doing things that were once pleasurable
- ❑ Disturbed sleep: insomnia, early waking, or oversleeping
- ❑ Disturbed eating: a loss of appetite, weight gain, or weight loss
- ❑ Decreased energy and constant fatigue
- ❑ Recurring aches and pains
- ❑ Restlessness and irritability
- ❑ Difficulty performing daily tasks, such as going to work
- ❑ Difficulty concentrating, remembering, or making decisions
- ❑ Neglect in personal appearance
- ❑ Thoughts of death or suicide

Seek professional help. An early diagnosis is important. Treatments have been very successful.

Some changes in lifestyle will help restore emotional health:

- ❑ Take time to pray each day and nurture your spiritual life.
- ❑ Join a support group.
- ❑ Get together with friends and have fun.

- ❏ Reduce stress and avoid overloading your schedule.
- ❏ Learn to recognize your negative thoughts and be positive.
- ❏ Identify problems and explore solutions and coping strategies.
- ❏ Look for something pleasant to do, and do it.
- ❏ Maintain your sense of purpose.
- ❏ Cherish family relationships.
- ❏ Exercise and eat healthy foods.
- ❏ Be patient with yourself.

Driving Skills Checklist

As explained in chapter 16, the aging process may affect your parent's ability to drive. You can expect a loss of hearing and visual acuity, changes in physical strength, and a slower reaction time. You may need to discuss driving with your parent. Here are some warning signs to look out for:

Driver errors:
❑ Trouble merging into traffic
❑ Difficulty seeing sides of the road
❑ Using incorrect signals
❑ Driving too fast or too slow
❑ Exercising poor judgment when making left turns
❑ Moving into the wrong lane
❑ Trouble staying in the proper lane
❑ Confusion at exits
❑ Tickets (moving violations or warnings)
❑ Failure to stop at signs or lights
❑ Stopping in traffic for no reason
❑ Failing to give the right of way

Problem behaviors:
❑ Riding the brake
❑ Hitting curbs
❑ Not parking between lines or using two spaces
❑ Agitation and irritation
❑ Difficulty turning corners
❑ Frequent close calls
❑ Getting lost in familiar places

❑ Confusing the gas and brake pedals or having trouble moving the foot from one pedal to the other

❑ Misinterpreting or disobeying traffic signs

❑ Forgetting to turn on the headlights

Underlying problems:

❑ Easily distracted

❑ Difficulty turning to look over the shoulder to change lanes and back up

❑ Delayed response to the unexpected: bikers, pedestrians, traffic signs, roadside activity, potential trouble

❑ Medical condition that may affect ability to drive safely

❑ Medication that may cause drowsiness

❑ Difficulty judging distance between one's own car and the car ahead

❑ Difficulty seeing lights at dusk or at night

❑ Ignoring potential mechanical trouble with the car

More clues that it's time to be concerned:

❑ Others not wanting to ride along

❑ Lack of confidence in abilities and nervousness when driving

❑ Increase in number of other drivers honking horns

❑ Dents and scrapes on car

❑ Using a copilot or asking passengers to help look out for cars

❑ Car accidents

Remember that you need to make sure alternative transportation is available if your parent is unable to drive. Now is the time for good planning.

Legal and Financial Paperwork Checklist

What paperwork and/or information do you need, and where is it kept? Everyone's situation will be unique. Here is a list of information that may be relevant to your parent's circumstances. Be sure to take notes as you find information. Don't depend on your memory.

Questions to ask:
- Does my parent have and/or need this item?
- Where is it?

Record the company name, address, phone numbers, Web site, e-mail address, and contact person, if appropriate.

Banks:
❑ Account numbers of all bank accounts
❑ Safety deposit box (Make sure you or someone else also has access to the box so that the material can be easily accessed if your parent is incapacitated or has died.)

Financial assets:
❑ Recent tax returns
❑ Savings bonds
❑ CDs
❑ IRAs
❑ Stock certificates
❑ Investment accounts
❑ 401(k), pension, company stock
❑ Accountant and/or financial planner

Property:
- ❏ Automobile title and registration
- ❏ Inventory of possessions
- ❏ Deeds of real estate and/or mortgage

Insurance policies:
- ❏ Life
- ❏ Disability
- ❏ Homeowner
- ❏ Renter
- ❏ Automobile
- ❏ Medical, vision, and/or dental
- ❏ Long-term health care

Identification:
- ❏ Social Security card
- ❏ Marriage certificate or divorce certificate
- ❏ Military discharge documentation, branch of service, military ID, dates of service
- ❏ Birth certificate
- ❏ Passport and/or citizenship card
- ❏ Medicare and/or Medicaid card
- ❏ Private health insurance card

Legal:
- ❏ Attorney
- ❏ Will
- ❏ Durable power of attorney for finances and property
- ❏ Guardianship
- ❏ Trust fund arrangement

Health:

❑ Medical coverage and ID number

❑ Advance directive for health care

❑ Living will

❑ Durable power of attorney for health care

❑ Do Not Resuscitate order

❑ Organ donor card

❑ Primary physician

❑ Dentist

❑ Physical therapist

❑ Other health-care providers

Debts:

❑ Credit card information, including companies, account numbers, and recent statements

❑ Loan information

Parish:

❑ Name, phone number, and location

❑ Priest

❑ Extraordinary minister of the Eucharist (if one visits your parent)

Final details:

❑ Funeral plans

❑ Funeral home

❑ Burial arrangement

❑ Cemetery information

Support:
❑ Social service agencies involved

❑ Visiting nurse

❑ In-home assistant

❑ Case manager

Elder Abuse Checklist

As mentioned in chapter 16, caregiver stress can lead to abuse. This subject should be looked at very seriously. If there is a danger that your behavior is inappropriate, get help immediately. If you are not the primary caregiver, watch for any evidence that your parent is in danger. Here are some basic facts:

Types of abuse:
- Physical abuse: inflicting physical pain or injury
- Sexual abuse: touching in a nonconsensual sexual way
- Emotional and psychological abuse: causing mental or emotional anguish
- Financial and material exploitation: using money or belongings without the consent of the owner
- Neglect: failing to provide care
- Abandonment: deserting a person under one's care
- Self-neglect: behaving in a way that threatens one's own health and safety

Possible causes:
- Caregiver stress: providing care for an elderly person is not an easy task
- Impairment of elder: the more impaired a person is, the higher the risk of abuse
- History of family violence
- Personal problems of abuser: problems with drugs or alcohol or financial difficulties

Getting Help

"If someone you care about is in imminent danger, call 911, police, or hospital emergency NOW." This is a quote from the National Center on Elder Abuse, an agency funded by the U.S. Administration on Aging.

Check www.elderabusecenter.org. This Web site has a list of abuse hotlines in every state.

If you have trouble finding the number you need, call the Eldercare Locator at (1-800) 677-1116, or look in your local phone directory for any of these programs:

- Adult protective services: a state agency that investigates reports of abuse for individuals over the age of eighteen
- State elder abuse hotline: A twenty-four-hour hotline for confidential reports
- Law enforcement: Your local police department or sheriff's office
- Long-term–care ombudsman: A state agency that investigates abuse in a nursing home setting
- Senior Information and Assistance: information on a wide range of services available in your area

If in doubt, report it.

Evaluating Housing Options

Many housing options are available for seniors. At one end of the spectrum is an *independent living facility* with residents in private apartments. This facility may provide a common dining area and basic housekeeping but no other services. An *assisted-living facility* has the same amenities, but a resident also has access to personal care assistance, such as help with bathing, dressing, and managing medication. The most extensive services are offered in a *nursing home,* where the residents are no longer able to be independent and need medical care. A first step is to determine which housing option best suits your parent's needs. See chapter 14 for a discussion of housing options.

Before you visit a housing facility, do some research:

❑ Contact the state ombudsman to ask for a copy of the latest review of the facility's license.
❑ Find out if the facility is for-profit or nonprofit.
❑ Find out if it is owned by an individual or a corporation.
❑ Find out where its home office and any other properties are located.

Checklists for evaluating an assisted-living facility or a nursing home follow. Make several photocopies of the appropriate checklist so that you can use a separate one for each facility you visit. It's best to visit each site more than once and to make your appointments at different times on different days to get a more accurate idea of how the facility is run. (For example, on-duty staff size may vary at different times of the day.)

Because there are many items to consider, take the time to review the checklist before you make your visit.

As you tour the facility with the admissions or marketing director (or other staff member), spend a few moments looking at your list to see if you missed something. Remember that you don't want to make any decisions on the spot and you can always call and ask questions after you get home. Ask for a copy of the facility's monthly calendar, activity schedule, and resident contract. Review these materials at home.

Evaluation of Assisted-Living Facility

Name of facility

Address

Phone

Contact name / Position

Date of visit / Day and time

Initial questions:
- ❏ Is Medicare accepted? Medicaid? Long-term–care insurance? Private pay?
- ❏ What are the levels of care (independent, assisted living, nursing)?
- ❏ Does the facility have a religious affiliation? Weekly church services? A chaplain? A Eucharistic minister?
- ❏ How long has the facility been under the present ownership/management?
- ❏ Are the patient's rights posted?
- ❏ Is the facility licensed by the state?
- ❏ Can you get a copy of the most recent state licensing review? Have all deficiencies listed on the review been corrected?

Treatment of residents:
- ❏ Does the staff respond quickly to a resident's call button?
- ❏ How do the staff and residents interact?
- ❏ Does your tour guide greet residents and know their names?

Staff:

❑ Are criminal history checks and drug tests done on all staff members?

❑ What are the staff positions (administrator, direct care providers, social worker, nutritionist)?

❑ How many RNs are on duty for each shift? LPNs? CNAs? Support staff?

❑ What is the staff-to-resident ratio for each shift?

❑ Do the staff members wear name tags?

Care:

❑ Does the facility develop a care plan for each resident? Who writes the care plan? Are the residents and their family involved? How often is the care plan reviewed?

❑ Is there a resident/family council? How often does it meet? What do they talk about?

❑ Are there planned activities? How many choices are there? Do you take trips? Are there opportunities for exercise?

❑ Is any therapy (physical, occupational, speech) available?

❑ Does the food look and taste good?

❑ Are the mealtimes flexible? How many meals and which meals are included?

❑ Is room delivery for meals available if your parent is sick?

❑ Are there choices for meals? Can special diets be accommodated? Are nutritious snacks provided? Can a resident select a portion size?

❑ Are seats assigned? What happens if a resident doesn't like his or her assignment?

❑ Are there arrangements for care with a local hospital? Is there a doctor on call for emergencies?

❑ How often is a registered nurse on site? How often is a physician?

❑ Who decides if a resident is no longer eligible to remain in this setting?

❑ Who determines the level of care, and how is it determined?

❑ Can services be added if the patient needs them?

Environment:

❑ What is your general first impression? Were you greeted?

❑ Is there a pleasant smell?

❑ Are accidents cleaned up promptly?

❑ Is the hallway clear for wheelchair and walker use?

❑ Is parking available? How much does it cost?

❑ Is there a common room? A living room? A den? A library? A snack area? A game room?

❑ Is the noise level in the halls, common rooms, and dining room comfortable?

❑ Are extra services, such as a beauty salon or café, available?

❑ Are there areas for visiting indoors? Outdoors?

❑ Is the dining room clean, nicely set up, and pleasant?

❑ What is your overall impression? Is it institutional? Homelike?

❑ What is provided in the apartments (TV, telephone, cable, Internet connection)?

❑ Are the rooms furnished or can residents bring in their own furniture?

❑ Do staff members treat one another with respect?

Policies:

❑ When are visiting hours?

❑ Who handles discharge planning? How is it handled?

❑ What is involved in the admissions process? Is there a waiting list?

❑ Is smoking allowed?

❑ Under what conditions would a resident be asked to leave? Would there be referral arrangements?

❑ Will a person's apartment be held if he or she has to be hospitalized? For how long?

❑ Are pets allowed?

Safety:

❑ Does a staff member check in on residents every day?

❑ Is there a sign-out and a sign-in sheet to help staff know who is not in the building?

❑ Are strangers prevented from entering without permission?

❑ Are there intercoms in each unit?

❑ Is there a twenty-four-hour emergency response system?

❑ Is the facility wheelchair accessible?

❑ Does it have well-lit halls?

❑ Are there marked exits?

❑ Are there handrails in the halls?

❑ Are there grab bars and call buttons in the bathrooms?

❑ Are there locks on doors and windows?

❑ Are fire systems, sprinklers, fire doors, and evacuation plans in place?

❑ Is there a generator if the power goes out?

❑ Are there locks and peepholes in the doors?

Apartments:

❑ Are several floor plans available (studio, one bedroom, two bedroom)?

❑ Is there a call button in the bathroom?

❑ Does the bathroom have grab bars? Is it wheelchair accessible?

❑ Is there a temperature control system in each room?

❑ Is additional storage space available?

❑ Is there a refrigerator? An oven? A stove? A dishwasher? A microwave? A sink?

Financial:

❑ Is there a buy-in fee?

❑ Is there a security deposit? Does it include first month's rent? Last month's?

❑ What is the monthly rate?

❑ What services (utilities, cable) are covered by the monthly rate?

❑ Are additional services available for an extra fee?

❑ Is there a sliding fee scale for low-income residents?

❑ Is there a financial qualification?

❑ How can payments be made?

❑ Is renter's insurance necessary?

Services:

❑ Is laundry service available?

❑ Are linens changed? How often?

❑ Is housekeeping available?

❑ Is dressing assistance available?

❑ Is eating assistance available?

❑ Is mobility assistance available?

❏ Is grooming and hygiene assistance available?

❏ Is bathing assistance available?

❏ Is toilet assistance available?

❏ Is there a shopping service?

❏ Is medication management assistance available? Who distributes medications?

❏ Can outside services (such as a visiting nurse) be brought in?

Location:

❏ Is the facility in a convenient location, near shopping, doctor, church?

❏ Is it close to public transportation?

❏ Is there a residence bus? Where will it go? How do you set it up? How much does it cost?

Evaluation of Nursing Home

Name of facility

Address

Phone

Contact name / Position

Date of visit / Day and time

Initial questions:

❑ Is Medicare accepted? Medicaid? Long-term–care insurance? Private pay?

❑ What are the levels of care (independent, assisted living, nursing)?

❑ Does the facility have a religious affiliation? Weekly church services? A chaplain? A Eucharistic minister?

❑ Are volunteers involved? In what capacity?

❑ How long has the facility been under the present ownership/management?

❑ Are the patient's rights posted?

❑ Is the facility licensed by the state?

❑ Can you get a copy of the most recent state licensing review? Have all deficiencies listed on the review been corrected?

Treatment of residents:

❑ Does the staff knock on the door before entering a patient's room?

❑ Is the door closed when a staff member is taking care of a patient's personal needs?

❑ Does the staff respond quickly to a resident's call button?

❑ How do the staff and residents interact?

❑ Does your tour guide greet residents and know their names?

Staff:

❑ Are criminal history checks and drug tests done on all staff members?

❑ What are the staff positions (administrator, direct care providers, social worker, nutritionist)?

❑ How many RNs are on duty for each shift? LPNs? CNAs? Support staff?

❑ What is the staff-to-resident ratio for each shift?

❑ Do the staff members wear name tags?

Care:

❑ Does the facility develop a care plan for each resident? Who writes the care plan? Are the residents and their family involved? How often is the care plan reviewed?

❑ Is there a resident/family council? How often does it meet? What do they talk about?

❑ Are patients clean, dressed, and groomed?

❑ Are there planned activities? How many choices are there? Are they age appropriate?

❑ Is any therapy (physical, occupational, speech) available?

❑ Is there fresh water in the rooms?

❑ Does the food look and taste good?

❑ Are the mealtimes flexible? How many meals and which meals are included?

❑ Is room delivery for meals available if your parent is sick?

❑ Are there choices for meals? Can special diets be accommodated? Are nutritious snacks provided? Can a resident select a portion size?

❑ Are seats assigned? What happens if a resident doesn't like his or her assignment?

❑ Is special care available for patients with special needs, such as dementia?

❑ Are there arrangements for care with a local hospital? Is preventive care (such as flu shots) provided?

❑ Is there a doctor who makes regular visits?

❑ Can a patient's current primary doctor continue to provide care?

Environment:

❑ Is there a pleasant smell?

❑ Are accidents cleaned up promptly?

❑ Is the hallway clear for wheelchair and walker use?

❑ Is the room temperature appropriate, not too hot or too cold?

❑ Is the noise level in the halls, common rooms, and dining room comfortable?

❑ Is storage space available?

❑ Are there windows that let in natural light?

❑ Is there a dining room?

❑ Are there areas for visiting indoors? Outdoors?

❑ What is your overall impression? Is it institutional? Homelike?

❑ What is provided in the apartments (TV, telephone, cable, Internet connection)?

❑ Are the rooms furnished or can residents bring in their own furniture and personal items?

Policies:

❑ When are visiting hours?

❑ Who handles discharge planning? How is it handled?

❑ What is involved in the admissions process? Is there a waiting list?

❑ Is smoking allowed?

❑ How are room assignments made? Can they be changed?

❑ What happens if items are stolen from a patient's room?

Safety:

❑ Are strangers prevented from entering without permission?

❑ Is the facility wheelchair accessible?

❑ Does it have well-lit halls?

❑ Are there marked exits?

❑ Are there handrails in the halls?

❑ Are there grab bars and call buttons in the bathrooms?

❑ Are there locks on doors and windows?

❑ Are fire systems, sprinklers, fire doors, and evacuation plans in place?

❑ Is there a generator if the power goes out?

Appendix III:
Traditional Prayers
of the Catholic Church

This section collects many of the traditional Catholic prayers. Many caregivers and parents pray them together.

Sign of the Cross

In the name of the Father, and of the Son, and of the Holy Spirit. Amen.
(To make the sign of the cross, use the right hand to touch the forehead when saying "Father," the chest when saying "Son," the left shoulder when saying "Holy," and the right shoulder when saying "Spirit.")

Apostles' Creed

I believe in God, the Father almighty,
creator of heaven and earth.
I believe in Jesus Christ, his only Son, our Lord.
He was conceived by the power of the Holy Spirit
and born of the Virgin Mary.
He suffered under Pontius Pilate,
was crucified, died, and was buried.

He descended to the dead.

On the third day he rose again.

He ascended into heaven,

and is seated at the right hand of the Father.

He will come again to judge the living and the dead.

I believe in the Holy Spirit,

the holy catholic Church,

the communion of saints,

the forgiveness of sins,

the resurrection of the body,

and the life everlasting. Amen.

Lord's Prayer

Our Father, who art in heaven, hallowed be thy name; thy kingdom come; thy will be done on earth as it is in heaven. Give us this day our daily bread; and forgive us our trespasses as we forgive those who trespass against us; and lead us not into temptation, but deliver us from evil. Amen.

Hail Mary

Hail Mary, full of grace, the Lord is with you. Blessed are you among women, and blessed is the fruit of your womb, Jesus. Holy Mary, Mother of God, pray for us sinners, now and at the hour of our death. Amen.

Glory Be to the Father

Glory be to the Father, and to the Son, and to the Holy Spirit. As it was in the beginning, is now, and ever shall be, world without end. Amen.

Memorare

Remember, O most gracious Virgin Mary,
that never was it known
that any one who fled to thy protection,
implored thy help, or sought thy intercession
was left unaided.

Inspired by this confidence,
I fly unto thee,
O Virgin of virgins my Mother;
to thee do I come,
before thee I stand,
sinful and sorrowful;
O Mother of the Word Incarnate,
despise not my petitions,
but in thy clemency hear and answer me.
Amen.

Angelus

V. The angel of the Lord declared unto Mary.

R. And she conceived of the Holy Spirit.

Hail Mary.

V. Behold the handmaid of the Lord.

R. May it be done unto me according to your word.

Hail Mary.

V. And the Word was made flesh,

R. And dwelt among us.

Hail Mary.

V. Pray for us, O holy Mother of God.

R. That we may be made worthy of the promises of Christ.

Let us pray.

Pour forth, we beseech thee, O Lord,

thy grace into our hearts;

that we, to whom the incarnation of Christ, thy Son,

was made known

by the message of an angel,

may by his passion and cross

be brought to the glory

of his resurrection

through the same Christ our Lord.

Amen.

Magnificat

My soul magnifies the Lord,
and my spirit rejoices in God my Savior,
for he has looked with favor on the lowliness of his servant.

Surely, from now on all generations will call me blessed;
for the Mighty One has done great things for me,
and holy is his name.

His mercy is for those who fear him
from generation to generation.

He has shown strength with his arm;
he has scattered the proud in the thoughts of their hearts.

He has brought down the powerful from their thrones,
and lifted up the lowly;
he has filled the hungry with good things,
and sent the rich away empty.

He has helped his servant Israel,
in remembrance of his mercy,
according to the promise he made to our ancestors,
to Abraham, and to his descendants forever.

Hail Holy Queen

Hail Holy Queen, Mother of mercy, our life, our sweetness, and our hope. To you do we cry, poor banished children of Eve; to you do we send up our sighs, mourning and weeping in the valley of tears. Turn, then, most gracious advocate, your eyes of mercy toward us, and after this, our exile, show unto us the blessed fruit of your womb, Jesus. O clement, O loving, O sweet Virgin Mary.

Pray for us, O holy Mother of God. That we may be made worthy of the promises of Christ.

Let us pray. O God, whose only begotten Son, by his life, death, and resurrection, has purchased for us the rewards of eternal life, grant, we beseech you, that meditating on these mysteries in the most holy rosary of the Blessed Virgin Mary, we may imitate what they contain, and obtain what they promise, through the same Christ, our Lord. Amen.

Peace Prayer of St. Francis

Lord, make me an instrument of your peace:
where there is hatred, let me sow love;
where there is injury, pardon;
where there is doubt, faith;
where there is despair, hope;
where there is darkness, light;
where there is sadness, joy.

O divine Master, grant that I may not so much seek
to be consoled as to console,
to be understood as to understand,
to be loved as to love.
For it is in giving that we receive,
it is in pardoning that we are pardoned,
it is in dying that we are born to eternal life.

Prayer to the Holy Spirit

V. Come, Holy Spirit, fill the hearts of your faithful.
R. And kindle in them the fire of your love.
V. Send forth your Spirit and they shall be created.
R. And you will renew the face of the earth.

Let us pray.

O God, who by the light of the Holy Spirit did instruct the
hearts of the faithful, grant that by that same Spirit, we may
be truly wise, and ever rejoice in your consolation. Through
Christ our Lord.
R. Amen.

Act of Contrition

Act of Contrition (1)
O my God, I am heartily sorry for having offended you,
and I detest all my sins because of your just punishments,
but most of all because they offend you, my God, who are

all-good and deserving of all my love. I firmly resolve, with the help of your grace, to sin no more and to avoid the near occasion of sin. Amen.

Act of Contrition (2)

O my God, I am heartily sorry for having offended you, and I detest all my sins because I dread the loss of heaven and the pains of hell, but most of all because they offend you, my God, who are all-good and deserving of all my love. I firmly resolve, with the help of your grace, to confess my sins, to do penance, and to amend my life. Amen.

Act of Contrition (3)

My God, I am sorry for my sins with all my heart. In choosing to do wrong and failing to do good, I have sinned against you whom I should love above all things. I firmly intend, with your help, to do penance, to sin no more, and to avoid whatever leads me to sin. Our Savior Jesus Christ suffered and died for us. In his name, my God, have mercy. Amen.

Act of Contrition (4)

O my God, I am sorry and beg pardon for all my sins, and detest them above all things, because they deserve your dreadful punishments, because they have crucified my loving Savior Jesus Christ, and, most of all, because they offend your infinite goodness; and I firmly resolve, by the help of your grace, never to offend you again, and carefully to avoid the occasion of sin. Amen.

Prayer to My Guardian Angel

Angel of God, my guardian dear, to whom God's love commits me here, ever this day be at my side, to light and guard, to rule and guide. Amen.

Grace before Meals

Bless us, O Lord, and these thy gifts, which we are about to receive from thy bounty. Through Christ our Lord. Amen.

Grace after Meals

We give thee thanks for all thy benefits. O almighty God who reignest forever; world without end. Amen.

The Universal Prayer, Attributed to Pope Clement XI

Lord, I believe in you: increase my faith.
I trust in you: strengthen my trust.
I love you: let me love you more and more.
I am sorry for my sins: deepen my sorrow.

I worship you as my first beginning.
I long for you as my last end.
I praise you as my constant helper,
and call on you as my loving protector.

Guide me by your wisdom,
correct me with your justice,
comfort me with your mercy,
protect me with your power.

I offer you, Lord, my thoughts: to be fixed on you;
my words: to have you for their theme;
my actions: to reflect my love for you;
my sufferings: to be endured for your greater glory.

I want to do what you ask of me:
in the way that you ask,
for as long as you ask,
because you ask it.

Lord, enlighten my understanding,
strengthen my will,
purify my heart,
and make me holy.

Help me to repent of my past sins
and to resist temptation in the future.
Help me to rise above my human weakness
and to grow stronger as a Christian.

Let me love you, my Lord and my God,
and see myself as I really am:
a pilgrim in this world,
a Christian called to respect and love

all whose lives I touch,
those in authority over me
or those under my authority,
my friends and my enemies.

Help me to conquer anger by gentleness,
greed by generosity, apathy by fervor.
Help me to forget myself
and reach out toward others.

Make me prudent in planning,
courageous in taking risks.
Make me patient in suffering,
unassuming in prosperity.

Keep me, Lord, attentive in prayer,
temperate in food and drink,
diligent in my work,
firm in my good intentions.

Let my conscience be clear,
my conduct without fault,
my speech blameless,
my life well-ordered.

Put me on guard against my human weaknesses.
Let me cherish your love for me,
keep your law,
and come at last to your salvation.

Teach me to realize that this world is passing,
that my true future is the happiness of heaven,
that life on earth is short,
and the life to come eternal.

Help me to prepare for death
with a proper fear of judgment,
but a greater trust in your goodness.
Lead me safely through death
to the endless joy of heaven.
Grant this through Christ our Lord. Amen.

Eternal Rest

Eternal rest grant unto them, O Lord, and let perpetual light shine upon them. May the souls of the faithful departed, through the mercy of God, rest in peace. Amen.

Rosary

"Saying a rosary" usually means reciting five decades, or sets of ten Hail Marys. An entire rosary is twenty decades. For each decade there is a "mystery," an event to be meditated on.

The rosary begins with the sign of the cross, the Apostles' Creed, an Our Father, three Hail Marys, and a Glory Be to the Father. Each decade is an Our Father, ten Hail Marys, and a Glory Be to the Father, followed by the Fátima Invocation. The rosary concludes with the Hail Holy Queen.

Sign of the Cross

In the name of the Father, and of the Son, and of the Holy Spirit. Amen.

Apostles' Creed

I believe in God, the Father almighty,

creator of heaven and earth.

I believe in Jesus Christ, his only Son, our Lord.

He was conceived by the power of the Holy Spirit

and born of the Virgin Mary.

He suffered under Pontius Pilate,

was crucified, died, and was buried.

He descended to the dead.

On the third day he rose again.

He ascended into heaven,

and is seated at the right hand of the Father.

He will come again to judge the living and the dead.

I believe in the Holy Spirit,

the holy catholic Church,

the communion of saints,

the forgiveness of sins,

the resurrection of the body,

and the life everlasting. Amen.

Our Father

Our Father, who art in heaven, hallowed be thy name; thy kingdom come; thy will be done on earth as it is in heaven. Give us this day our daily bread; and forgive us our trespasses as we forgive those who trespass against us; and lead us not into temptation, but deliver us from evil. Amen.

Hail Mary

Hail Mary, full of grace, the Lord is with you. Blessed are you among women, and blessed is the fruit of your womb, Jesus. Holy Mary, Mother of God, pray for us sinners, now and at the hour of our death. Amen.

Glory Be to the Father

Glory be to the Father, and to the Son, and to the Holy Spirit. As it was in the beginning, is now, and ever shall be, world without end. Amen.

Fátima Invocation

O my Jesus, forgive us our sins, save us from the fires of hell, and lead all souls to heaven, especially those most in need of thy mercy.

Hail Holy Queen

Hail Holy Queen, Mother of mercy, our life, our sweetness, and our hope. To you do we cry, poor banished children of Eve; to you do we send up our sighs, mourning and weeping in the valley of tears. Turn, then, most gracious advocate, your eyes of mercy toward us, and after this, our exile, show unto us the blessed fruit of your womb, Jesus. O clement, O loving, O sweet Virgin Mary.

Pray for us, O holy Mother of God. That we may be made worthy of the promises of Christ.

Let us pray. O God, whose only begotten Son, by his life, death, and resurrection, has purchased for us the rewards of eternal life, grant, we beseech you, that meditating on these mysteries in the most holy rosary of the Blessed Virgin Mary, we may imitate what they contain, and obtain what they promise, through the same Christ, our Lord. Amen.

The Joyful Mysteries

First: The Annunciation

In the sixth month the angel Gabriel was sent by God to a town in Galilee called Nazareth, to a virgin engaged to a man whose name was Joseph, of the house of David. The virgin's name was Mary. And he came to her and said, "Greetings, favored one! The Lord is with you." But she was much perplexed by his words and pondered what sort of greeting this might be. The angel said to her, "Do not be afraid, Mary, for you have found favor with God. And now, you will conceive in your womb and bear a son, and you will name him Jesus. He will be great, and will be called the Son of the Most High, and the Lord God will give to him the throne of his ancestor David. He will reign over the house of Jacob forever, and of his kingdom there will be no end." Mary said to the angel, "How can this be, since I am a virgin?" The angel said to her, "The Holy Spirit will come upon you, and the power of the Most High will overshadow you; therefore the child to be born will be holy; he will be called Son of God. And now, your relative Elizabeth in her old age has also conceived a son; and this is the sixth month for her who was said to be barren. For nothing will be impossible with God." Then Mary said, "Here am I, the servant of the Lord; let it be with me according to your word." Then the angel departed from her. (Luke 1:26–38)

Second: The Visitation

In those days Mary set out and went with haste to a Judean town in the hill country, where she entered the house of Zechariah and greeted Elizabeth. When Elizabeth heard Mary's greeting, the child leaped in her womb. And Elizabeth was filled with the Holy Spirit and exclaimed with a loud cry, "Blessed are you among women, and blessed is the fruit of your womb. And why has this happened to me, that the mother of my Lord comes to me? For as soon as I heard the sound of your greeting, the child in my womb leaped for joy. And blessed is she who believed that there would be a fulfillment of what was spoken to her by the Lord."

And Mary said,

"My soul magnifies the Lord,
    and my spirit rejoices in God my Savior,
for he has looked with favor on the lowliness of his servant.
    Surely, from now on all generations will call me blessed;
for the Mighty One has done great things for me,
    and holy is his name.
His mercy is for those who fear him
    from generation to generation.
He has shown strength with his arm;
    he has scattered the proud in the thoughts of their
    hearts.
He has brought down the powerful from their thrones,
    and lifted up the lowly;
he has filled the hungry with good things,
    and sent the rich away empty.

He has helped his servant Israel,

in remembrance of his mercy,

according to the promise he made to our ancestors,

to Abraham and to his descendants forever."

And Mary remained with her about three months and then returned to her home. (Luke 1:39–56)

Third: The Nativity

In those days a decree went out from Emperor Augustus that all the world should be registered. This was the first registration and was taken while Quirinius was governor of Syria. All went to their own towns to be registered. Joseph also went from the town of Nazareth in Galilee to Judea, to the city of David called Bethlehem, because he was descended from the house and family of David. He went to be registered with Mary, to whom he was engaged and who was expecting a child. While they were there, the time came for her to deliver her child. And she gave birth to her firstborn son and wrapped him in bands of cloth, and laid him in a manger, because there was no place for them in the inn.

In that region there were shepherds living in the fields, keeping watch over their flock by night. Then an angel of the Lord stood before them, and the glory of the Lord shone around them, and they were terrified. But the angel said to them, "Do not be afraid; for see—I am bringing you good news of great joy for all the people: to you is born this day in the city of David a Savior, who is the Messiah, the Lord. This will be a sign for you: you will find a child wrapped in bands of cloth and lying in a manger." And suddenly there was with the angel a multitude of the heavenly host, praising God and saying,

"Glory to God in the highest heaven,
    and on earth peace among those whom he favors!"

When the angels had left them and gone into heaven, the shepherds said to one another, "Let us go now to Bethlehem and see this thing that has taken place, which the Lord has made known to us." So they went with haste and found Mary and Joseph, and the child lying in the manger. When they saw this, they made known what had been told them about this child; and all who heard it were amazed at what the shepherds told them. But Mary treasured all these words and pondered them in her heart. The shepherds returned, glorifying and praising God for all they had heard and seen, as it had been told them. (Luke 2:1–20)

Fourth: The Presentation

When the time came for their purification according to the law of Moses, they brought him up to Jerusalem to present him to the Lord (as it is written in the law of the Lord, "Every firstborn male shall be designated as holy to the Lord"), and they offered a sacrifice according to what is stated in the law of the Lord, "a pair of turtledoves or two young pigeons."

Now there was a man in Jerusalem whose name was Simeon; this man was righteous and devout, looking forward to the consolation of Israel, and the Holy Spirit rested on him. It had been revealed to him by the Holy Spirit that he would not see death before he had seen the Lord's Messiah.

Guided by the Spirit, Simeon came into the temple; and when the parents brought in the child Jesus, to do for him what was customary under the law, Simeon took him in his arms and praised God, saying,

"Master, now you are dismissing your servant in peace,
　　according to your word;
for my eyes have seen your salvation,
　　which you have prepared in the presence of all peoples,
a light for revelation to the Gentiles
　　and for glory to your people Israel." (Luke 2:22–32)

Fifth: The Finding of Jesus in the Temple

Now every year his parents went to Jerusalem for the festival of the Passover. And when he was twelve years old, they went up as usual for the festival. When the festival was ended and they started to return, the boy Jesus stayed behind in Jerusalem, but his parents did not know it. Assuming that he was in the group of travelers, they went a day's journey. Then they started to look for him among their relatives and friends. When they did not find him, they returned to Jerusalem to search for him. After three days they found him in the temple, sitting among the teachers, listening to them and asking them questions. And all who heard him were amazed at his understanding and his answers. When his parents saw him they were astonished; and his mother said to him, "Child, why have you treated us like this? Look, your father and I have been searching for you in great anxiety." He said to them, "Why were you searching for me? Did you not know that I must be in my Father's house?" But they did not understand what he said to them. Then he went down with them and came to Nazareth, and was obedient to them. His mother treasured all these things in her heart.

And Jesus increased in wisdom and in years, and in divine and human favor. (Luke 2:41–52)

The Luminous Mysteries

First: The Baptism of Jesus in the River Jordan

And when Jesus had been baptized, just as he came up from the water, suddenly the heavens were opened to him and he saw the Spirit of God descending like a dove and alighting on him. And a voice from heaven said, "This is my Son, the Beloved, with whom I am well pleased." (Matthew 3:16–17)

Second: The Wedding Feast at Cana

And Jesus said to her, "Woman, what concern is that to you and to me? My hour has not yet come." His mother said to the servants, "Do whatever he tells you." (John 2:4–5)

Third: The Proclamation of the Kingdom of God

Now after John was arrested, Jesus came to Galilee, proclaiming the good news of God, and saying, "The time is fulfilled, and the kingdom of God has come near; repent, and believe in the good news." (Mark 1:14–15)

Fourth: The Transfiguration

And while he was praying, the appearance of his face changed, and his clothes became dazzling white. Suddenly they saw two men, Moses and Elijah, talking to him. They appeared in glory and were speaking of his departure, which he was about to accomplish at Jerusalem. Now Peter and his companions were weighed down with sleep; but since they had stayed awake, they saw his glory and the two men who stood with him. Just as they were leaving him, Peter said to Jesus, "Master, it is good for us to be here; let us make three dwellings, one for you, one for Moses, and one for Elijah"—not knowing what he said. While he was saying this, a cloud came and overshadowed them; and they were terrified as they entered the cloud. Then from the cloud came a voice that said, "This is my Son, my Chosen; listen to him!" (Luke 9:29–35)

Fifth: The Institution of the Eucharist

While they were eating, Jesus took a loaf of bread, and after blessing it he broke it, gave it to the disciples, and said, "Take, eat; this is my body." Then he took a cup, and after giving thanks he gave it to them, saying, "Drink from it, all of you." (Matthew 26:26–27)

The Sorrowful Mysteries

First: The Agony in the Garden

They went to a place called Gethsemane; and he said to his disciples, "Sit here while I pray." He took with him Peter and James and John, and began to be distressed and agitated. And he said to them, "I am deeply grieved, even to death; remain here, and keep awake." And going a little farther, he threw himself on the ground and prayed that, if it were possible, the hour might pass from him. He said, "Abba, Father, for you all things are possible; remove this cup from me; yet, not what I want, but what you want." He came and found them sleeping; and he said to Peter, "Simon, are you asleep? Could you not keep awake one hour? Keep awake and pray that you may not come into the time of trial; the spirit indeed is willing, but the flesh is weak." And again he went away and prayed, saying the same words. And once more he came and found them sleeping, for their eyes were very heavy; and they did not know what to say to him. He came a third time and said to them, "Are you still sleeping and taking your rest? Enough! The hour has come; the Son of Man is betrayed into the hands of sinners. Get up, let us be going. See, my betrayer is at hand." (Mark 14:32–42)

Second: The Scourging at the Pillar

Then Pilate took Jesus and had him flogged. (John 19:1)

Third: The Crowning with Thorns

Then the soldiers led him into the courtyard of the palace (that is, the governor's headquarters); and they called together the whole cohort. And they clothed him in a purple cloak; and after twisting some thorns into a crown, they put it on him. And they began saluting him, "Hail, King of the Jews!" They struck his head with a reed, spat upon him, and knelt down in homage to him. After mocking him, they stripped him of the purple cloak and put his own clothes on him. Then they led him out to crucify him. (Mark 15:16–20)

Fourth: The Carrying of the Cross

As they led him away, they seized a man, Simon of Cyrene, who was coming from the country, and they laid the cross

on him, and made him carry it behind Jesus. A great number
of the people followed him, and among them were women
who were beating their breasts and wailing for him. But
Jesus turned to them and said, "Daughters of Jerusalem, do
not weep for me, but weep for yourselves and for your children. For the days are surely coming when they will say,
'Blessed are the barren, and the wombs that never bore, and
the breasts that never nursed.' Then they will begin to say to
the mountains, 'Fall on us'; and to the hills, 'Cover us.' For if
they do this when the wood is green, what will happen when
it is dry?" (Luke 23:26–31)

Fifth: The Crucifixion

Then he handed him over to them to be crucified.

So they took Jesus; and carrying the cross by himself,
he went out to what is called The Place of the Skull, which
in Hebrew is called Golgotha. There they crucified him,
and with him two others, one on either side, with Jesus
between them. Pilate also had an inscription written and
put on the cross. It read, "Jesus of Nazareth, the King of the
Jews." Many of the Jews read this inscription, because the
place where Jesus was crucified was near the city; and it was
written in Hebrew, in Latin, and in Greek. Then the chief
priests of the Jews said to Pilate, "Do not write, 'The King
of the Jews,' but, 'This man said, I am King of the Jews.'"
Pilate answered, "What I have written I have written."
When the soldiers had crucified Jesus, they took his clothes
and divided them into four parts, one for each soldier. They
also took his tunic; now the tunic was seamless, woven in
one piece from the top. So they said to one another, "Let us

not tear it, but cast lots for it to see who will get it." This was to fulfill what the scripture says,

"They divided my clothes among themselves,
and for my clothing they cast lots."

And that is what the soldiers did.

Meanwhile, standing near the cross of Jesus were his mother, and his mother's sister, Mary the wife of Clopas, and Mary Magdalene. When Jesus saw his mother and the disciple whom he loved standing beside her, he said to his mother, "Woman, here is your son." Then he said to the disciple, "Here is your mother." And from that hour the disciple took her into his own home.

After this, when Jesus knew that all was now finished, he said (in order to fulfill the scripture), "I am thirsty." A jar full of sour wine was standing there. So they put a sponge full of the wine on a branch of hyssop and held it to his mouth. When Jesus had received the wine, he said, "It is finished." Then he bowed his head and gave up his spirit. (John 19:16–30)

The Glorious Mysteries:
First: The Resurrection

For I handed on to you as of first importance what I in turn had received: that Christ died for our sins in accordance with the scriptures, and that he was buried, and that he was raised on the third day in accordance with the scriptures, and that he appeared to Cephas [Peter], then to the twelve. Then he appeared to more than five hundred brothers and sisters at one time, most of whom are still alive, though some have died. Then he appeared to James, then to all the apostles. Last of all, as to one untimely born, he appeared also to me. (1 Corinthians 15:3–8)

Second: The Ascension
Then he led them out as far as Bethany, and, lifting up his hands, he blessed them. While he was blessing them, he withdrew from them and was carried up into heaven. And they worshiped him, and returned to Jerusalem with great joy; and they were continually in the temple blessing God. (Luke 24:50–53)

Third: The Coming of the Holy Spirit
When the day of Pentecost had come, they were all together in one place. And suddenly from heaven there came a sound like the rush of a violent wind, and it filled the entire house where they were sitting. Divided tongues, as of fire, appeared among them, and a tongue rested on each of them. All of them were filled with the Holy Spirit and began to speak in other languages, as the Spirit gave them ability. (Acts 2:1–4)

Fourth: The Assumption of Mary
Listen, I will tell you a mystery! We will not all die, but we will all be changed, in a moment, in the twinkling of an eye, at the last trumpet. For the trumpet will sound, and the dead will be raised imperishable, and we will be changed. For this perishable body must put on imperishability, and this mortal body must put on immortality. When this perishable body

puts on imperishability, and this mortal body puts on immortality, then the saying that is written will be fulfilled:

"Death has been swallowed up in victory."
"Where, O death, is your victory?
    Where, O death, is your sting?"

The sting of death is sin, and the power of sin is the law. But thanks be to God, who gives us the victory through our Lord Jesus Christ. (1 Corinthians 15:51–57)

Fifth: The Coronation of Mary

A great portent appeared in heaven: a woman clothed with the sun, with the moon under her feet, and on her head a crown of twelve stars. She was pregnant and was crying out in birth pangs, in the agony of giving birth. Then another portent appeared in heaven: a great red dragon, with seven heads and ten horns, and seven diadems on his heads. His tail swept down a third of the stars of heaven and threw them to the earth. Then the dragon stood before the woman who was about to bear a child, so that he might devour her child as soon as it was born. (Revelation 12:1–4)

Index

A

AARP, 257
ABLEDATA, 244
abuse, by parent, in childhood, 206–9
abuse, elder, 242, 288–89
activities of daily living, assessment
    checklist, 271–74
Act of Contrition. *See* Contrition, Act of
Administration on Aging, 245
adult family home, 170
advance directives, 189
Agency of Healthcare Research and
    Quality, 246
AgingStats.gov, 246
Aging with Dignity, 243
Al-Anon, 125
Alcoholics Anonymous, 125, 253. *See also*
    alcoholism
alcoholism. *See also* Alcoholics
    Anonymous
    aging body, impact on, 123
    difficulty diagnosing in elder
        persons, 124
    disease *vs.* moral weakness, 123
    ignoring parent's, 124
    National Clearinghouse for Alcohol
        and Drug Information, 242
    prayer for, 125
    professional help for, 124–25
    Serenity Prayer, 123
    Substance Abuse and Mental Health
        Services Administration,
        243
    warning signs, 124–25

Alzheimer's disease. *See also* dementia
    Alzheimer's Association, 253
    Alzheimer's Disease Education and
        Referral Center, 257
    Alzhome, 258
    Alzinfo.org, 258
    ALZwell Caregiver Support, 258
    diagnosis, 5
    fear of, 115
    personality changes, 209
    second opinion for, 116
Alzhome, 258
Alzinfo.org, 258
American Association for Geriatric
    Psychiatry, 251
American Association of Suicidology, 252
American Bar Association, 251
American Cancer Society, 253
American Council of the Blind, 253
American Diabetes Association, 253
American Federation for Aging
    Research, 258
American Foundation for the Blind, 253
American Heart Association, 253
American Hospice Foundation, 254
American Liver Foundation, 254
American Lung Association, 254
American Medical Association: Older
    Driver Safety, 242
American Pain Foundation, 254
American Parkinson Disease
    Association, 254
American Psychological Association
    Office on Aging, 252

American Red Cross. *See* Red Cross
Americans for Better Care of the Dying, 243
American Stroke Association, 254
Amyotrophic Lateral Sclerosis Association, 255
angels, guardian, 164
Angelus, 306
anger, 34–35
anniversaries, 133–36
anointing of the sick, 156–58
annunciation, 317
Anxiety Disorders Association of America, 252
Apostles' Creed, 303–4, 315
Area Agency on Aging, 42, 58
arthritis, 6
Arthritis Daily, 255
Arthritis Foundation, 255
assessment
    changing needs of, 64
    checklist, 269–301
    emotional/social health, 61–63
    mental, 60–61
    overview, 57–59
    physical, 59–60
    prayer, for conducting, 59, 60, 61, 63, 65
    solutions, choosing, 65–66
    spiritual life, 63
assisted-living facility evaluation checklist, 292–97
Augustine, St., 153
awareness of God, 22–23

B

basics of Catholic caregiving, 14–16
BenefitsCheckUp.org, 260
birthdays, 133–36
Blessings of Age: A Pastoral Message on Growing Older within the Faith Community, 28–29, 30
Borromeo, St. Charles, 143
burden, parent's worry over being, 80–81

C

canes. *See* mobility issues
Caregiver Assistance Network of Catholic Social Services, 239
caregiver's prayer, 22–23

caregiving
    Catholic, basics of, 14–16
    defining, 11
    difficulty of (hard work), 18
    end of, through death of parent, 13
    end of role (through death). (*see* death)
    long-distance, 196–98
    prayer, journey as, 13–14
    realities of, 21–22
    sandwich generation. (*see* sandwich generation)
    spouse of. (*see* spouse of caregiver)
    stages, 11–13
    stress, signs of, 267–68
    tips for, 266
Caregiving.com, 237
Caring Connections, 244
Caring to Help Others, 237
case manager, 181–83
CatholicCaregivers.com, 237, 239
Catholic Charities USA, 239
Catholic Health Association of the United States, 239
Catholic Information Network, 239
Catholic Medical Association, 239
Catholic News Service, 240
Catholic Online, 240
Centers for Disease Control and Prevention, 246
Centers for Medicare and Medicaid Services, 246
checklists
    assessment, 269–74
    depression, 280–81
    driving skills, 282–83
    home safety, 275–79
    legal and financial paperwork, 284–87
children
    death of grandparents, dealing with, 216–18
    grandparents, nurturing relationship with, 136–37
    prayer, 49
    preparing for visits with parent, 48–49
Children of Aging Parents, 238
Christian Burial, Mass of, 230–31
Church, the, returning to, 149–50

church militant, 233
church suffering, 233
church triumphant, 233
closed captioning television, 101
communication
    breakdown in, 83–84
    dementia's impact on, 118–19
    importance, 15
    long-distance, 196–98
    prayer for, 85
    secrets within family, 200–3
    suggestions for improving, 84–85
Communion, Holy. *See* Holy
    Communion
communion of saints, 232–35
comparisons to other parents, avoiding,
    6–7
Consumer Consortium on Assisted
    Living, 250
Contrition, Act of, 147, 152, 154, 309–10
control, importance to parent, 71–72
counseling, 43, 120, 215
crabby parents, 206–9
Creighton University Online Ministries,
    240
cremation, 226–27
cross, sign of, 303, 315

D
death
    caregiving role ends, 13, 221–23
    careless words of others, dealing
        with, 218–19
    children, preparing for, 216–18
    cremation. (*see* cremation)
    euphemisms, avoiding, 217
    funerals, memorial services. (*see*
        funerals, memorial services)
    good-bye, saying, 215
    overview of preparation for, 213–16
    prayer, end of life, during, 206, 218,
        219, 221, 223, 230, 232
    relief, complex feelings of, 36
dementia. *See also* Alzheimer's disease
    accepting, 117
    assessing, 60–61
    communicating with parent suffering
        from, 84–85
    communication, effects on, 117–18
    definition/description, 115

dementia (*continued*)
    medical tests for, 116
    memory loss associated with, 115
    personality changes, 116
    prayer regarding, 118
    reasons for, 5–6
    support when dealing with, 116–17
dental problems, 102–3
    prayer, for dental issues, 103
Department of Health, 172
depression, 61. *See also* suicide
    checklist, assessment, 280–81
    Church's teaching on, 112
    counseling, 120
    Depression and Bipolar Support
        Alliance, 255
    prayer for, 122
    signs of, 119–20
    suggestions for dealing with,
        121–22
Depression and Bipolar Support
    Alliance, 255
diabetes
    American Diabetes Association,
        253
    vision loss, 97
DisabilityInfo.gov, 244
DNR. *See* Do Not Resuscitate order
doctor, parent's. *See* physician, parent's
Do Not Resuscitate order, 89, 189–90
driving
    encouraging stopping, 99
    overview of problem, 193–94
    skills assessment, 282–83
    suggestions, 194–95
durable power of attorney, 187
dying. *See* death

E
Eldercare.gov, 180
Eldercare Locator, 260
ElderCare Online, 238
emergency response system, 161–62
emotional/social health
    assessment, 61–63
    fun, need for, 129–31
    isolation, 131–33
    leisure activities, 140–41
    memoirs, writing, 137–39
    prayer for, 131

emotions of caregiver, 12
   anger. (*see* anger)
   exhaustion. (*see* exhaustion)
   expressing, 43–44
   frustration, 4–5
   grief. (*see* grief)
   guilt. (*see* guilt)
   self-doubt, 3–4
end-of-life issues, 89, 188–90
Environmental Protection Agency, 249
EPA. *See* Environmental Protection
   Agency
Epilepsy Foundation, 255
ethnic prejudices, 203–4
Eucharist, 154–56
   receiving at home/hospital if unable
     to attend Mass, 144–45
euphemisms for death, avoiding, 217
euthanasia
   Charter for Health Care Workers,
     204–5
   Declaration on, 158
   message of, 204
evaluations
   assisted living facility, 292–97
   housing options, 290–301
   nursing home, 298–301
exhaustion
   definition, 38
   prayer for help, 40
   strategies for handling, 39–40
   symptoms, 39

F
Family Caregiver Alliance, 238
family home, leaving, 178–80. *See also*
   housing
Fátima Invocation, 316
FDA. *See* Food and Drug Administration
Federal Emergency Management
   Agency, 164, 165, 246
Federal Trade Commission: Consumer
   Information, 246
FedWorld.gov, 246
FEMA. *See* Federal Emergency
   Management Agency
fighting, between parents, 209–11
   prayer, for dealing with, 211
finances
   checklist for assessment, 284–87
   management, 185–87

finances (*continued*)
   prayer for, 187
FirstGov for Seniors, 247
Food and Drug Administration, 249
Food Research and Action Center, 258
food stamps, 258
Foundation for Grandparenting, 250
Francis de Sales, St., 33
Francis of Assisi, St., 11, 266, 308–9
Friends of St. John the Caregiver, 238,
   240
frustration, 4–5
funerals, memorial services. *See also* death
   Church's role, 225–26
   cremation. (*see* cremation)
   importance of burial service, 227–28
   Mass, 230–31
   overview, 225–26
   parent, discussing with, 226
   vigil, 229–30

G
generation, parent's
   overview of history, 67–70
Generations United, 250
geriatric case manager. *See* case manager
Geriatric Mental Health Foundation, 252
glorious mysteries. *See* mysteries, glorious
Glory Be to the Father, 305, 316
God, understanding and knowing of,
   17–19
Gospel of Life, The, 150–51
   prayer on value of elderly, 151
grace, God's, 20, 112
grandparenthood, 136–37
grief. *See also* death; loss
   avoiding change during, 78
   death, inevitability of, 5
   prayer for, 78–79
   spouse, death of, 75–76
   stages, 76–77
   suggestions for handling, 77–78
   uniqueness of process for each
     individual, 77
Guardian Angel prayer, 311
guilt, 35–38
   prayer for relief from, 38

H
Hail Holy Queen, 308, 316–17
Hail Mary, 25, 26, 304, 316

healing, 157
HealthandAge.com, 258
health-care agent, 189
health-care power of attorney, 189
Health Compass, 258
Healthfinder, 247
Health.gov, 247
Health Resources and Services
    Administration: Division of
    Facilities Compliance and
    Recovery, 247
Healthy People (organization), 247
hearing aid, 6, 100
hearing loss, 100–2
    prayer for, 102
Holy Communion, 21
Holy Spirit, strength from, 19
hospice, 205
    American Hospice Foundation, 254
    finding, 220–21
    goal and purpose of, 220
    history of, 219–20
    Hospice Association of America, 255
    Hospice Education Institute, 259
    Hospice Foundation of America, 255
    Hospice Net, 244
    Hospice Web, 259
Hospice Association of America, 255
Hospice Foundation of America, 255
Hospice Net, 244
hospitals
    overview, 93–94
    paperwork, 93–94
    suggestions for easing experience,
        94–96
housing
    evaluation checklists, 290–301
    family home, leaving, 178–80
    moving in. (see moving in, parent's)
    nursing home. (see nursing home)
    overview of options, 169–71
    prayers for choosing options, 171,
        174, 176, 178
Huntington's Disease Society of
    America, 255

I

identity theft, 164
incontinence, 60
    difficulty in addressing topic, 109–10
    prayer regarding, 110

incontinence (continued)
    warning signs, 110
independence
    importance, 71
    preserving, 184
Indian Health Service: Elder Care
    Initiative, 244
individualization, 14–15
informed consent, 188–89
informed refusal, 188–89
in-home care, 170
in-law, stepparent, caring for, 51–53
instrumental activities of daily living,
    assessment checklist, 271–74
Internet
    prayers on, 24
    resources on, 237–60
isolation, 131–33
    prayer for help regarding, 133

J

John, St.
    Christ's request that he care for
        Blessed Mother, 17, 20
    patron saint of caregivers, 17
    prayer to, 22
John Paul II
    art of prayer, 27
    final years, death, as example, 205
    human life, on the value of, 150–51
    prayer, on, 145–46
    purgatory, teaching on, 234
John XXIII Medical-Moral Research
    and Education Center, 240–41
journaling, 24

K

Knights of Columbus, 240
Kübler-Ross, Elisabeth, 76–77

L

last will and testament. See will
legal matters, 185–91
    prayer for wisdom concerning, 190,
        191
leisure-time activities, 140–41
    prayer regarding parent's, 141
Leukemia and Lymphoma Society, 256
Library of Congress: THOMAS:
    Legislative Information, 247
Lifeline, 260

Liturgy of the Hours, 24
living will, 189
long-distance caregiving, 196–200
    prayer for, 200
Lord's Prayer. *See* Our Father
loss, 73–75. *See also* grief
    prayer for support during, 75
love and respect, 14
luminous mysteries. *See* mysteries,
        luminous
Lupus Foundation of America, 256

M

Magnificat, 307
Mass
    attending, 24
    Christian Burial, of, 230–31
Mayo Clinic Senior Health Center, 259
Meals on Wheels, 181
Medicare, 247
medications
    safety issues, 160–61
    supplies on hand during emergency,
        165–66
Medline Plus, 259
memoirs, writing, 137–39
    prayer when writing, 139
Memorare, 305
memorial services. *See* funerals, memorial
        services
memories, prayer for creating positive, 136
memory loss, 115, 117. *See also* dementia
mental health
    assessment, 60–61
    Church's teaching on, 112
    depression. (*see* depression)
    diagnosis, 113
    euphemism's for, 112
    fostering good mental health, 114
    incapacity, 190–91
    National Institute of Mental Health,
        248
    National Mental Health Association,
        252
    National Mental Health Consumers'
        Self-Help Clearinghouse,
        252
    overview, 111–12
    prayer regarding, 114
    stigma, 112–13

mental health (*continued*)
    warning signs, 113
minimum to maximum, 15
mobility issues
    overview, 106
    prayer regarding, 109
    resistance to aids, 106–7
    suggestions for handling, 106–8
    wheelchairs, walkers, canes, 108–9
moving in, parent's
    overview, 174–75
    prayer regarding, 176, 178
    suggestions for easing transition,
        176–78
mysteries, glorious, 326–28
mysteries, joyful, 317–22
mysteries, luminous, 322–23
mysteries, sorrowful, 323–26
myziva.net, 250

N

National Alliance for Caregiving, 238
National Alliance on Mental Illness, 252
National Asian Pacific Center on Aging,
        245
National Association of Area Agencies
        on Aging, 259
National Association of Catholic
        Chaplains, 240
National Association of Professional
        Geriatric Care Managers, 182,
        260
National Cancer Institute, 256
National Catholic Bioethics Center,
        240–41
National Caucus and Center on Black
        Aged, 245
National Cemetery Administration, 247
National Center on Elder Abuse, 242
National Clearinghouse for Alcohol and
        Drug Information, 242
National Family Caregivers Association,
        238
National Handbook on Laws and
        Programs Affecting Senior
        Citizens, 251
National Highway Traffic Safety
        Administration: Older Road
        Users, 243
National Hispanic Council on Aging, 245

National Hospice and Palliative Care Organization, 256
National Indian Council on Aging, 245
National Institute of Arthritis and Musculoskeletal and Skin Diseases, 256
National Institute of Mental Health, 248
National Institute on Aging, 248, 259
National Institute on Drug Abuse, 248
National Institutes of Health, 248
National Library of Medicine, 248
National Mental Health Association, 252
National Mental Health Consumers' Self-Help Clearinghouse, 252
National Mental Health Information Center, 248
National Multiple Sclerosis Society, 256
National Osteoporosis Foundation, 256
National Parkinson Foundation, 257
National Pastoral Life Center, 241
National Resource Center on Native American Aging, 245
National Respite Locator Service, 260
National Senior Citizens Law Center, 243, 251
National Strategy for Suicide Prevention: Suicide Among the Elderly, 243
National Stroke Association, 257
Nativity, 319–20
Need to Promote the Consistent Use of Catholic Funeral Rites, The, 227–28
New Advent Catholic Supersite, 241
Niebuhr, Reinhold, 123
normalization, 14
nursing home
    certification, 172
    choosing, 171–74
    evaluation checklist, 298–301
    online guide, 250
nutrition, 104–5
    prayer for food issues and, 105

O
OncoLink, 259
online resources, 237–60
Order of Christian Funerals, The, 228–32
Osteoporosis and Related Bone Diseases—National Resource Center, 257

Our Father, 25, 26, 27, 304, 315

P
pain, controlling, 205
parish
    involvement in parent's spiritual life, 145
    prayer for, 31
    responsibilities of, toward caregivers, 28–29
    support from, 30–31
Patient Self-Determination Act, 188
Peace Prayer of St. Francis, 308–9
personality changes, 116, 209. See also dementia
physician, parent's. See also hospitals
    choosing, 87–88
    communicating with, 6, 88
    disagreements with, 92–93
    end-of-life issues, 89
    prayer for, 89–90
    second opinion, obtaining, 90–91
    visiting alone, 88–89
Pontifical Council for Health Pastoral Care, 241
prayer. See also prayers
    art of, 27
    beginning dialogue with God, 20–21
    caregiver, as, 25–27
    contemplation, 26, 27
    importance, 16, 23, 145–46
    meditation, 26, 27
    parish community, from, 24
    tool when dealing with abusive or crabby parent, 208
    vocal, 26
prayers, 7, 11, 19, 27, 29, 53, 81. See also prayer
    acceptance, for, 16
    alcoholism, for, 125
    Angelus, 306
    Apostles' Creed, 303–4, 315
    assessment, for conducting, 59, 60, 61, 63, 65
    caregiver, journey as, 13–14
    children, for preparing for visit, 49
    communication, for better, 85
    death, end of life, during, 206, 218, 219, 221, 223, 230, 232
    dementia and mental illness, for, 118

prayers (*continued*)
  dental issues, for, 103
  depression, for, 122
  emotional/social health, for, 131
  Eternal Rest, 314
  Eternal Rest, of, 231
  exhaustion, for relief from, 40
  Fátima Invocation, 316
  fighting parents, for dealing with,
      211
  finances, for, 187
  food issues and nutrition, for, 105
  Glory Be to the Father, 305, 316
  God's will, for, 66
  grace, 311
  Greater Awareness of the Presence of
      God, A Prayer for, 22–23
  grief, 78–79
  Guardian Angel, to My, 311
  guilt, for relief from, 38
  Hail Holy Queen, 308, 316–17
  Hail Mary. (*see* Hail Mary)
  hearing loss, for, 102
  Holy Spirit, to, 309
  housing options, for choosing, 171,
      174, 176, 178
  incontinence, for dealing with, 110
  isolation, for help regarding, 133
  legal matters, for wisdom
      concerning, 190, 191
  leisure, regarding parent's, 141
  life story, for help learning, 139
  long-distance caregiving, for, 198,
      200
  Lord's Prayer. (*see* Our Father)
  loss, for support during, 75
  Magnificat, 307
  medical wisdom, for, 91
  medical workers, for, 96
  Memorare, 305
  memoirs, when writing, 139
  memories, for creating positive, 136
  mental health, for, 114
  mobility issues, for, 109
  Our Father. (*see* Our Father)
  parishes, for, 31
  Peace Prayer of St. Francis, 308–9
  physicians, for, 89–90, 93
  piety, for, 63
  reconciliation and forgiveness, for, 154
prayers (*continued*)
  respite care prayer, 43
  rosary, 314–28
  safety, for, 162, 164, 167
  saints, for, 234
  Serenity Prayer. (*see* Serenity Prayer)
  siblings, for wisdom to work
      together, 47
  sign of the cross, 303, 315
  smoking, for help quitting, 128
  spiritual life, on, 146, 148, 150
  spouse of caregiver, 51
  St. John, to, 22
  support, for persons to give, 44
  support options, for choosing, 181,
      183, 184
  understanding, for, 71
  Universal Prayer (attributed to Pope
      Clement XI), 311–14
  value of elderly, on, 151
  vision loss, for, 99
  wisdom, for, 72
  worry, for parents who do so
      chronically, 83
priest, counsel from, 44
purgatory, 233–34

Q
quality of life, 204

R
racism, 203–4
reading, suggested, 261–64
Red Cross, 164, 165, 254
resistance to help, 183–84
resistance to help, parent's, 12
resources for caregivers
  caregiver, 237–38
  Catholic, 239–42
  critical issues, 242–43
  death and dying, 243–44
  disability, 244
  diversity, 244–45
  government, 245–50
  grandparents, 250
  housing, 250
  legal, 251
  mental health, 251–52
  national organizations, 252–57
  resource information, 257–59

resources for caregivers (*continued*)
    support, 260
    use of, 16
respect and love, 14
respite care, 29
    frequency of, 41–42
    guilt over, 42
    importance, 41
    overview, 40–41
    prayer for, 43
    social service agencies, 42
    wise use of time, 42
Resurrection, symbols of, 230
retirement community, 170
retirement home, 170–71
right to die movements, 204. *See also*
        euthanasia
role reversal, 79–80
rosary, 314–28

S
sacraments
    anointing of the sick, 156–58
    Eucharist. (*see* Eucharist)
    overview, 151
    penance and reconciliation, 152–54
Sacred Space, 241
safety
    disaster or emergency, during,
        164–67
    home, 159–62, 275–79
    personal, 162–64
    prayer for, 162, 164, 167
Saltarelli, Michael A., 227
sandwich generation
    description, 9
    suggestions for dealing with pressure
        of, 10–11
Saunders, Cicely, 219
scams, 163–64
Scripture
    reading together with parent, 26
    spiritual nourishment, as, 23
second opinion, obtaining, 90–91
self-determination, 14, 72, 188
self-doubt, 3–4
self-sufficiency, 80
SeniorHealth.gov, 248
Senior Information and Assistance, 42,
        58, 180

Serenity Prayer, 123
siblings
    conflicts, 45, 46
    help, asking for, if primary caregiver,
        47
    overview, 45
    prayer for, 47
    working together, 46
sign of the cross, 303, 315
Sirach, 47–48
smoking
    prayer for quitting, 128
    quitting, arguments for, 125–26
    suggestions regarding quitting,
        126–28
social health. *See* emotional/social health
Social Security, 249
solutions, 15
sorrowful mysteries. *See* mysteries,
        sorrowful
Spirit, Holy. *See* Holy Spirit
spirituality. *See* prayer, prayers, spiritual
        life
spiritual life
    assessing parent's, 63–64
    assessment, 63, 143–44
    Church, returning to, 149–50
    Eucharistic minister if unable to
        attend Church, 144–45
    nourishing, 23–24
    parish involvement, 145
    peace, forgiveness, 147–48
    prayer. (*see* prayer)
    sacraments. (*see* sacraments)
    suggestions for fostering, 144–46
spouse of caregiver
    overview, 50
    prayer for, 51
    suggestions for, 50–51
stepparent, in-law, caring for, 51–53
stress, signs of, 267–68
Substance Abuse and Mental Health
        Services Administration, 243
suicide, 120–21. *See also* depression
    National Strategy for Suicide
        Prevention: Suicide Among
        the Elderly, 243
support, 15
support groups
    feelings, as place to express, 44

support groups (*continued*)
importance, 10
starting, 31
Supportive Care of the Dying: A
Coalition for Compassionate
Care, 244

T
Thérèse of Lisieux, St., 213
terminal illness
secretive, 200–3
tobacco use. *See* smoking

U
Universalis Publishing: Liturgy of the
Hours, 241
Universal Prayer (attributed to Pope
Clement XI), 311–14
Untangling the Web: Where Can I
Go to Get Information about
Disabilities?, 244
U.S. Conference of Catholic Bishops,
241–42
U.S. Consumer Product Safety
Commission, 249, 250
U.S. Department of Health and Human
Services, 249
U.S. Department of Veterans Affairs,
249
U.S. Food and Drug Administration,
249

U.S. Senate Special Committee on
Aging, 250

V
Vatican, 242
vigil, 229–30. *See also* funerals, memorial
services
vision loss
common complaints/symptoms, 98
overview, 97–98
prayer for, 99
tips for coping with, 98–99
visitation, the (of the angel to Mary),
318–19
Visiting Nurse Association of America,
260
visits, 198–200
preparing children for, 48–49
vitamins, 105

W
walkers. *See* mobility issues
Well Spouse Association, 260
wheelchairs. *See* mobility issues
will, legal, 190
worrying, chronic, 82–83
prayer for parents who do so, 83

Y
Your Aging Parent, 238
Your Aging Parent Web site, 242

A Special Invitation

Loyola Press invites you to become one of our Loyola Press Advisors! Join our unique online community of people willing to share with us their thoughts and ideas about Catholic life and faith. By sharing your perspective, you will help us improve our books and serve the greater Catholic community.

From time to time, registered advisors are invited to participate in online surveys and discussion groups. Most surveys will take less than ten minutes to complete. Loyola Press will recognize your time and efforts with gift certificates and prizes. Your personal information will be held in strict confidence. Your participation will be for research purposes only, and at no time will we try to sell you anything.

Please consider this opportunity to help Loyola Press improve our products and better serve you and the Catholic community. To learn more or to join, visit **www.SpiritedTalk.org** and register today.

—The Loyola Press Advisory Team

FACING PAIN, FINDING HOPE

A Physician Examines Pain, Faith, and the Healing Stories of Jesus

Daniel Hurley, MD

ISBN-13: 978-0-8294-1780-7
ISBN-10: 0-8294-1780-X
6" x 9" Hardcover
224 pages • $22.95

In *Facing Pain, Finding Hope,* Dr. Daniel Hurley explores what he calls "the intimacy of suffering and faith." It is a place where afflicted people encounter the Jesus of the Gospels. Dr. Hurley shows how an intimate reading of the gospels can open new horizons of healing for people in pain. He invites sufferers—and those who live with them—into a dialogue with Jesus the healer.